A WORLD BANK COUNTRY STUDY

Poland

Policies for Growth with Equity

The World Bank
Washington, D.C.

2-1-95

World Bank Country Studies are among the many reports originally prepared for internal use as part of the continuing analysis by the Bank of the economic and related conditions of its developing member countries and of its dialogues with the governments. Some of the reports are published in this series with the least possible delay for the use of governments and the academic, business and financial, and development communities. The typescript of this paper therefore has not been prepared in accordance with the procedures appropriate to formal printed texts, and the World Bank accepts no responsibility for errors. Some sources cited in this paper may be informal documents that are not readily available.

The World Bank does not guarantee the accuracy of the data included in this publication and accepts no responsibility whatsoever for any consequence of their use. The boundaries, colors, denominations, and other information shown on any map in this volume do not imply on the part of the World Bank Group any judgment on the legal status of any territory or the endorsement or acceptance of such boundaries.

The complete backlist of publications from the World Bank is shown in the annual *Index of Publications*, which contains an alphabetical title list (with full ordering information) and indexes of subjects, authors, and countries and regions. The latest edition is available free of charge from the Distribution Unit, Office of the Publisher, The World Bank, 1818 H Street, N.W., Washington, D.C. 20433, U.S.A., or from Publications, The World Bank, 66, avenue d'Iéna, 75116 Paris, France.

ISSN: 0-0253-2123

Library of Congress Cataloging-in-Publication Data

Poland, policies for growth with equity.
p. cm. — (A World Bank country study, ISSN 0253-2123)
ISBN 0-8213-3158-2
1. Poland—Economic policy—1990- 2. Poland—Economic conditions—1990- 3. Economic stabilization—Poland.
I. International Bank for Reconstruction and Development.
II. Series
HC340.3.P64395 1994
338.9438— dc20 94-48162
CIP

CONTENTS

Figures

Tables

Boxes

ABSTRACT

This Country Economic Memorandum is based on the findings of an economic mission that visited Poland in February 1994. It provides an analysis of recent economic developments and a discussion of policy choices facing the country as it tries to capitalize on its recent good economic performance to reduce poverty and to move towards integration with the European Union.

The mission, led by Luca Barbone, included Christine Allison, Gerardo Corrochano, Jean-Jacques Dethier, Vincent Gouarné, James Hicks, Daniel Oks, Witold Orłowski, Alexander Preker and Jaime Vazquez-Caro. Contributions were also received from Henk Busz, Jinyong Cai, Christian Duvigneau, Yves Duvivier, Olivier Godron, Barbara Nunberg, and Margaret Thalwitz. The report benefited from the results of ongoing work sponsored by the Council of Ministers on central and local public investment decision-making, and from the recently-issued poverty assessment. Research assistance was provided by Mira Kuczyńska and Agnieszka Strzelec. The report was processed by Sahra Harbi.

The Department Director is Kemal Derviş, the Lead Economist is Christine Wallich and the Division Chief is Michel Noël. Alan Gelb was the peer reviewer.

CURRENCY AND EQUIVALENT UNITS

Currency Unit = Złoty (Zł)

	1989	1990	1991	1992	1993	Oct 1994
US$1 =	5565	9500	10583	13631	18145	23100

ACRONYMS AND ABBREVIATIONS

ARR	Agencja Rynku Rolnego (Agency for Agricultural Market)
BGZ	Bank Gospodarski Żywościowej (Bank for Food Economy)
CEE	Central and Eastern Europe
CEFTA	Central European Free Trade Agreement
CHP	Combined Heat and Power
CIT	Corporate Income Tax
CMEA	Council for Mutual Economic Assistance
CUP	Centraly Urząd Planowania (Central Office of Planning)
EBRD	European Bank for Reconstruction and Development
EBRP	Enterprise and Bank Restructuring Program
EFA	External Funding Agency
EFTA	European Free Trade Agreement
EIB	European Investment Bank
EU	European Union
FP	Fundusz Pracy (Labor Fund)
FUS	Fundusz Ubezpieczenia Społecznego (Fund for Social Protection)
GDP	Gross Domestic Product
GJ	Gigajoule
GNP	Gross National Product
GUS	Głowny Urząd Statystyczny (Central Statistical Office)
KRUS	Farmers' Pension Fund
LSGA	Local Self-Government Act
PGiG	Polskie Górnictwo Naftowe i Gozownictwo (Polish Oil and Gas Company)
RPI	Regional Privatization Initiative
SIR	Strategic Investment Review
SME	Small and Medium-size Enterprises
SOE	State-owned Enterprise
TOCB	Treasury-owned Commercial Bank
VAT	Value added tax

Fiscal Year
January - December 31

EXECUTIVE SUMMARY

At the end of the 1980s Poland took the lead among former socialist countries in rejecting the centrally planned system's attempts to introduce reform at the margin while keeping the old political and economic infrastructure in place. With rare determination, the new leaders engaged in radical economic and political reform, casting aside the 45-year legacy of an oppressive regime. Turning its back on the old eastward orientation, the new government aimed for membership in the European Union by the turn of the millennium — a watershed decision of political, economic, and cultural significance.

No one underestimated the daunting task the country had set for itself. Not only had Poland inherited an economy weakened by stagnation, inefficiencies, and distortions and incapable of change; but the very institutions so common in Western Europe and so necessary for a modern economy had to be invented from scratch in Poland. Throughout difficult years, Poland has shown a remarkable ability to stick to its vision, despite recession in the first two years and Europe's sometimes cautious attitude. Even the recent change in governing coalition, which some feared would mean a reversal of policies, has confirmed that the path to reform is irreversible. Economic success is beginning to reward this remarkable effort, and unification with the European family of nations in the not-so-distant future now seems increasingly likely.

Poland's positive economic performance in 1993 continues in 1994. Nearly written off as the new sick man of Europe — and further evidence that shock therapies do not work — the country is now in its third year of industrial recovery. Projected GDP growth of 4.5 percent for 1994 looks realistic and could even be bettered. Policies to sustain recovery and allow Poland to complete her transformation into a modern, market-oriented, democratic society must capitalize on the strengths of recent performance, and remedy emerging weaknesses. The strengths are impressive:

- The recovery is marked by strong growth of the private sector, which now accounts for more than a third of industrial activity and half or more of all GDP and employment.
- Productivity has increased substantially in the private sector and in many state enterprises.
- Progress has been made in reducing inflation and external reserves have improved.
- Unemployment appears to have peaked.

But weaknesses could undermine growth and stability:

- Recovery has been driven by strong growth of domestic demand, especially consumption. As a result, national savings have declined for the third year in a row. This trend cannot be sustained without hurting macroeconomic stability and competitiveness.
- A powerful group of large, mostly capital-intensive state-owned enterprises (employing perhaps 15 to 20 percent of the industrial labor force) is still postponing painful but needed adjustment measures. These enterprises represent a severe burden now and a policy dilemma for years to come. Their size and importance makes the resolution of their financial problems essential for Poland's long-term health.
- Social strains have emerged and intensified, driven by the perception of segments of society that the fruits of recovery have not been shared equitably. The consensus for reform is weakening.

How can policies build on the strengths of the recovery? The government's program emphasizes the right priorities: the importance of safeguarding macroeconomic stabilization, the reform of public finances, continued privatization and the reform of governance in state enterprises, and the development of financial markets.

Macroeconomic Stabilization

Stabilization has succeeded in the past two years largely because explosive tendencies in the 1991-92 fiscal accounts have been contained. Poland can take pride in this accomplishment, on which a stronger program of public finance reform can now be built. Public sector demands on credit have been kept within limits compatible with reduced inflation and a generally stable macroeconomic environment. Relatively moderate wage increases helped keep Polish exports competitive, thereby minimizing the European recession's effects on growth and on the current account. Stable real incomes (and increasing incomes for new private activities), together with a rebound in confidence and business expectations, have contributed to the pick-up in consumption and investment.

But there are reasons for concern:

- There is a risk of *slippage in fiscal reform*. The budget approved by Parliament in March 1994 projects a substantial increase in public sector demands on domestic credit and a return to gross dissaving. Although the deficit is slated to remain relatively low as a share of GDP, it will absorb more than 60 percent of credit, and should not be increased.
- Financial markets, and hence domestic credit, remain small in Poland, magnifying how public deficits crowd out credit to the productive sector. Interest rate policy should aim at continued financial deepening, but after the *interest rate reductions* by the National Bank of Poland in mid-1994 and the recent increases in inflation, real yields on złoty assets are low or negative. There is a risk that, if growth of real money demand halts or is reversed as a result of the low returns on domestic assets, as happened in 1993, either the fiscal accounts must contract further, or significant crowding out of the private sector would become inevitable, possibly with a further increase in inflation.
- Recent *wage developments* are disturbing. The void in wage control legislation has already resulted in several wage awards out of line with inflation objectives. Lack of wage discipline could quickly undermine confidence in macroeconomic objectives, and lead to strong pressures on the external accounts. An appropriate framework must be developed to bring policy and wage developments in line with projected growth in productivity.

Defusing short-term risks will require strong fiscal management and appropriate monetary policy. Cautious monetary and fiscal policies and greater wage discipline need not lead to a slowdown in the economy, even if growth of consumption were to slow down. With Western Europe now beginning to resume growth, Poland seems able to take advantage of increased external demand, which would lead toward more balanced growth. The government should renew its efforts to steer public opinion toward support of sustainable reform. Implementation of the agreements in the State Enterprise Pact would be a good basis for renewing consensus.

Achieving popular support for reform is important because in the medium term what Poland needs most for sustainable high growth is a commensurate increase in productive capacity. The resources now devoted to capital formation must be increased, even though growth may be faster in sectors of less capital intensity. The downward trend in national savings must be reversed, or at least halted. Public policy will be important not only *directly* to generate savings to finance public investment requirements, but *indirectly* to stimulate savings through appropriate tax policy, social security reform, and development of the financial market.

Investment prospects hinge as much on a turnaround in savings as on improved external capital flows. With completion of the second phase of the Paris Club debt reduction and of the agreement with the London Club, Poland no longer has arrears as a financing option; *paid* debt service will increase as a result of the debt settlements. Poland's challenge is now to gain more access to international private capital markets. Prospects are encouraging: Hungary, with a considerably smaller economy, attracts substantially higher private capital flows. Policies that safeguard economic stability, remove impediments to foreign direct investment, and eliminate uncertainty about property rights will help Poland get the external financing it needs for growth.

Policymakers face important tests. In other European nations that over the past decades joined the European Union, the real exchange rate appreciation that accompanied an increased inflow of capital caused a narrowing of per capita income differentials, but at the cost of high unemployment, as the economies were not flexible enough. This need not happen in Poland, if the reforms already begun are pursued with determination, so that productivity growth continues and offsets the effects on competitiveness of large capital inflows.

Public Sector Reform: Reducing the Size of the State

The government recognizes that fundamental reform of public finance beyond the emergency measures of the past years is essential for sustained growth. Poland's financial markets are too limited to finance large public deficits as well as provide enough credit to finance production growth. Net external financing of the budget deficit is expected to be minimal or negative in the next few years and the structure of foreign obligations will become inflexible when the debt reduction agreements are finalized, so financing for the budget deficit must come from domestic financial markets. In order not to further reduce real credit to the productive sector, public sector deficits in the second half of the 1990s must be contained to between 0.5 percent and 3 percent of GDP, with the 3 percent assuming strong growth in the demand for monetary aggregates.

Further increases in tax pressure may not be feasible and are not economically desirable. Even if tax revenues could be increased, it would not be in Poland's long-term interest for the state to continue to grow. The high-productivity, private sector-based growth that Poland should aim to achieve is probably incompatible with the public sector absorbing half of GDP, as it presently does. International data show that, on average, a 10-percent increase in public spending as a share of GDP is associated with a 1-percent reduction in the long-run growth rate of output. High priority must be given to cutting spending programs, to liberate resources for private sector development and to finance investments essential to economic change.

Broadening the Tax Base

Poland faces two challenges with respect to the modern tax system it has built: coping with the disappearance of tax revenues from state enterprises and other temporary sources of revenue; and strengthening tax administration, so the tax system is reliable and collects revenues from large sectors of the economy — especially the emerging private sector— that now escape the system.

Tax policy should emphasize broadening the tax base. Some measures connected with the 1994 budget move in this direction: a presumptive income tax was introduced to capture certain hard-to-tax sectors, thresholds were lowered to include more taxpayers in the tax system, and incentives were introduced to discourage the underreporting of investment expenditures and of profits and the overreporting of costs. There should now be a thorough reexamination of the rationale for tax exemptions — especially for the value-added tax — that reduce revenues and may be abused.

Policymakers must resist the temptation to increase revenues by hiking direct tax rates — that is, by extracting more revenues from those already caught in the tax net. The economic costs of punitive rates are well documented and the national savings would be especially ill-served by punitive taxes on savings, which are needed for investment. The proposal to bring marginal tax rates in the personal income tax back to their 1993 levels in 1995 is a step in the right direction.

Improving Tax Administration

The task of the Polish tax administration in the last four years has been arduous, but its continued reform and strengthening are essential. The initial honeymoon between taxpayers and authorities may come to an abrupt end if taxpayers detect administrative incapacity and become convinced that tax evasion gives them a competitive edge. Poor enforcement of compliance provides ammunition for those who argue for punitive taxation of the private sector, whose reputation for avoiding taxes has created resentment among complying taxpayers.

In developing a strategy for reforming tax administration, policymakers should focus on improving the *capacity to ensure compliance*. The next stage of tax reform should develop along four complementary lines:

- A *strategy for increased compliance* must encompass procedural rules, administrative functions, and the organizational changes needed to improve tax auditing. The administration should develop computer applications and become knowledgeable about key, hard-to-tax sectors.
- Increased *automation and computerization* should carry tax administration beyond mere collection activities, to expand capabilities for tax auditing and inspections.
- *Training* is needed to bring tax administration personnel up to date on operations and technical content and on dealing with day-to-day questions from, and problems posed by, taxpayers.
- Taxpayer services must be developed to improve outreach to taxpayers and thereby reinforce the legitimacy of the tax system, public confidence in which is essential.

Reforming Public Spending

Total government spending in Poland has remained roughly constant as a proportion of GDP (at somewhat less than half), but its structure has changed substantially with the economic transformation. The sharp decline in subsidies (especially to state enterprises) has been matched by an equally sharp increase in cash benefits to the population. These cash benefits include unemployment benefits and heavier pension outlays, as the state has absorbed most of the costs of the transformation.

These shifts in the composition of spending have not been painless. The reallocation of expenditures has taken place in a context of restraint, with continuous struggles for increased funding to programs or sectors. Ad hoc reactions to the crisis in Poland's public finances in 1991-92 must now be replaced by a more structured approach to spending reform. In the next few years, spending programs will be under pressure on many fronts:

- More resources will be needed to eliminate the quasi-fiscal deficits that linger in the enterprise and financial sectors, and to finance the social costs of restructuring. Tackling the sources of quasi-deficits is essential to the health of public finance.
- Payments on external and domestic debt will absorb proportionately more spending after debt restructuring, and given the increase in domestic debt servicing (for deficit financing and from absorbing the costs of bank recapitalization programs).
- More resources will be needed to modernize Poland's infrastructure, and to preserve and increase Poland's most valuable resource, her human capital.

A clash between demands on public resources and available financing is inevitable, unless reform goes deep, especially into social transfer programs.

Reforming Social Security

The growth of social security expenditures lies at the heart of Poland's fiscal problem. Excessive entitlements and a swelling in the ranks of pensioners (because of lax early-retirement policies) have enlarged the deficit of the main social funds. Based on current policies, spending for social funds will escalate beyond levels manageable on the emergency basis that has prevailed since 1990. The Government should move beyond the short-term fixes of the past few years to address the problems of Poland's pension system at their core. Immediate work must be done to eliminate provisions that undermine the financial viability of the current pension system and there should be a gradual move toward a multi-tier pension system. To make the pension system financially viable requires:

- Abolishing most remaining early retirement schemes.
- Revising the formula for determining individual pensions, with a view to reducing replacement rates.
- Moving back pensionable ages, and putting stricter limits on maximum benefits.
- Reducing pension benefits on an actuarial basis for early retirees, or if the retiree continues to work after becoming eligible for a pension.
- Changing the formulas for indexation to link pension increases to the consumer price index rather than to wage growth.
- Developing a better system for collecting contributions and eliminating arrears, and improving the administration of the Fund for Social Protection (FUS) and the Farmers' Pension Fund (KRUS).

A second set of measures, to be phased in over a longer period, would replace the current, defined-benefit system with:

- A first-tier pension scheme providing a fixed minimum social pension for all those eligible (financed from general revenues).
- A second pay-as-you-go tier providing earnings-related benefits, with strict caps.

- A fully-funded tier, based on individual savings retirement accounts, which would supplement the first two tiers and provide benefits proportional to the amounts contributed over the individual's working life.

These reforms could help strengthen public finances, develop capital markets, and provide new vehicles for private savings. Additional reform of the administration of, and entitlement to, other social benefits (sickness, maternity leave, and so on) — separating them from pension-related schemes — would also improve the use of public resources.

Strengthening the Social Safety Net

The economic transformation of the past four years entailed important social costs, manifested in increased poverty and unemployment. An adequate safety net to minimize the consequences of social dislocation must be a priority. Poverty[1] (defined as per capita spending below the minimum pension) affects some 14 percent of the population. Poverty is overrepresented among the long-term unemployed and families with more than four children. The poverty gap (the additional expenditures that would be needed to raise the poor above the poverty line) averages less than one-fifth of the minimum pension. Poverty is differentiated less by region than by socioeconomic group, but varies considerably between rural villages and large urban areas.

How can public policy directly address and reduce poverty? Most important, sustained growth will greatly reduce unemployment and poverty, especially in Poland, where poverty is "shallow" and there are no great socioeconomic differences between poor and nonpoor. Continuing reforms that have increased output in the past two years is the best way to alleviate poverty. But public policy should also directly address the problems of the poor through programs aimed at protecting the welfare of the most vulnerable groups. In theory, it should be possible to eliminate poverty by guaranteeing a "social minimum" to everybody. This would be inadvisable not only because of huge budgetary costs, but also because of the disincentive effects such a policy would generate. Many social programs already exist in Poland. The question is how to make them more effective by reducing "leakage" — resources spent on beneficiaries who are not poor — while preventing the emergence of adverse incentives or poverty traps.

One proposal is to improve targeting to families with many children (a proxy for poverty). Clearly targeting the family allowance to poor families would finance an increase in the family allowance for large, poor families (doubling the amount per child), a system of day-care coupons, and a school lunch program for poor children. The resources to fund benefit increases would also come from limits in entitlements. Families would be entitled to allowances only if their income were to fall below a certain threshold — say, 50 percent of the average wage. Simulations based on the current structure of income and expenditures indicate that this package could result in budgetary savings (of some 0.4 percent of GDP), while reducing the incidence of poverty by 3.3 percent of total population, or *one quarter of all currently poor.* Other, more aggressive, alternatives may be conceived, with higher budgetary costs and greater impact on poverty. The choice between cost and poverty reduction must be part of a national consensus on priorities, subject to the reality of budget constraints.

---

1 See "Poverty in Poland", World Bank report n. 13051-POL, September 1994.

Improving the Management of Public Investment

Capital expenditures have been compressed in the transition, because of the need for budgetary savings as social expenditures rapidly overtook revenues. But the changing role of the state has exerted as much pressure for change as budgetary stringency. Areas in which, under communism, it was natural for the state to direct investment and thus contribute public funds, are now part of the private sector. Even where the public sector still plays an important role, it is seeking partnerships with the private sector in the funding and the operation of investment projects.

Two tasks are essential to the reform of public investment:

- Resources must be used efficiently. This is presently not the case, largely because of an inadequate management system for public investment, which results in too many underfunded projects.
- Public policy must continually redefine the role of the state, and delegate to the private sector in whole or in part responsibility for the investments that were once traditionally considered part of the public domain.

To strengthen management of the public investment program (PIP), building on the impressive achievements of the past few years, the following should be priorities:

- Setting medium-term resource ceilings under which budgetary units would frame their investment objectives.
- Establishing a process for review and rationalization of sectoral investment programs, assigning greater strategic emphasis to higher levels of government.
- Introducing procedures for identifying, preparing, appraising, and screening new projects.
- Strengthening the database on PIP projects.

Given the unmanageable number of underfunded projects now supported by the public investment program, sectoral reviews should be undertaken in 1994 and 1995 with the objective of refocusing public investment on high priority areas, matching the portfolio of investment projects to available financing, and regrouping site-specific investments into major projects and subsectoral programs.

There is an urgent need to clarify the institutional framework for PIP coordination and management among central economic management agencies. We recommend locating management either within a restructured and strengthened Central Office of Planning or under a separate unit established within Ministry of Finance.

Even with better management of the public investment program, it would be impossible to meet all of Poland's public investment needs from budgetary resources alone. Modernizing and upgrading key infrastructure sectors such as energy, roads, ports, telecommunications, and water supply and sewerage will cost tens of billions of U.S. dollars. And a backlog of investment in social infrastructure areas must be accommodated. Budgetary resources will not meet all these needs, so it is essential to leverage public resources with far more private investment flows. There are several options for organizing and financing the provision of infrastructure services, ranging from total government ownership and control to total privatization. In between are various forms of public/private partnership, including contracting out, management contracts, and various types of private concessions.

To attract private sector participation, however, institutional arrangements must be devised that release operators from unnecessary, burdensome controls and regulations. At the same time, the interests of end users must be protected. Activities where competition is possible should be clearly separated from those calling for monopoly privileges. Appropriate tariff, interconnection, and distribution regulatory systems should be established, service goals clarified, and cost containment targets and incentives developed. A regulatory capability must be created or reinforced to oversee concessions and to ensure that concessionaires fulfill their obligations.

Stimulating the Supply Response

Much of the progress in the supply response observed over the last two years is attributable to expansion of the private sector. The government's program of reform continues to assign high priority to facilitating the growth of private sector initiatives. This is to be done by continuing to improve the legal and regulatory framework and to privatize state enterprise assets and by reforming the financial sector. Among problems that must be addressed:

- Privatization has proceeded more slowly than desired; it needs a decisive push forward, to prevent stalling.
- A number of loss-making enterprises, which have not been dealt with in the commercial bank recapitalization exercise, continue to operate in a void, increasing the potential costs of their work-outs, and creating negative demonstration effects.
- Although considerable progress has been made in financial sector reform, potential losses in the specialized banks are great and, unless problems are confronted decisively, may result in substantial budgetary costs and threaten the stability of the financial sector.

Privatization

Despite significant progress in the privatization of state enterprises, unless decisive steps are taken, Poland's privatization program may be completed later than those elsewhere in the region. Improving existing approaches will not be sufficient. It is time for Poland to update her privatization strategy comprehensively, with a time-bound plan encompassing all remaining enterprises. The momentum for launching this plan may well come from the long-awaited implementation of the mass privatization program (MPP). In parallel with its execution, the government should:

- Clearly define criteria under which the state will maintain ownership in a number of enterprises for a longer period.
- Set up a program, with dated objectives by category and type of enterprise, through which all other state enterprises should be privatized or — in the case of nonviable enterprises — liquidated, with their assets made available for transfer to private owners. This was the strategy espoused in the state-owned enterprises pact, and it is still valid.

The multi-track approach followed so far is flexible enough to remain the main plan for a significantly strengthened privatization effort, provided individual "tracks" are adjusted as needed:

- The *liquidation privatization* approach now has a track record: it could be applied to many small and medium-size state enterprises, which would appeal to investors. The cash constraints and under-capitalization that often weaken employee buyouts could be alleviated through a variety of schemes. The availability of *post-privatization restructuring assistance* could significantly encourage investors.

- Less attractive state enterprises (with reasonable prospects for turnaround after managerial or other defensive restructuring) that fail to attract investors, could be handled through management contracts with options to purchase within a specified time-frame, following up on the experience gained in the first *restructuring privatization* experiences.
- *Debt-equity swaps* in the framework of external debt reduction would provide another tool to encourage risk-taking and investment in complex enterprise restructuring.
- As the mass privatization program is being implemented and its benefits appreciated by enterprises and individual investors, the Ministry of Privatization should organize *additional waves of mass privatization*, with different characteristics. Some could focus, for example, on medium-size enterprises and others on public utilities.
- *Capital privatization* has been quite successful, but its effectiveness has been hampered by waning political support and excessive turnover of competent personnel in the Ministry of Privatization. Correcting these shortcomings would give new impetus to this important track.

Adopting an ambitious, definitive privatization program will require popular support. Poland now has enough experience with privatized enterprises and foreign investment to know first-hand the net benefits of privatization. Comprehensive post-privatization analysis should be carried out under the auspices of the Ministry of Privatization and its results widely communicated through a systematic public relations campaign. Similarly, a campaign for foreign investors could be targeted at persuading medium-size companies to invest in small and medium-size Polish enterprises, the economic sector that generates the most growth and employment worldwide.

Dealing with Loss-Makers

Loss-making state enterprises that have postponed adjustment account for perhaps 15 percent of industrial employment. They are concentrated in large capital intensive factories which have lost their economic viability after the dissolution of the old system as well as coal mining and the railways. Government strategy for this group has come slowly and problems have compounded. In three large sectors (coal, steel, and the railways) restructuring plans include substantial downsizing, coupled with aid to displaced workers for severance, retraining, and relocation. There has been substantial progress, but key decisions must be made. The focus should shift now to finding appropriate vehicles to cushion the social impact of restructuring so that cumulative losses are gradually brought under control.

A number of state enterprises in a precarious financial situation do not necessarily belong to sectors in crisis but have been put in bankruptcy by banks or other creditors for a variety of reasons. The Treasury and ZUS (the main pension fund) are now the main creditors for most of these enterprises, as they have substantial tax arrears. The government intends to take the lead in a bankruptcy-like procedure for these enterprises, along the lines the Enterprise and Bank Restructuring Program is now executing. Through its Treasury Chambers, the government will negotiate plans with individual enterprises to enable them to become current in their tax obligations, and eventually to repay arrears. One of the schemes being put forward is to convert outstanding obligations into convertible bonds, which would be called at the moment of privatization. This strategy of restructuring is worth supporting, provided certain principles are maintained:

- Restructuring plans, including commercialization of the enterprise before sale of its assets, should be time-bound. No new investments should be made before privatization.
- Enterprises unable to come up with an acceptable plan, or unable to enter any of the privatization tracks after a certain period, would automatically enter a streamlined liquidation program.

Reforming the Financial Sector

Financial sector reform is crucial to Poland's becoming a market economy. Reallocating real resources is virtually impossible without credit. Efforts to bring financial discipline and a hard budget constraint to the state enterprises are pointless if financial markets are not developed. The government's strategy has been to bring competition and private sector activity to the financial markets; to strengthen both the central bank and the nine Treasury-owned banks that resulted from the break-up of the old monobank at the end of the 1980s; to create a framework for resolving portfolio problems inherited from the past; and to establish the regulatory and institutional framework for a securities market.

The main constraints on developing financial intermediation and increasing credit to the productive sectors are the high rate of inflation, low demand for domestic-denominated monetary aggregates n relation to GDP, and the government's heavy borrowing requirements. Macroeconomic stabilization and public finance reform are essential to the reform of the financial sector.

The problems inherited from the past have required active government involvement. The program to recapitalize the Treasury-owned commercial banks started well. Most of the bad loans identified have been assigned to one of the avenues spelled out in the Enterprise and Bank Reconciliation Procedures Law, and the commercial banks have shown progress in internal restructuring. But several problems need tackling:

- Portfolio problems in much of the banking sector (private and public) have recently intensified, particularly in the specialized banks, despite some progress in restructuring and privatizing the commercial banks. The agricultural credit system is in a state of crisis, and substantial budgetary support may be required to restructure BGZ (the Bank for the Food Economy) and some of the cooperative banks. Several private banks have also required intervention from the National Bank of Poland.
- The strategy for privatizing the remaining commercial banks must be reaffirmed, avoiding unnecessary delays.
- The legal framework, particularly for executing loan collateral, needs upgrading to permit lending to creditworthy private borrowers.

The government realizes how serious these problems are and is continuing to work on its program. In dealing with BGZ and the cooperative banks, the government should recognize existing losses in BGZ and in the troubled cooperative banks; reorganize BGZ, by substantially redefining its activities and its relationship with the cooperative banks; create affiliation or other arrangements that would allow effective supervision of the many already independent cooperative banks. A well-designed work-out is urgently needed, as the losses incurred by BGZ and some of the cooperatives are large and growing. Inaction could undermine confidence in banking.

Reform of the other specialized banks should also be accelerated. Bank Handlowy, whose position in trade finance is shrinking, should diversify into domestic operations and develop or preferably acquire a branch network, in preparation for its privatization. One option worth exploring further would be to merge with PKO SA, which collects most foreign-exchange deposits. As for PKO BP (the savings and mortgage bank), there may be no immediate solution to problems with outstanding housing loans, but one option is to spin off the commercial loan portfolio, and part of the large branch network, into a new entity that would be capitalized by the Treasury and later privatized.

The government program of continued privatization of Treasury-owned commercial banks should be pursued as rapidly as possible with the aim of reaching an ownership structure conducive to effective governance — either through strategic bank investors or a core of stable investors. Selected Treasury-owned commercial banks should be encouraged or directed to merge, preferably with privatized banks taking over public ones.

The problem of the smaller private banks should be addressed on two fronts. First, the deposit insurance scheme under preparation should be implemented to allow the smooth liquidation of some private banks and to level the playing field for the others. At the same time, private banks need both to strengthen their capital base and to reach a critical mass. The National Bank of Poland could devise an attractive package of financial and regulatory incentives to attract private and foreign capital to this market and increase competition.

The first priority in improving the supervisory and regulatory framework is to gather the technical and financial means to enhance central bank capabilities for resolving bank failures. This means finalizing the deposit insurance scheme, making broader use of available technical assistance, and devising financial or regulatory incentives for domestic or outside investors to take over troubled banks. Second, while maintaining the orthodox regulatory stance of the past two years, the current regulations should be better phased in, so private banks have a credible incentive to build up their capital base. Third, bank supervision must be strengthened more quickly by decentralizing the central bank's regional agencies and delegating supervision of the cooperative banks to their regional or national leadership.

To improve the legal environment for lending to nongovernment entities, the government could finalize the draft collateral law and submit it to Parliament. Under that law, new instruments of collateralization would be introduced, such as floating charges; mandatory registration would prevent conflicts between creditors; and there would be procedures for direct foreclosure in case of default.

Sectoral Reforms

Reforming the Energy Sector

To make the energy sector more competitive and viable, the government strategy has been to narrow the gap between tariffs and economic costs and to restructure the sector to introduce more competition and allow — even encourage — private sector participation. Under a comprehensive restructuring program, most subsectors (except gas) have been demonopolized and restructured and many state enterprises have been commercialized. The levels and structure of energy prices (extremely low in 1989) have been greatly adjusted. The direct subsidy to households for district heating is expected to be phased out by the end of 1994.

Energy price adjustments and the elimination of subsidies have been impressive, but further steps must be taken to bring energy prices up to their economic levels. Network fuel prices average about 60 percent of economic levels, but individual fuels range from 45 percent to 91 percent of economic levels, depending on tariff category. The government is fully aware of the need to raise prices but must reconcile that objective with the need to reduce measured inflation and protect the vulnerable. It is now developing a long-term strategy for the energy sector, including a program of price adjustments. Bridging the gap to economic prices in a reasonable period is the only way to attract the resources needed (foreign or domestic) to upgrade infrastructure and move toward meeting environmental standards. Effective protection of poor households can be provided through differentiated tariffs, coupons, or other targeted compensation schemes. The government is considering a draft Energy Law, which would provide for an appropriate regulatory framework; completing its preparation should be given a high priority.

Reforming Agricultural Policies

Like the rest of the economy, agriculture changed drastically in the 1990s. The previous regime supported heavy subsidies for food, exports, and imports, as well as low-interest credit combined with guaranteed farm prices; some 10 percent of GDP was allocated to subsidies for agriculture. Reform has reduced this tenfold, to about 1 percent of GDP, setting the stage for major restructuring, and leading to price signals for farmers that are not generally distorted.

After a period of essentially hands-off policies *vis-á-vis* the sector, in the past three years successive governments have shifted toward more active intervention, both in tariff policy and in domestic price stabilization. The major objectives of policies have been alleviation of rural poverty by increasing farmers' incomes and reducing price fluctuations, and the promotion of modernization of agro-industrial sectors as well as reform and divestiture of state farms. It should be stressed that, overall, relatively few budgetary resources have been allocated to the pursuit of these objectives: in a macroeconomic sense, the negative effects of distortive policies in the sector is bound to have been limited, particularly if compared to the situation in the neighboring European Union.

Nevertheless, it should also be recognized that the results of government policies have been mixed, with unintended effects and unforeseen economic and social costs. Repeated increases in tariff protection for different products have resulted in distorted rates of effective protection and increased costs to consumers. The introduction of a variable levy system, which is bound to be dismantled in 1995 under GATT rules, has been cited as one of the causes of high growth of prices for certain commodities during 1994. It also signals the intention to attempt to impose prices above international levels rather than counter the negative effects of cyclical price fluctuations that are typical for a number of agricultural commodities. These contradictory signals, coupled with inaction that has left a number of money-losing agroprocessing plants operating, have impeded progress on privatization and on establishing competitive conditions in a number of agro-processing sub-sectors (grains, dairy, sugar, tobacco, etc.) which are still largely in state hands.

A series of actions should thus be considered to re-focus agricultural policies in ways that will further stimulate change while taking into account the social dimensions of rural restructuring, rather than attempting to maintain a status quo that will not solve existing problems. More specifically, the government should consider to:

- Adhere to its intentions to phase-out variable levies and replace them with tariffs bound under the GATT framework.
- Mitigate the social costs of adjustment for specific social groups through social policies (such as pensions for retiring farmers, social assistance, regional infrastructural initiatives) rather than agricultural policies that distort prices.
- Develop the physical and social infrastructure needed for growth, especially in regions where there is heavy rural unemployment.
- Take decisive action to solve sectoral uncertainties and adopt sectoral policies (in sugar, tobacco, grains, etc.) that will foster competition and lead to rapid privatization.

Reducing rural poverty. Many of the poor live in villages and small cities. Rural poverty accounts for a disproportionate 60 percent of poverty, (the rural population is only 38.9 percent of the whole). Interestingly, rural poverty is not necessarily *agricultural* poverty. Far too many farmers are poor, but fewer than half of the rural poor are farmers or farm workers. That poverty is overrepresented for nonfarmers in rural areas indicates a lack of economic opportunities, which adds another dimension to the adjustment in agriculture. Modernizing the sector will reduce the agricultural labor force. Avoiding more poverty in rural areas means finding alternative employment for the workers and farmers leaving the sector. It means developing infrastructure, trade, and services, and eliminating impediments to regional mobility, especially rigidity in the housing market. Demographic trends will influence agricultural modernization and rural revival — which in Western Europe has taken several generations — but well-designed, well-implemented policies can accelerate change.

Conclusions

Poland's recent achievements are truly remarkable. Despite many problems and difficulties, the current recovery and enormous social changes (especially evident to observers returning to Poland after a few years' absence) show that the basic promise of the *big bang* strategy is being fulfilled. Courage in implementing painful measures upfront is being rewarded with growth and increased welfare. The lessons are clear for other countries in the region that are still struggling with indecision about the basic direction of reform.

But Poland cannot afford to be complacent; economic policies and institutions must be constantly updated to meet emerging challenges. The reform agenda is not yet complete, and complex policy issues must be solved. Sustainability of growth over the medium-term will ultimately depend on the success in the implementation of major reforms in public finances and in the enterprise and banking sectors. Consensus for reform must be constantly reaffirmed. If these important tests are met, however, the country should be a credible candidate for full membership in the European Union in the next decade. The government is well aware of these challenges. This document is intended to provide support and constructive criticism to strengthen the course of reform.

CHAPTER 1: BUILDING ON THE STRENGTHS OF THE RECOVERY

An encouraging development has taken place in central Europe. Poland, the first country in the old socialist bloc to undertake radical political and economic transformation, has begun to show positive economic results. Nearly written off as the new sick man of Europe — and as evidence that shock therapies do not work — Poland has enjoyed eleven quarters of industrial recovery after the trough of the recession in late 1991. This translated into modest growth in 1992 and estimated GDP growth for 1993 of 3.8 percent. Recovery has been accompanied by a slow decline in inflation, to 35 percent in 1993 (table 1.1). Hyperinflation and stagnation seemed only too possible two years ago but that threat seems to have disappeared. Poland is viewed increasingly as an emerging market: Foreign investors' interest is strong, and full integration into the European Union in the not-so-distant future looks increasingly realistic. Most observers agree, however, that Poland still has a considerable socioeconomic agenda to complete. The impressive reforms begun in 1990 are still being implemented, new needs and priorities have emerged, and doubts have been voiced about the quality and sustainability of recovery.

Table 1.1: Four Years of Reforms - Main Economic Indicators

	1990	1991	1992	1993
GDP growth rate	-11.9	-7.6	1.5	3.8
Private Cons. per capita growth	-16.3	6.5	5.3	5.4
Index, 1989=100	83.7	89.1	93.8	98.9
Exports (US$billion)	10.9	12.8	14.0	13.6
Imports (US$billion)	8.6	12.7	13.5	15.9
Current Account Balance (US$billion)	0.6	-0.8	-0.3	-2.3
(percent of GDP)	1.0	-1.0	-0.3	-2.6
Change in Intnl. Reserves (US$billion)	-4.4	-1.3	-1.6	-0.6
Inflation (Consumer Prices)	585.8	70.3	43.0	35.3
Inflation (Producer Prices)	622.4	48.1	28.5	31.9
Real Exchange Rate, PPI (1989=100)	81.9	106.5	97.9	102.2
Unit Labor Cost US$ (1989=100)	81.3	107.2	102.5	99.0
Real Wage Index (1989=100)	75.6	75.3	73.3	72.3

Source: GUS; World Bank estimates.

This chapter provides an overview of the main economic issues Poland faces. The three main messages of this report, in a nutshell, are as follows:

- The prospects for output growth are good, but recent developments, particularly on the inflation and wage front, are worrisome. With the inflation rate for 1994 likely to overshoot its target by a few percentage points, restraint in wage behavior becomes all the more important. Continued excessive wage awards could fuel inflation and undermine the strong external performance. To avoid this trap, macroeconomic policies should remain cautious. As wage controls expire, they should be replaced by convincing arrangements aimed at moderation in wage demands. Efforts should be made to achieve social consensus on economic stability and on public finance reform as the key to sharing in the fruits of growth.

- In the medium term, Poland's external financing from private sources can be expected to grow, perhaps even considerably. But sustained recovery requires reversing the downward trend in national savings, so necessary for funding investment. The growth in consumption that fueled recovery from the 1990-91 recession should give way to a more balanced growth path.

- Medium-term policies to shore up recovery and encourage savings and investment must emphasize, above all, the reform of public finance, especially of social spending.

Strengths and Weaknesses of Recovery

What went wrong in the 1990-91 recession, and why is Poland growing now? There is no consensus on *all* the reasons for the contraction in output in the first two years of the transition. Most agree, however, that disappointing performance was attributable largely to two economic shocks experienced in 1990 and 1991.[1] The first was the shock therapy applied to break hyperinflation and rid the economy of distortions inherited from the socialist system. The sharp reduction in real wages that followed price liberalization and the abolition of subsidies led to a sharp contraction in domestic demand, and the collapse of consumption and investment by state-owned enterprises (SOEs). The external balance, on the other hand, improved as the reorientation of trade toward the West began in earnest. By contrast, as a result of the second shock — the dissolution of the CMEA in 1991 — the economy suffered on the external side. The CMEA collapse left many state enterprises with no market for their products. Investment continued to decline as state enterprises, unable to improve their financial position,

Figure 1.1 - GDP Growth and Savings

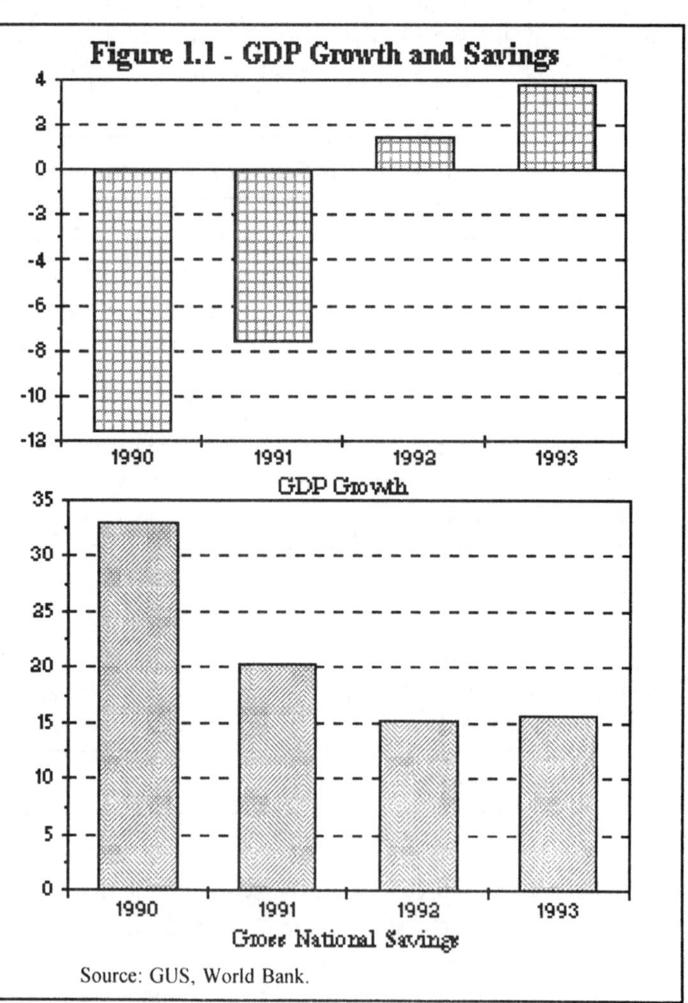

Source: GUS, World Bank.

[1] Part of the reason facts are disputed is the relatively backward state of Polish national account statistics. Even with recent advances, substantial discrepancies occur between different sources (particularly trade data), so any interpretation of facts is subject to wide margins of error.

adopted a defensive attitude. Despite the expansion of exports to Europe and a rebound in consumption, output continued to fall, for a two-year decline of almost 20 percent.

Once it absorbed the CMEA shock, the economy responded positively to the changed environment. Initially, expanded exports to Europe spurred growth. Soon, however, recovery was driven largely by *increasing domestic demand*, particularly consumption. External trade stimulated growth in late 1991 and the first half of 1992, but the European recession dampened (recorded) export growth, especially from mid-1992 to mid-1993. Exports of goods and services declined an estimated 4 percent in 1993.

Poland's relatively large domestic market (domestic demand accounts for some 86 percent of supply) allowed it to expand GDP without unsustainable consequences on the external accounts. Consumption — private and public — fed the rebound of 1991, rising a strong 5 to 6 percent in 1992-93, despite slow or no growth in real incomes for some parts of the population (reported real wages and pensions declined somewhat in 1992 and 1993). As 1994 began, private per capita consumption, measured in constant prices, was almost back at late 1980s levels. (In 1992 and 1993, substantial unrecorded exports — an estimated 1.5 percent of GDP in 1993 — may have occurred, producing an overestimate of consumption growth.)

Growth of investment in fixed capital also turned positive, driven largely by private sector activity, although the extent of its rebound is debated.[2] Trade statistics show investment in machinery and equipment to have been especially strong, indicating that expanding sectors are re-tooling to meet higher demand. Housing construction (as captured by official statistics, which may substantially underestimate individual activity) has continued to decline. Overall, investment is substantially below 1980s levels, as a percentage of GDP. To some extent, the high investment ratios of the old regime reflected inefficient use of capital resources and the distorted price of capital goods. Still, resources devoted to investment, even allowing for underreporting to evade taxes, appear lower than in countries that have experienced prolonged economic growth.

Increased real consumption, together with substantial price changes for consumption goods, were mirrored by a marked decline in national savings, from exceptionally high levels before the transition. At current prices, national savings as a proportion of national product may have declined one-fourth between 1991 and 1993 (from about 20 percent to about 15 percent). The decline is equally noticeable at constant prices (from 23.8 to 19.5 percent of GNP).

In 1993, as domestic demand outpaced supply, the external accounts deteriorated. The current account (on a recorded BOP basis) worsened by some US$2 billion between 1992 and 1993, or the equivalent of 2.3 percent of GDP (allow again for statistical uncertainty). However, net international reserves continued to *rise* in 1993. Possibly exports along the German border were underreported, by as much as US$1.2 billion net. (The number of visits German citizens make to Poland has grown to over 30 million a year and most visits are very short.)

The Private Sector Responds

During the recession of 1990-91, most performance indicators for state-owned enterprises deteriorated. The private sector seized opportunities for trading and profit early in the transition, but the state

---

2 Preliminary GUS statistics point to 6-percent growth in capital formation in 1992, and only a moderate increase in 1993 — although other indications (including trade data) suggest strong investment growth, particularly among small and medium-size enterprises. Tax-evading behavior may explain conflicting data; there is ample anecdotal evidence that enterprises have been charging the acquisition of investment goods to current costs to defray tax payments. As a result, both investment and GDP are probably underestimated for 1993. A polite guess would put investment growth at 6 to 8 percent, and GDP growth at 4.5 to 5 percent in 1993.

enterprises adjusted slowly, sowing the seeds of a crisis that would reach commercial bank portfolios. In 1991, some sectors fared better than average, reflecting the CMEA-induced nature of the shock. As the recession ended, the recovery became more broad-based. Important gains in productivity were registered across sectors, with few (but significant) exceptions. Substantial downsizing of manpower occurred in all sectors of the economy, even in 1993.

From the start, the recovery was led largely by strong growth in the private sector. Private sector activity as a share of GDP continues to increase, standing now at more than one-third in industry and three-fourths in construction. The private sector, which began with mostly trade-related, quick-return activities, is now firmly established in most sectors and accounts for most investment. Although it is still mainly in small- and medium-size enterprises, some relatively large firms have also been privatized. Despite statistical uncertainties, the private sector has been considerably more productive than the state enterprises (table 1.2). Continued low profits in the private sector are puzzling, but may merely reflect profit-hiding to avoid taxes.

Table 1.2: Indicators of Supply Response, 1990-93
(In Percent)

	1990	1991	1992	1993
Industrial output growth	-24.2	-11.9	3.9	6.2
SOEs	..	-19.4	-3.3	-6.5
Private sector	..	25.2	23.4	34.6
Productivity growth	-19.7	-4.2	13.7	11.3
SOEs	..	-4.2	10.0	4.6
Private sector	..	14.0	26.4	27.7
Profits/sales		6.2	2.2	6.4
State enterprises	..	6.4	3.1	6.8
Private sector	..	0.1	0.0	5.1
Gross losses/GDP	..	5.6	6.5	4.9
State enterprises	..	4.5	4.9	3.5
Private sector		1.1	1.6	1.4

Note: Private sector growth includes also the effect of the privatization if state enterprises.
Source: GUS and World Bank estimates.

The weaker *output* performance of public enterprises is partly attributable to privatization, which now accounts for 15 percent of manufacturing production: part of the state enterprises sector (and its output) have been reclassified as private. But the slower supply response of state enterprises is not simply a statistical phenomenon: it reflects a real, continued burden on society. As the recession ended, two patterns of enterprise behavior emerged. Many state enterprises were able to restructure their operations and to adapt, to some extent, to the new market conditions. Their improved performance was a reaction to the generally tougher credit market after bank restructuring began in 1992, and to the credible end of direct government subsidies. Those enterprises are now the best candidates for privatization.

But a second, powerful group of large, mostly capital-intensive state enterprises (employing perhaps 15 to 20 percent of the industrial labor force) adopted a more defensive attitude. Using their political clout, those state enterprises — concentrated in steel, shipbuilding, transportation, and coal mining — have refused to carry out the painful adjustment needed. In 1993, the subsectors most beset by losses accounted for only 15 percent of sales, but a substantial 45 percent of losses (about 2.1 percent of GDP). With credit from the banking sector virtually halted, financing for their continued operations has come from the nonpayment of tax obligations combined with outright decapitalization (the selling off of assets and the spinning off of productive activities to joint ventures). The change-resistant enterprises represent a burden and a considerable policy dilemma for years to come. The size and importance of these enterprises makes the resolution of their financial problems, while difficult, essential for the long-term health of the country. (A solution is proposed in Chapter 3.)

The extent of industrial recovery and strong growth in the private sector are surprising in view of Poland's lack of credit. Credit to the productive sector decreased in real terms over 1992-93; working capital credit in particular fell 40 percent in real terms for all enterprises (and 25 percent for private enterprises) between end-1991 and end-1993. The industrial recovery appears to have been largely self-financed. The potential for growth and investment would be even greater if the right financing mechanisms were in place.

The Costs of the Economic Transformation

That the resumption of growth was uneven across regions and social sectors is not surprising; it is a sign of structural adjustment. But the social consequences of emerging inequalities must be addressed if reform is to have popular support.[3]

Figure 1.2: Unemployment Rate by Region (June 1994)

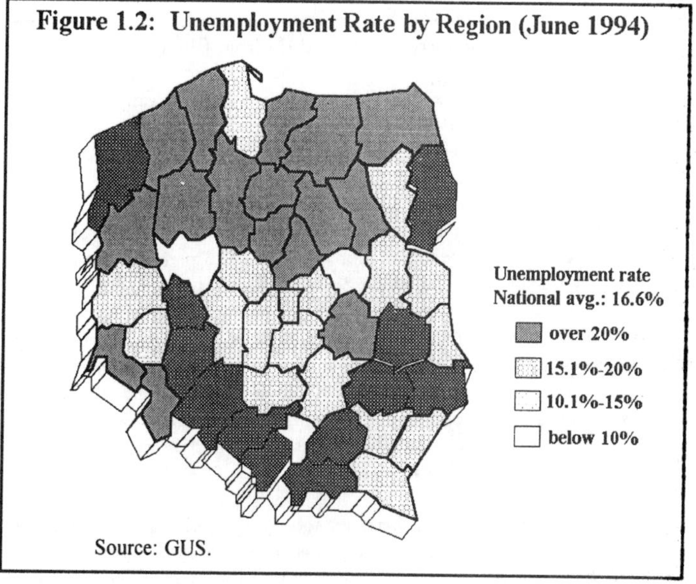

Source: GUS.

Unemployment has been higher in some regions than others. Unemployment grew rapidly in the two years of the recession, then at a much reduced pace, and recently it has stabilized (at about 16 percent of the labor force), as the economy has begun to generate more jobs than it sheds. Regional variations in unemployment (see figure. 1.2) reflect the decline of some highly concentrated industries. In certain regions, high unemployment rates have persisted, reflecting the emergence of pockets of structural unemployment. Growth has been slowest where traditional industry was strong and in some rural areas in north and north-central Poland. Restructuring in several large loss-making sectors is likely to increase the regional disparities in unemployment. Many of the problems encountered in Europe in the 1970s and 1980s are emerging with a vengeance in Poland, compounded by the immobility of the Polish labor force (because of the rigid housing market), and the disproportionate amount of aging industry.

However the poverty line is defined, in the past three years poverty has increased across the board in Poland as a result of the recession and rising unemployment. If the poverty line is defined as consumption of US$70 per month per equivalent adult (corresponding roughly to Poland's minimum pension), 5-6 million people (about one-seventh of the population) are poor. Most at risk are the long-term unemployed and children in large families, especially those in which the head of the family no longer work (box 1.1).

---

3 These issues are reviewed in detail in the recent World Bank report, "Poverty in Poland" (Report No. 13051-POL, June 1994).

Box 1.1: Poverty in Poland, 1993

Poverty is measured against the minimum pension and the minimum wage. In 1993, 14.4 percent of the population had expenditures (per equivalent adult) below the minimum pension, and 26.3 percent had expenditures below the minimum wage.

Poverty Profile

The highest and lowest incidence of poverty occurs in two new ***socioeconomic groups*** that have emerged in the transition: households whose main income source is social transfers other than pensions or whose main earnings come from casual work ("social income recipients") and "self-employed" households whose main earnings come from self-employment in the nonagricultural private sector. The transition has apparently widened the distribution of poverty, extending both ends of its distribution. The second lowest incidence of poverty occurs among pensioners and workers, of whom about 11 percent live below the minimum pension. For pensioners, this is a reversal of how things were before the transition, when they consistently had the highest incidences of poverty. For groups actively connected to the labor market, the most poverty is now recorded among farmers.

The ***regional variation*** in poverty incidence is less pronounced than the incidence across socioeconomic groups. The Warsaw region has the lowest poverty incidence, followed by the South. The highest poverty incidence is in the Southeast and Central-west, the two regions where 30 percent of the poor live. The absence of strong regional variation in poverty incidence is surprising because different regions in Poland have been affected very differently by the economic transition. This could be a testimony to the functioning of the safety net which, especially through unemployment benefits and pensions, has largely been able to compensate people for the costs of the transition and prevented many of them from falling into poverty.

Still, there is a ***spatial dimension*** to poverty. Its incidence is much higher in villages and in small cities. In large cities (of more than 200,000 inhabitants), only 5.5 percent of people live below the minimum pension. This percentage uniformly rises with smaller city size, and reaches 22 percent in villages. There is a similar pattern for the minimum wage.

Demographic characteristics are important indicators of poverty in Poland. Only 3.4 percent of childless couples fall below the minimum pension; many of these households are pensioners. The incidence of poverty rises steadily with the number of children. Among households with four or more children, 42.6 percent have an expenditure level per equivalent adult below the minimum pension, and 60.8 percent fall below the minimum wage.

One corollary of this is that ***poverty among children*** is high in Poland - one in five children lives in a household with an expenditure level below the minimum pension. By contrast, the ***poverty rate among elderly people*** (60 and older) is only 7.6 percent - one-half the national average. The strong correlation between poverty and the presence of children in the household makes the presence of children an important indicator for targeting social transfers. Currently, only the family allowance and maternity care are based on this criterion. The social safety net seems quite effective at protecting elderly people against poverty, so further old-age-based interventions do not seem warranted at this time.

There is a strong inverse link between ***poverty and education***. Where the head of household has only a vocational or elementary education, poverty incidence is twice as high as in households with more education. Almost two-thirds of the Polish population live in households where the head has only vocational or elementary education.

One remarkable feature of the poverty profile in Poland is the relatively low ***poverty gap*** and its even distribution across all socioeconomic groups, regions, and types of households. The average poverty gap is 22 percent of the minimum wage and 19 percent of the minimum pension and varies by no more than two to three percentage points regardless of classification. This indicates that no single group or region in Poland forms a pocket of deep poverty (at least at the level of aggregation considered in this study). The sole exception is the social income recipients who not only have the highest poverty incidence but whose poverty is also more severe than any other group.

Poverty and Unemployment

Unemployment is a major cause of poverty in Poland. The poverty rate among households in which there is at least one unemployed person is 27.8 percent - almost twice the national average. Over one-third of all poor live in households where there is an unemployed member. The link between poverty and unemployment is strongest in worker and pensioner households, and in social income recipient households, where 80 percent of poverty is linked to unemployment. But the regional structure of poverty has the most pronounced link with unemployment. In the five regions with the lowest poverty incidence, the structure of poverty is virtually the same, save for poverty due to unemployment. In the other four regions, differences in poverty among children and the elderly explain most of the differences in total poverty.

The best remedy both for high regional unemployment and for pockets of poverty is continued high growth as it would enable more people to return to jobs that allow them to escape poverty. The poor fall into "poverty traps" for a variety of reasons and restructuring in some economically depressed areas is likely to increase short-term unemployment, so it essential that policies to relieve extremes of poverty are carefully targeted and funded. (These policies are discussed in Chapter 2.)

Economic Policies in the Transition

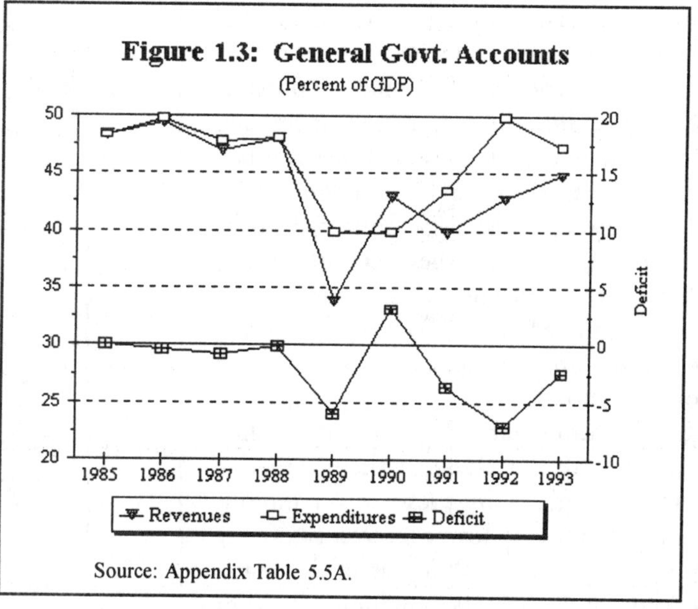

Source: Appendix Table 5.5A.

The 1992 Country Economic Memorandum called for fiscal responsibility and caution in the execution of economic policies. At a time when a fiscal stimulus package had been publicly declared to be the only way to restore growth, the Country Economic Memorandum pointed out the very limited scope for domestic financing of a substantially increased government deficit, and the serious possibility of a setback in stabilization should such an increase be contemplated. Considering the resistance to a policy of fiscal restraint, policy conduct has been remarkable. Not only did the deficit not increase, but the public sector accounts have been more or less brought under control, with a deficit of only 2.4 percent of GDP in 1993 (figure 1.3). Public savings have turned positive, partly offsetting the sharp drop in savings for the rest of the economy. The public sector has also reduced its demands on domestic credit. Fiscal consolidation has been the result of both declining expenditures and increased revenues. Expenditures declined in real terms (and as a percentage of GDP) partly because the treasury had difficulty getting financing from the banking sector at the interest rates it was offering in mid-1993[4]. Revenues were stronger than expected, reflecting both the strong economic growth, and the better-than-expected initial implementation of the value-added tax (VAT).

This fiscal progress was a key factor in Poland's success at stabilization, but that success may be ephemeral. Great strides have been made in tax reform, but important structural problems have been postponed rather than resolved. Many ad hoc taxes have been replaced by modern broad-based taxes, VAT was successfully implemented in July 1993, and Poland is closer to having a European tax structure. Many of the old state spending functions have been discontinued, but outlays under Poland's generous social programs have grown rapidly. The state has absorbed a disproportionate share of the cost of adjustment and of reductions in the labor force. Decisive reform must be brought to public finance both to prevent the exploding costs built into current programs and to improve the delivery and targeting of social services and transfers.

---

[4] Treasury bills are offered at a fixed price, with quantity adjusted to clear the market if demand is lower than supply.

The need to rein in the deficit is underscored by a look at behavior of monetary and credit aggregates and the problems created for the conduct of *monetary policy*. At 35 to 39 percent of GDP for broad money (including dollar-denominated deposits) and 25 to 29 percent for M2, Poland's monetary aggregates are relatively narrow compared to those of most industrial countries. After substantial real increases in broad money in 1991-92 — which paradoxically made possible declining inflation despite increasing government deficits — real broad money declined in 1993, and its composition shifted toward dollar-denominated deposits (figure 1.4). Under these circumstances, the risks to economic stability and growth are heightened by large public sector demands on financing. To expand domestic credit within limits compatible with inflation targets, monetary policy must squeeze out credit to the productive sector and maintain pressure on interest rates. Attempts to lower interest rates may cause the public to shift out of domestic-denominated assets, which further complicates monetary management.

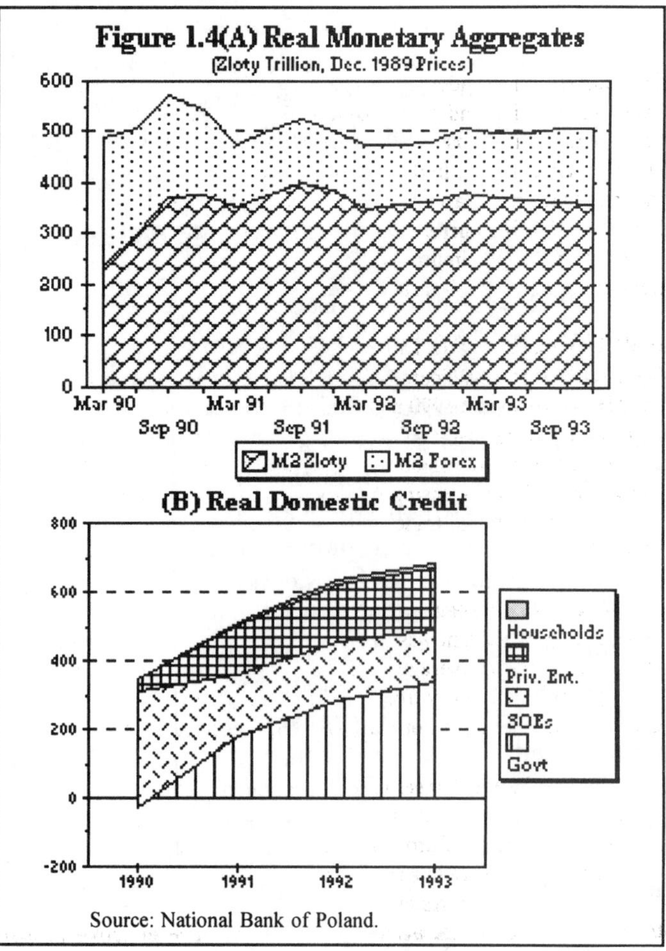

Source: National Bank of Poland.

This was what happened in 1993. Monetary policy was still being conducted in the framework of the crawling peg exchange rate policy implemented in 1991. The pace of the crawl and the expansion permitted in domestic credit have provided two nominal anchors for reducing inflation. After a step devaluation in July 1993, the crawl was reduced further to send a stronger anti-inflationary signal. Overall, policy was successfully executed, as shown by the slow but continued decline in inflation (except for the abnormal November-December 1993 price increases), gains in external reserves, and the continued competitiveness of Polish exports. But even though Poland maintains controls over capital transactions, a crawling-peg policy limits the central bank's ability to influence short-term interest rates, as the National Bank of Poland learned in 1993 when it tried to reduce interest rates. The public's reaction (particularly toward the middle of the year, when expectations of a step devaluation increased) was to shift out of złoty-denominated assets.[5] For the year as a whole, M3 declined 1.1 percent in real terms (deflated by CPI), and złoty money declined 6.4 percent. The real decline in credit to the productive sector was limited to 2.6 percent only because of the Treasury's unexpectedly low demand for credit, which reflected both a lower-than-expected deficit and the banks' reluctance to buy Treasury bills at the lower rates.

---

5 Of course, this was complicated by the emergence of the stock market as a possible alternative source of funds (see Chapter 3).

Box 1.2: Trade Policy

For almost four decades, more than half of Poland's foreign trade was with CMEA countries, on the basis of bilateral export-import lists and prices fixed by the governments. Foreign trade was administratively controlled and subordinated to a central plan. Most of this trade was cleared in transferable rubles and the former Soviet Union (FSU) was Poland's largest trade partner. In the 1980s, Poland implemented reform aimed at establishing closer links between domestic and international prices, a more realistic exchange rate, an allowance to keep part of foreign exchange earnings to finance imports, a foreign currency auction to importers, and relaxed conditions for issuing foreign trade licenses. Although export performance improved, the trading environment was still burdened by costly administrative procedures, limited freedom of entry, high tariffs and nontariff barriers (NTBs), and a non-convertible exchange rate.

1990 Unilateral Trade Liberalization. On January 1, 1990, Poland 's trade policy underwent radical changes. Domestic prices were liberalized and most tariff and NTBs were unilaterally eliminated or sharply reduced. The average tariff between August 1990 and August 1991 declined to 5.5 percent from 18.3 percent in early 1989. Import and export licensing was drastically reduced to cover relatively few products (mainly imports of cigarettes, alcohol, dairy products, natural gas, oil, and some sensitive products). The exchange rate was sharply devalued and the złoty declared convertible. Trade licensing was liberalized. As a result of these policy changes, Poland at the beginning of 1990 had one of the most liberal trade regimes in Europe according to GATT's 1992 Trade Policy Review. Exports boomed in 1990.

1991 Tariff Adjustments. After significant deterioration of the trade balance in the first half of 1991, a new, more restrictive, tariff system was introduced in August 1991. Suspended tariffs and NTBs were reimposed and many tariffs were increased; the average tariff rose from 5.5 percent in mid-1991 to 18.4 percent in 1992. The increase in tariffs accompanied a shift away from unilateral trade liberalization to bilateral negotiations for future mutual reductions in tariff and NTBs in the context of free trade agreements.

1992-93 Free Trade Agreements. Three major multilateral free trade agreements, covering from 70 to 75 percent of Poland's trade flows, were signed in 1991-93. By far, the most important was the European Association Agreement (EAA) signed with the European Union in late 1991 and made effective in March 1992. The main objective of the EAA was to create a free trade zone for industrial goods for a 10-year period. Other trade agreements signed in 1993 were aimed at creating free trade zones with EFTA and CEFTA countries (Hungary, Poland, and the Czech and Slovak Republics). The EFTA agreement, which became effective in November 1993, is similar to the EAA regulations, allowing for the liberalized trade of industrial goods and giving only limited concessions for food and sensitive sectors. The CEFTA agreement, implemented in April 1993, was also similar to the EAA. Initially, tariff reductions applied only to raw materials and finished goods not in direct competition with domestic products. Tariffs on other industrial goods will be reduced gradually.

Unfavorable external circumstances could make monetary policy more important in 1994 and beyond. The scope for further declines in interest rates is limited by the pace of fiscal adjustment. Attempts to prematurely reduce real returns on domestic instruments may prove counterproductive and ultimately contribute to greater instability and lower growth. NBP's May 15 decision to lower its two key refinancing and rediscount rates may have stretched to the limit its room for maneuver.

Wage policy was governed until March 1994 by a tax on excessive wage increases, or *popiwek* (PPWW). This policy of wage restraint, in place since 1989, replaced the former wage determination system and was to be the framework for introducing the free determination of wages within an enterprise. This legislation addressed the possibility that state enterprises might grant wage increases incompatible with controlling inflation and might decapitalize the enterprises, transferring as many assets as possible to workers (through higher wages) before privatization. Wage controls set ceilings on the total wage bill for an enterprise, allowed for only partial monthly indexation to inflation and adjustment (at a rate determined by the Council of Ministers), and relied on stiff tax penalties payable on excessive wage increases. The theory was that, by increasing the cost of excessive wage awards, the popiwek would give managers and workers an incentive for wage moderation. The policy has been modified several times in the last three years, and was increasingly questioned in 1993. Unions and workers argued that it should be replaced by a system of tripartite wage negotiations (involving unions, management, and the state). During negotiations between the Government and unions that led to the signing of the State Enterprises Pact in February 1993, it was agreed that the *popiwek* would be replaced by such a system. A law to replace the expiring *popiwek* was approved by Parliament in early 1994, but was vetoed by the president because, among other things, it would have empowered the executive to impose wage controls on private enterprises under certain circumstances. A new law, approved later, took only effect in August 1994. In the meanwhile, on several occasions state enterprises awarded large wage increases. This may have contributed to the apparent overshooting of the inflation target now likely for 1994.

Has the *popiwek* been an effective tool for fighting inflation and decapitalization? From 1990 to 1993, wage developments were broadly compatible with plans for inflation reduction. Nominal wage awards tended to follow the path prescribed by the wage law. After a sharp reduction at the beginning of 1990, *real* wages have fluctuated considerably. Deflated by the consumer price index, however, they have remained at roughly two-thirds of 1989 levels.[6] Deflated by the producer price index, real wages have by now returned almost to pre-transition levels. Increases in unit labor costs have been more moderate because of productivity gains in the past two years. Still, some firms chose to be taxed as "offenders" and awarded higher wages. In 1990-93, Zł 55 trillion was incurred in excess wage taxes. The "offenders" have been concentrated in certain sectors, and much of the Zł 16 trillion in outstanding arrears to the Treasury at end-1993 was from the firms with significant losses. For those firms at least, the tax-based wage control scheme is apparently not binding. It is too early to tell whether there has been a change in attitude, but substantial wage increases in late 1993 and in March 1994 suggest a relaxation of discipline in some enterprises. More worrisome, high wages were awarded in health sectors as well as loss-making sectors. Seasonal factors traditionally inflate wage growth in those months, but the real wage increases observed go beyond seasonal changes.

Positive developments affecting both demand and supply would not have been possible if Poland's incentive structure had not been improved by the reforms begun in 1990. Poland seems to have made more progress than other Central European countries in getting the private sector involved in production and in credibly tackling the immense problems in the banking sector. The "structural" package of the 1990 Economic Transformation Program included action on economic incentives (through the liberalization of prices and interest rates), on property rights (through privatization), and on the general economic environment (through trade liberalization, deregulation, and the establishment of a framework for private sector activity). By and large, progress has been continuous, though not without setbacks.

There have been signs of increasing disenchantment with some policies, however, the reasons for which must be understood if backtracking is to be avoided. Some of the criticism of reform policies reflects a legitimate concern for their social consequences (actual or perceived). The negotiations that led to the signing of the State Enterprises Pact in early 1993 addressed the concerns of workers opposed to accelerated privatization. All provisions in the pact (including the enterprises' compulsory declaration of a path to privatization) remain as valid today as they were a year ago. In

---

6 Real wage comparisons based on CPI deflation do not reflect the scarcity of consumer goods under the previous regime and thus overestimate how much the purchasing power of wages has fallen.

Box 1.3: The European Association Agreement (EAA)

Previous European Union Concessions. In the 1980s, Poland had most favored nation (MNF) status in the EU, meaning that Poland was subject to the same tariffs as EU imports from non-European industrial economies which, in turn, were considerably higher than those applied on imports from developing countries or European OECD countries. The Polish radical reform program fostered better treatment of Polish exports by the EU. In 1990, the EU granted GSP (General System of Preferences) status to Poland. This implied lower tariffs, the removal of specific quantitative restrictions, the suspension of nonspecific restrictions in 1990-91, the elimination of quantitative restrictions on steel and iron exports to EC countries (excluding Germany and Italy) and larger quotas for textile exports. Polish suppliers had considerable tariff preferences in the EC over exports from non-European OECD countries.

Objectives and Phase-in Period. The EAA aims to create a free trade zone over a 10 year transition period during which mainly industrial tariffs will be gradually eliminated. The EAA also covers various other areas including trade in agricultural goods and services, movement of factors, foreign investment regulations, competition policy, convergence of legislation and cooperation. The treaty was signed at the end of 1991, and the first tariff reductions came into effect in March, 1992 under an Interim Agreement. Implementation of the EAA was speeded up at the November, 1993 EU Copenhagen Summit.

Industrial Goods. Tariffs for about 50 percent of Polish exports of industrial goods were abolished; access for other goods was improved through tariff reductions of 15-50 percent, preferential ceilings and increased quotas. NTBs were maintained in the case of sensitive export goods (food, textiles, coal, and steel) but were eliminated otherwise. In turn, Poland has liberalized around 37 percent of industrial imports from the EU, and introduced a large duty-free quota for cars (30,000 the first year) which is increased (3,000) every year. Based on the "asymmetry" principle, Poland's trade concessions in the years 1992-94 were much smaller than EC concessions. Poland obtained a 3-year grace period: massive tariff reductions will not take place before 1995-96. Poland granted tariff and/or tariff and ceiling quota concessions on various industrial imports which were previously under NTBs. As a result of the Copenhagen Summit, beginning in January, 1995, all Polish industrial exports except steel (subject to duties) and textiles (subject to QRs and duties) will be granted free access to the EU. Full liberalization of market access for industrial products to the EU will be granted in March, 1997.

Agricultural Goods. There were few changes in agricultural tariffs. Some agricultural import quotas were removed or will be gradually liberalized under the recent Uruguay round of GATT. Growth of imported agricultural goods, though, cannot exceed 10 percent per year during the first five years of the EAA. Under the EAA, the average weighted tariff for processed and unprocessed agricultural products became 21 percent, making this sector the most protected. The EU lowered NTBs on imports of various agricultural goods originating in Poland.

Cross-border Services. The EAA calls for a progressive liberalization of cross-border services. However, with few exceptions, there are no specific time commitments. The parties will permit the temporary admission of persons offering the service, provided business is not solicited. In the case of maritime transportation, access to the market is unrestricted.

Foreign investment restrictions. Establishment of firms is to be granted in terms no less favorable than those established by nationals. However, permits are required for establishment in the following sectors: mining; armaments; pharmaceuticals; some chemicals; most services (particularly, financial services); acquisition of state-owned assets under privatization; ownership, deal, use, sale or rental of real estate; legal services; high voltage power lines; and pipeline transportation. Restrictions on these sectors will be lifted gradually, at the latest by the end of the ten-year transition period. Foreign direct investment is subject to relatively stringent rules of origin. Polish goods have to undergo "sufficient working or processing", meaning a non EU content requirement not exceeding 40 percent.

Regulatory framework. Poland is given three years to implement changes in its pro-competition legislation to make it compatible with existing EU legislation. More generally, Poland will, over the 10 year transition phase, approximate its laws to those prevailing in the EU in the following areas: customs law, company law, banking law, company accounts and taxes, intellectual property, protection of workers at the workplace, financial services, health, consumer protection, standards, transport, and the environment.

Safeguard Clauses. The EAA contains several important safeguard clauses which allow, at least temporarily, the contracting parties to step back from some of the concessions. Apart from sector-specific safeguards, there are two general safeguards. First, during the twelve months that follow the first stage of EAA (first five years), the Association Council will decide, based on performance under the first stage, whether the EAA will proceed to its second stage and, if so, which changes may be imposed. Second, administrative procedures can be started to interrupt trade flows, "where any product is being imported in such increased quantities and under such conditions as to cause or threaten to cause: i) serious injury to domestic producers of like or directly competitive products in one of the contracting parties, or ii) serious disturbances in any sector of the economy or difficulties which could bring about serious deterioration in the economic situation of a region.

some areas, however, setbacks in the implementation of policies may be the result of successful lobbying by special interest groups. The most worrisome of these is agricultural policy. Variable levies have been passed for certain key agricultural products, and restructuring in key agroindustrial sectors appears to be aimed at preserving the status quo. Some agricultural policies seem to arrest rather than favor the transformation of this important sector.

An Agenda for Growth

The key to Poland's successful stabilization has been its ability to limit the explosive tendencies of the fiscal accounts in 1991-92. The public sector's demands on credit have been kept within bounds compatible with reduced inflation and a stable macroeconomic environment. The exchange rate policy, together with moderate wage increases, helped keep Polish exports competitive, thereby minimizing the European recession's effect on growth and on the current account. Stable (or, for new private sector activities increasing), levels of real income, together with a rebound in business confidence and expectations, have contributed to the recovery in consumption and investment.

Short-Term Risks

Poland's economic targets for 1994 are continued growth in output (4.5 percent), 23-percent inflation by year's end, and the further accumulation of international reserves. The instruments announced to support these targets are a slightly expansionary fiscal stance (with the deficit targeted to increase by about 1 percent of GDP), a monetary policy aiming at increased domestic credit (compatible with macroeconomic targets), lower interest rates (in line with inflation reduction), and an exchange rate policy that would maintain the crawl at a pace slightly below the rate of inflation.

Can Poland attain these ambitious objectives and expect continued growth in the next few years? There are four short-run risks: possible slippage on budget targets because of strong demands for more public spending, continued demonetization, an unfavorable external environment, and excessive wages.

It is crucial that Poland adhere to budget targets approved by Parliament in March 1994, which already project a substantial increase in public sector demands on domestic credit and a return to gross dissaving. The deficit is slated to remain relatively low as a share of GDP, but will still absorb more than 60 percent of credit. Only if there is real growth in broad monetary aggregates will it be possible to reconcile financing of the projected deficit with declining inflation and enough domestic financing for the targeted increase in output. If there is less growth in broad monetary aggregates, either the fiscal accounts must contract further (as in 1993), or significant crowding out of the private sector is inevitable. The demand for broad monetary aggregates has been unstable recently (because of enormous structural changes in the economy), but the National Bank of Poland should consider that further reductions in interest rates might become counterproductive by causing the amount of available credit to contract. Interest rate policy could become the first line of defense against inflation fed by high wage settlements. Policies need to shift direction even if prudent fiscal management continues.

Poland's current account position in 1993 was probably stronger than balance-of-payments statistics indicate, and there are few indications that the country's export competitiveness has significantly deteriorated. But if growth does not resume in Europe (especially Germany) in 1994, strong domestic demand may become incompatible with available external financing. Poland's relatively comfortable external reserve position could permit a transitory cushioning of the anti-cyclical growth pattern (compared with Europe), but this option cannot be carried too far. A sustained loss of reserves could destroy confidence and escalate demand for złoty assets. There may be a need for a corrective slowdown, probably as expenditure reduction or switching (through a combination of tightening monetary policy and adjusting the exchange rate). The affect on output would be magnified if domestic sources of inflation were not under control.

Recent wage developments must be viewed with apprehension: A wage-price spiral could overwhelm action on the exchange rate front and undermine confidence. Wage and policy developments should be brought in line with projected growth potential.

Medium-Term Growth Scenarios

Navigating policy options for 1994 will not be easy, but relative stability and a favorable business environment improve the prospects for achieving government objectives. More fundamental challenges and policy decisions lie ahead, however. Poland must sustain and even improve on its 1993 growth rate if it is to find the resources needed to meet social demands and to be able to join the European Union by the turn of the century.

To maintain rapid growth Poland must increase its productive capacity, while maintaining a stable economy. To upgrade Poland's production infrastructure requires increasing current ratios of investment to GDP, even though growth may be faster in less capital-intensive sectors (especially services). If Poland is to increase its productive potential and address environmental concerns, it is necessary to introduce new technologies in privatized enterprises and to upgrade such public infrastructure as telecommunications, water treatment plants, and energy production and distribution.

Increasing investment requires reversing, or at least halting, the decline in private savings. A turnaround in savings will depend largely on external capital flows. Since 1990, Poland has relied on two main sources to finance her external account deficit: loans from international financial institutions and the rescheduling or reduction of debt and other obligations (table 1.3). Private capital flows (both debt-creating and direct foreign investment) have been negligible. With the second phase of the Paris Club debt reduction behind it, the agreement with the London Club executed, and with good prospects for a satisfactory agreement with other creditors, Poland will no longer be able to consider arrears a financing option, and interest payments will increase as a result of these settlements. If official sources remain Poland's main source of credit, financing for continued growth will be tight indeed, and Poland will have to rely on continued expansion of exports together with slower growth in consumption. The resulting growth path will be radically different from that of the past two years, and to improve its market share abroad Poland will have to reduce its labor costs.

It is difficult, if not impossible, to project external financing from private sources in the medium term, but there are grounds for optimism. In several countries that have reduced or rescheduled their external debt (especially but not only in Latin America), heavy capital inflows have resulted, in the form of substantially increased investment. Hungary, with a considerably smaller economy, has attracted substantially more private capital flows, and there is now great interest in Poland, which may have great investment potential. On the other hand, Poland does not have a stock of domestic capital parked abroad that can easily be repatriated, as has happened in several Latin American countries; the gestation period for direct foreign investment (DFI) is relatively long; the underdevelopment of Poland's financial markets may be a formidable hurdle for potential investors; and regional considerations may inhibit investors' willingness to substantially increase their Polish exposure.

That is not to say that Poland can do nothing to influence these patterns; policymakers can create an environment more likely to attract foreign flows (see Chapter 3). Privatization (and debt-equity swaps after debt reduction agreements) have been a main avenue for increased private inflows. Financial market development, and the removal of restrictions on investment in the services sector, can stimulate direct participation in financial institutions as well as portfolio investment.

Table 1.3: Sources of External Financing

	1990-93			1994-97			1998-01			1994-01		
	US$b	(%)	% GDP	US$b	(%)	% GDP	US$b	(%)	% GDP	US$b	(%)	% GDP
I. Uses of Funds	18.8	100.0	6.0	18.0	100.0	4.5	21.3	100.0	4.0	39.3	100.0	4.2
1. NICA deficit	-5.0	-26.3	-1.6	3.1	16.8	0.8	3.1	14.8	0.6	6.2	15.7	0.7
2. Factor Payments Due 1/	17.8	94.3	5.7	12.6	69.5	3.1	15.8	74.4	3.0	28.4	72.1	3.1
o/w Paris Club	6.9	36.3	2.2	3.0	16.7	0.8	4.9	23.2	0.9	7.9	20.2	0.9
London Club 2/	6.6	35.0	2.1	3.9	21.7	1.0	2.2	10.4	0.4	6.1	15.6	0.7
CMEA	1.4	7.3	0.4	0.8	4.5	0.2	0.7	3.3	0.1	1.5	3.9	0.2
New Bilateral Loans	0.0	0.0	0.0	0.2	1.1	0.0	1.4	6.4	0.3	1.6	4.0	0.2
Other Multilateral Loans	0.0	0.0	0.0	0.2	1.3	0.1	0.8	4.0	0.2	1.1	2.7	0.1
Other Commercial	0.0	0.0	0.0	0.2	0.9	0.0	1.5	7.1	0.3	1.7	4.2	0.2
IBRD	0.1	0.5	0.0	1.4	7.4	0.3	2.6	12.3	0.5	4.0	10.1	0.4
IMF	0.4	1.9	0.1	1.1	6.3	0.3	1.0	4.7	0.2	2.1	5.4	0.2
Other	2.5	13.3	0.8	1.7	9.6	0.4	0.6	3.0	0.1	2.4	6.1	0.3
3. Change in Gross Reserves	6.1	32.0	1.9	2.5	13.7	0.6	2.3	10.8	0.4	4.8	12.1	0.5
II. Sources of Funds	18.8	100.0	6.0	18.0	100.0	4.5	21.3	100.0	4.0	39.3	100.0	4.2
1. Official Sources	3.5	18.7	1.1	6.7	37.2	1.7	8.1	38.1	1.5	14.8	37.7	1.6
o/w IBRD	1.1	5.6	0.3	2.7	14.8	0.7	2.6	12.2	0.5	5.3	13.4	0.6
IMF	0.8	4.4	0.3	1.2	6.5	0.3	0.0	0.0	0.0	1.2	3.0	0.1
Others	1.6	8.7	0.5	2.9	15.9	0.7	5.5	25.9	1.0	8.4	21.3	0.9
2. Private Sources	3.0	15.8	1.0	10.7	59.2	2.7	13.2	61.9	2.5	23.8	60.7	2.6
DFI	1.0	5.3	0.3	3.2	17.8	0.8	5.0	23.5	0.9	8.2	20.9	0.9
Other Flows 3/	2.0	10.5	0.6	7.5	41.5	1.9	8.2	38.4	1.5	15.6	39.8	1.7
3. Arrears/Forgiveness	12.3	65.5	4.0	0.6	3.5	0.2	0.0	0.0	0.0	0.6	1.6	0.1

1/ Includes all payments due on ongoing schedules with the Paris Club and commercial creditors. Assumes completion of all debt agreements.

2/ Includes the estimated total outflow of the commercial DDSR.

3/ Includes private commercial credits, and capital not elsewhere identified.

Source: World Bank estimates.

Fuller trade integration will be needed to expand Poland's access to markets, especially the European Union, while Poland waits for full membership. The European Association Agreement (box 1.3) is a good basis for such access (except for agricultural trade, whose complexities are discussed in Chapter 3). Poland has also accepted the results of GATT's Uruguay Round. These agreements complement a trade policy that, while not eschewing selective concessions to attract foreign direct investment or selective help to domestic industries, has created an environment for expanded trade opportunities.

In building our central macroeconomic scenario for the next few years, we have made two crucial assumptions about external financing. First, private sector flows will be substantially more important than they have been for financing the current account deficit. But second, the increase in private flows and the more unfavorable (paid) debt service profile (after the debt reduction agreements) will have little impact on net resources available to finance the non-interest current account deficit.

In our scenario for 1994-2001, we assume that growth can be maintained at an average 5 percent of GDP in the last half of the 1990's, although per capita income in Poland will rise to only US$3,800, or about one-fifth of the projected per capita income of the European Union. Poland's inflation rate should converge fairly quickly toward the European norm. Progress on curbing inflation has been steady but gradual. Although the 1994 target of 23 percent might not be achieved, appropriate financial policies could help reduce inflation to below 10 percent by 1997 and move it toward the European norm before the turn of the century.

Under these assumptions and the external financing scenario of table 1.3, the recent decline in national savings would be gradually corrected, and investment would increase to an average 23 percent of GDP by the end of the decade. By that time, Poland would rely less on external savings and the current account deficit would be reduced to slightly over 1 percent of GDP. Per capita consumption growth would slow down early in the period, but would later catch up with the growth rate of GDP (table 1.4). The public sector would play an important role in the projected turnaround in savings and investment. Public sector savings would become and remain positive and public investment spending would increase about one-third from present levels, to 4 percent of GDP (see Chapter 2). At the end of the period, Poland would be on a sustainable growth path, having achieved a better balance between investment and consumption, and having decreased to more sustainable levels her reliance on external financing.[7]

Table 1.4: A Medium-Term Growth Scenario, 1993-2001

	1993 e	1994 p	1995-97 p	1998-01 p
GDP growth rate	3.8	4.5	5.0	5.0
Inflation (avg.)	35.3	39.8	12.9	5.0
(percent of current GDP)				
Total Investment	19.1	20.0	22.0	22.7
Private Investment	16.4	17.5	18.5	18.2
Public Investment	2.8	2.6	3.5	4.5
National Savings	15.6	17.2	19.6	20.4
Private Savings	15.3	18.2	18.3	18.0
Public Savings	0.4	-1.0	1.3	2.4
Foreign Saving	3.5	2.8	2.4	2.2
Current Account Balance (US$ billion)	-2.3	-1.9	-1.7	-1.9

Source: World Bank estimates.

Alternative Scenarios. There are several possible — perhaps equally plausible — alternative scenarios. Two alternatives are relevant in the next few years. The first scenario would result from unfavorable developments in the short run, such as wage and price inflation, which would probably cause a short-run output decline and reduced private capital inflows. External adjustment would have to be rapid. Growth could resume only with strong export performance, which would probably require substantial real depreciation. The subsequent path of low growth and/or low real wages — while similar in many ways to the initial expansion path of many East Asian economies that later took off — might in Poland further disturb social cohesion, and could eventually lead to a reversal of reform.

A second, more intriguing scenario could materialize if, paradoxically, foreign capital inflows were to increase substantially, after the London Club agreement and integration with the European Union. Higher capital inflows could boost investment and balanced growth and, in a virtuous cycle, lead to EU-level per capita income through appreciation of the real exchange rate, as has happened to other countries that joined the EU. Real appreciation would not reduce competitiveness if productivity continued to improve. But productivity will continue to improve only if restructuring and

---

7 This would permit Poland to tackle the bunching of repayment obligations to official and private creditors early in the next century.

privatization are pursued with determination. If they are not, increased capital flows might encourage a further reduction in national savings, as consumption growth would be the prime motor of demand. This scenario would replay the negative features of the economic performance of some smaller European nations after they joined the EU in the 1960s and 1970s. Savings would be down but large capital inflows would not be sustainable forever. Per capita income differentials might well be reduced, but at the cost of prolonged increasing unemployment.

Medium-Term Policies for Growth

Which scenario is most likely? That depends on the structural policies Poland pursues. Poland is now at a critical stage in its economic transformation. Macroeconomic management alone will not suffice: Poland has to choose between increased consumption in the short run (at the risk of a lower growth path) and increased investment in infrastructure. Once the initial push for reform is exhausted, the consolidation of economic gains and continued reform depends on having the support of the voters, who could choose new leaders if social tensions mount. Large segments of the population feel excluded from the economic recovery and many Poles feel insecure about those segments of industry that have yet postponed adjustment. Meeting the demands of those who want to share the fruits of recovery, and mitigating the effects of the transition yet to be experienced, must be part of any program for economic growth.

Past and present governments have tried to resolve social conflicts and gain support for reforms. The State Enterprises Pact signed in February 1993 — by emphasizing the workers' involvement in privatization and by giving workers an interest in the financial health of enterprises — provided the right framework to encourage continued reform. Poland must continue the search for consensus, by broadening the spectrum of issues to confront. Workers that participate in privatization and the new wage bargaining mechanism is not enough. Poland must also deal with the inevitable costs of *restructuring obsolete industries*, must *make its social safety* net adequate for adjustment, and must agree to a policy of moderate growth for real incomes, compatible with increased national savings.

It is essential to reform public finances. By limiting demands on available savings through prudent fiscal management, public sector reform will contribute to macroeconomic stability and will not crowd out credit to the private sector. By adapting public spending to the needs of a modern society, reform can contribute directly to savings, can provide vehicles for increased private savings (through pension reform and other policies), and can leverage public investment resources through increased private sector participation in building and providing infrastructure. Public sector reform must also address the need for better, more efficient protection of the poor and others displaced by the transition.

Nor can those aspects of implementation that have stimulated a supply response be neglected. Private sector development can continue through *accelerated privatization*, and by removing lingering legal impediments and regulatory uncertainties. Among other things, restrictions on foreign investment in services should be reduced or eliminated and property rights and markets (including court procedures for foreclosure) should be clarified.

To further encourage the supply response, there should be concerted action to curb losses in certain sectors of the economy, and to *strengthen financial markets*, where reform is in many ways incomplete. Increasing the breadth of financial markets, and the ability of financial institutions to assess risks and opportunities, will provide better opportunities for financing productive investment. Attention must also be paid to the lingering quasi-fiscal deficits in the enterprise and financial sectors; neglected, these could lead to catastrophic problems in the fiscal accounts, with many fewer options than are available now.

CHAPTER 2: PUBLIC SECTOR REFORM: REDUCING THE SIZE OF THE STATE

The public sector in Poland has gone through extraordinary changes in the last four years, producing a radical turnaround in the composition of financial flows in and out of government, and major changes in the role of government and the organization of the state. A modern tax system is gradually being built, replacing the ad hoc and arbitrary taxation of the old regime and the transitional taxes aimed at state enterprises. The state has almost doubled its outlays for the social safety net, while dramatically reducing direct intervention in the productive sector. Public investment has been drastically reduced. Finally, decentralization has changed decision-making about revenues and spending as well as the relationship between citizens and the state.

As expected, the transformation has not been without problems. At first, the combination of a recession and a rapidly changing economic base led to deficits that seemed destined to grow and to threaten macroeconomic stability. From the surplus of 1990 (in itself largely illusory, reflecting the hyperinflation of 1989), the public sector accounts plunged rapidly into the red, reaching an alarming deficit of 6.7 percent of GDP in 1992. In 1993, however, economic activity accelerated and substantial progress was made toward restoring fiscal balance, by reducing real expenditures and increasing revenues. The general government deficit, targeted at 5 percent of GDP, was instead reduced to less than 3 percent of GDP (table 2.1). This achievement, for which Poland deserves credit, has greatly facilitated macroeconomic stabilization. The government balances are now close to levels sustainable with stabilization and growth objectives.

Table 2.1: General Government Accounts, 1990-93

	1990		1991		1992		1993	
	Trillion Zl.	% GDP	Trillion Zl.	% GDP	Trillion Zl.	% GDP	Trillion Zl.	% GDP
Revenues	263.4	44.5	341.9	41.5	503.0	44.0	708.3	44.8
Expenditures	244.2	41.3	395.8	48.0	579.3	50.7	746.1	47.2
Current Expenditures	222.6	37.6	369.7	44.9	544.6	47.7	695.2	44.0
Capital Expenditures	21.6	3.7	26.1	3.2	34.7	3.0	59.1	3.2
Public Sector Saving	40.8	6.9	-27.8	-3.4	-41.6	-3.6	3.1	0.2
Primary Balance	21.3	3.6	-41.4	-5.0	-45.0	-3.9	21.8	0.2
Surplus (+)/ Deficit (-)	19.1	3.2	-53.9	-6.5	-76.3	-6.7	-37.9	-2.4

Source: Ministry of Finance; IMF, World Bank calculations.

That success is only temporary, however; more must be done. Polish society is expressing unmet needs, partly related to the pains of the transformation, and partly to the legitimate aspirations of important segments of the population, who want to partake of the fruits of economic growth. These demands increase pressure on state spending. And some key programs (especially pensions) have explosive tendencies that must be reversed. Meanwhile, there is a widespread perception that the burdens of taxation are unequally shared.

This chapter presents a broad strategy for reforming public finances. We discuss the limits of deficit financing, its effect on credit to the productive economy, the limited scope for further tax increases, the possibilities for redistributing the tax burdens more equitably, and issues associated with decentralization. We argue that even if taxes could be increased, it would not be in Poland's long-term interest to increase the size of the state. Poland cannot achieve high productivity and private sector-based growth at the same time that half of GDP is absorbed by the public sector, as is presently true. International experience shows that, on average, a 10-percent increase in public spending as a share of GDP is associated with a 1-percent reduction in the long-run growth of output. We argue that there is ample scope for restructuring Poland's spending programs. Rationalizing expenditure should be the main way to meet society's legitimate social demands and to help *reduce* the size of the state. Income transfers and income maintenance programs are the prime candidates for structural reform, which will over the years provide substantial savings and improved services. Public investment now absorbs a much lower share of resources than a decade ago, but substantive changes in the public investment program could lead to stronger social and physical infrastructure.

The Limits of Deficit Financing

The main problem with the general government absorbing so much domestic credit is that it crowds out credit available to private enterprises and state-owned enterprises. The scenario of high private sector-driven growth is unlikely to materialize if real credit to the productive sector does not increase, along with activity and investment.

What deficit is an appropriate target in the next few years? What factors must be considered in projecting an economically viable deficit level? First, any deficit requires some financing, whether foreign or domestic, voluntary or involuntary. But in the next few years, the potential for external financing is limited. With the successful renegotiation of its Paris Club and London Club debt, Poland assumes a fairly inflexible schedule of external payments. Sovereign borrowing is likely to remain limited to official sources (although Poland may well attract substantial private financing). Loans from multilateral and bilateral institutions are likely to shift away from general-purpose deficit financing toward project financing. Realistically, Poland's public sector cannot count on substantial external flows and our projections are that external financing of the public sector will be negative, particularly toward the end of the decade. Most deficit financing in this decade must come from domestic financial markets.

The resources needed to finance investment ultimately come from either domestic or foreign savings, but available credit and the degree of financial intermediation help determine what level of activity is compatible with a given level of savings. In a barter economy, there is no credit, so for each act of saving there must be a counterpart investment by the same economic unit, and producing goods and services is difficult because producers cannot borrow against future earnings to finance production. As economies become more sophisticated, economic units increase their holdings of domestically denominated financial assets, which makes it easier to allocate savings across sectors. For a given level of savings, the amount of credit available is a function of the degree of financial intermediation. The narrower the financial markets, the less new credit generated each year, and the greater the competition among sectors. If domestic credit is the intermediate objective of monetary policy (as in Poland), competing claims on available credit are resolved through either rationing or changes in interest rates.

For a given target of external reserves buildup (or decrease), the flow of credit available to the economy is the result of any change in the real demand for broad monetary aggregates, and of the inflation rate. For example, if the real demand for money is constant, the stock of money is 20 percent of GDP, and the inflation rate is 10 percent, then additional monetary instruments equivalent to 2 percent of GDP will be required each year to maintain a constant real stock of money. Through balance-sheet identities, the resulting flow of new credit can be calculated by subtracting the equivalent of the planned increase in international reserves from the 2-percent expansion of money. As is well known, reducing inflation paradoxically makes it more difficult to finance the public sector, as it reduces the "inflation tax" component of the demand for money. On the other hand, credible reductions in inflation can substantially increase the demand for domestically denominated assets, and therefore increase available credit.

In the first stage of calculating the desirable level of the public sector deficit for the next few years we create three hypothetical scenarios of financial deepening: (A) that it will resume at the 1991-1992 pace — that is, that each year broad monetary aggregates will increase 5 percent of GDP; (B) that they will increase by 2 percent of GDP; and (C) that they will remain constant in real terms (table 2.2). *Then*, assuming a high-growth economic path, we posit that it will be necessary to increase real credit to the nongovernment sector if credit is to remain constant in relation to total output. *Finally*, we take our best estimates of external credit flows that might become available to the public sector, as well as reasonable targets for increases in external reserves. The data in table 2.2 are striking.

Assuming the macroeconomic scenario described in Chapter I, domestic financing of the deficit must be limited, for the rest of this decade, to between ½ and three and a half percent of GDP, on average. Even so, domestic financing of three and a half percent of GDP would require increasing broad money as a percentage of GDP from 37 percent to almost 50 percent by the year 2000. These magnitudes have been observed elsewhere, but the growth in intermediation they signal would be unprecedented for Poland, and would depend on hugely successful financial reform. Since external financing of the deficit is likely to be zero or modestly negative for the 1990s, the room for maneuver on targets for the fiscal deficit is very limited indeed, if crowding out of nongovernment activity is to be avoided.

Table 2.2: Calculating a Desirable Budget Deficit
(Trillion Złoty)

Item	Scenario	1994	1995-97	1998-2001
Broad money (% of GDP)	A	37.2	41.0	48.7
	B	36.1	37.6	40.3
	C	35.4	35.4	35.4
Demand for money (flow)	A	200.4	198.8	271.3
	B	178.3	154.8	179.4
	C	147.3	127.9	130.1
Change in reserves		-9.1	16.4	26.4
New credit to non-govt. b/		98.1	97.3	85.2
Domestic financing of deficit	A	111.4	85.1	159.7
	B	89.3	41.0	67.7
	C	19.5	14.1	18.5
Deficit as % of GDP	A	5.2	2.8	3.6
	B	4.2	1.4	1.5
	C	0.7	0.5	0.4

a. A = 5% increase in broad money/GDP ratio per year; B = 2% increase; C = 0% increase.
b. Credit flow required to limit the credit/GDP ratio to acceptable levels.

Source: World Bank calculations.

The figures in table 2.2 relate to the bottom line of the government accounts. We will argue that Poland's tax pressure, at a time when tax reform is well advanced, is already extraordinarily high, and — if anything — will be difficult to maintain. Public spending is also very high, and the excessive resources intermediated by the public sector may well be an impediment to growth. A strategy for public finance reform may try to safeguard public revenues and reduce tax inequities and inefficiencies, but above all it should reform and reduce spending programs. That will be the main challenge for the second half of the 1990s.

Improving the Tax System

Poland moved quickly, early in the 1990s, to enact a modern tax structure. In doing so, it closely followed the Western European pattern — combining personal and corporate income tax with a value-added tax (VAT) and some excise taxes — and the advice of international agencies. After four years, the legislative work is largely done. The two main challenges now are coping with the effects of the disappearing state enterprises taxes (as privatization progresses and state enterprise-specific taxes are abolished) and developing sound tax administration. Compensating for the loss of state enterprise-specific taxes (and other transitional sources of revenue) will require broadening the tax base for basic taxes, a short-term measure. In the medium term, it is essential to reform tax administration so revenue is collected from large sectors of the economy (especially the emerging private sector) that now elude taxation.

Revenue Performance

General government revenues improved in the last three years after erratic behavior in 1988-90 (table 2.1). As revenues stabilized, the government got a big share of national income: with 1993 revenues at 47 percent of GDP, Poland is one of the most heavily taxed countries in the world (table 2.3). It would rank eighth among OECD countries, is far more heavily taxed than most countries at a comparable income level, and has reduced revenues less than other former socialist countries after economic and political liberalization.

Figure 2.1: Composition of Revenues

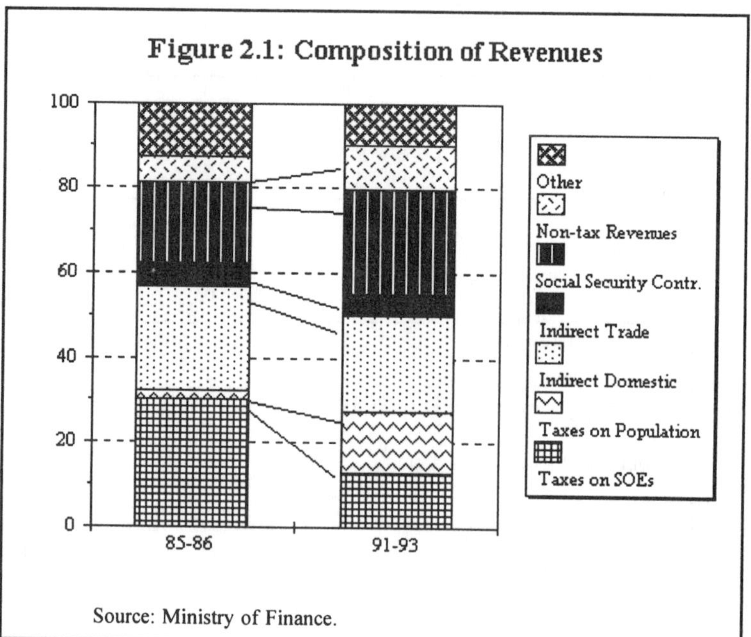

Source: Ministry of Finance.

Revenues have been consolidated as the result of reforms that substantially altered the shape of Poland's public finances (figure 2.1). Taxes directly levied on state and private enterprises have declined from about one-third of total revenues to less than 15 percent (or from about 50 percent of revenues, including social security contributions, to about 36 percent). The share of indirect taxes has remained roughly constant, but direct taxes increased substantially after the personal income tax was introduced in 1992. Taxes specifically designed to affect the behavior of state enterprises (the tax on excessive wage increases and the *dywidenda*) declined in importance but continued to produce a substantial share of total revenue in 1993.

New Western-style taxes have performed well but with less net effect on public finances than raw data suggest. The personal income tax (PIT) elevated the contribution to revenues from personal-income-related taxes from 3.5 percent of GDP in 1985-86 to 9 percent of GDP in 1993. But of this impressive increase, some 3 to 4 percent of GDP is attributable to an increase in the tax base (through including pensions and the salaries of public employees) which was ultimately financed by higher government outlays. The net effect on public finances was only 1 to 2 percent of GDP.

Direct tax payments from (public and private) enterprises under the corporate income tax (CIT) have declined dramatically since the 1980s, but have stabilized on the high side of OECD levels. This phenomenon, directly linked to the transition itself, happened in most former socialist economies. The high profitability of state enterprises, and hence the high level of corporate income tax, was a function of heavy subsidies to state enterprises. These subsidies were needed to compensate for the distorted prices under central planning and the resulting losses for many enterprises. Losses in some enterprises were compensated for by large profits in others, but once subsidies were eliminated (in January 1990), profits shrank and revenues disappeared. In net terms, however, the fiscal sector was a winner as the cut in subsidies has more than compensated for lower revenues.

The introduction of the value-added tax in July 1993 was the last building block of a Western-style tax system. That reform has also been successful. The VAT was set relatively high (22 percent), with exemptions that conform to international standards and a complement set of excise taxes on "vice" goods and other easy-to-tax goods.[1] The VAT quickly produced revenues (in the second part of 1993) that made it a major tax earner. Implementation has not been problem-free. The VAT status of energy and energy products, for example, is in flux because of the need to substantially raise relative energy prices and at the same time protect vulnerable parts of the population.

In short, after four years of reform, the following picture emerges. The general *tax pressure* has eased somewhat from high 1980s levels, largely by eliminating the "double counting" generated by central planning. Net resources absorbed by the government have not changed substantially. This puts Poland way above comparator countries with a market-based economy. The *composition of taxes*, on the other hand, has changed considerably. What used to be a payroll tax, largely invisible to the workers on which it was levied, has now become a personal income tax, the personal responsibility of the taxpayer. Similarly, the system of opaque turnover taxes has been replaced by a VAT the consumer can easily identify.

These changes have had important consequences. Making taxes explicit is an important step toward building democracy and making public officials accountable. It focuses public discussion on such issues as equity in the allocation of the tax burden. In Poland as elsewhere much resentment has been expressed about the private sector's perceived underparticipation in the formal tax system. This perception is based on impressions, as little data is available on tax collection by type of ownership; the tax administration is not yet equipped to provide such data. But it appears that the new private sector may be more difficult to tax than the state enterprises. Data on tax payments by medium-size and large enterprises show that, whereas payment of indirect taxes may be roughly similar among public and private taxpayers, the payment of corporate income taxes tends to decline in the private sector, reflecting a lower declared rate of profitability.

---

1 Excise taxes are levied on alcoholic beverages, wine and spirits, beer, tobacco products, perfumes, fuels and oils, boats, and certain electronic equipment.

Box 2.1: Poland's Public Revenue System - 1994

Poland's public revenue system comprises several taxes accruing partially or totally to the state budget; a number of quasi-tax payments, also accruing to the budget; a payroll tax earmarked for social funds; a series of taxes and non-tax revenues administered and collected locally, accruing to municipalities.

Main Taxes

Personal income tax. Effective January 1, 1992, and levied on all personal incomes (except some agricultural incomes). Withheld at the source for wage income at a rate of 21 percent (for incomes over Zł 1,212,000), 33 percent (for incomes over Zł 90,800,000), 45 percent (for incomes over Zł 181,600). (Tax rates were raised in 1994 from 20, 30, and 40 percent). Some deductions are allowed, and joint returns are possible. Proceeds of the tax are divided between the state (85 percent) and local governments (15 percent).

Corporate income tax. Effective January 1, 1989. Levied on all legal entities (whether state-owned, cooperative, or private). Rate 40 percent. Proceeds divided between state budget (95 percent) and local governments (5 percent).

Small taxpayer turnover presumption. Presumptive tax assessed as a proportion of sales if the previous year's turnover is less than Zł 1.2 billion (2.5 percent for trade; 7.5 percent for services 5.0 percent for production)

Value added tax (VAT). Introduced July 5, 1993 to replace turnover tax. Rates: 22 percent (general rate), 7 percent (energy products, construction, some consumption goods), 0 percent (exports and associated services). Exemptions include agricultural goods, some processed goods, and financial services. Revenues accrue entirely to the state budget.

Excises. Introduced with the VAT, and applicable to several vice and luxury goods and to petroleum products.

Customs duties. The tariff code ranges from 0 to 40 percent, and there are exemptions and tariff quotas. An across-the-board 6 percent customs surcharge was added in 1993. In 1994, the surcharge was transformed into a 6 percent tax on import and tariffs.

State Enterprises-based Taxes and Duties:

Tax on excessive wage increases (popiwek) (abolished as of April 1, 1994). Applicable to state-owned enterprises, cooperatives, and joint ventures with state participation of more than 50 percent. Provided for sharply increasing tax rates for wage awards above a given norm.

Dividend tax. Compulsory payment from state enterprises based on the re-evaluated value of "founding organ" contribution to enterprise capital. Rate varies by class and vintage of assets.

Main Local Taxes:

Real Estate Tax. Levied on urban and rural property at a rate established yearly by the Ministry of Finance (but not to exceed 0.1 percent for housing and 2 percent for commercial buildings) on assessed value (which is not yet related to market value).

Table 2.3: Revenues in Poland and Selected Countries
(As Percentage of GDP, 1991-93)

	Estimate of GDP per capita a/	Total revenues	Total tax revenues	Tax on goods & services	of which VAT	Tax on corporate income	Tax on personal income	Social security contributions	Tax on property
OECD total	17,928	44.5	38.4	11.7	5.5	2.9	11.4	9.0	2.1
Denmark	20,780	57.7	49.9	16.5	9.1	2.1	26.0	1.2	2.2
Netherlands	19,110	51.7	46.0	12.0	7.5	3.5	9.7	18.9	1.7
France	18,990	48.3	43.8	12.6	8.3	2.4	5.2	19.2	2.2
Germany	21,130	46.8	38.1	9.7	5.9	2.1	11.2	13.8	1.2
POLAND	4,720	46.0	42.5	12.7	-	5.3	9.1	8.4	0.9
Italy	15,960	45.1	37.8	10.2	5.3	3.8	10.1	12.5	0.9
Portugal	7,730	42.5	35.1	15.8	7.0	1.4	4.9	9.2	0.5
Spain	13,760	39.7	34.4	9.9	5.6	3.0	7.9	11.9	1.3
United States	22,130	30.8	30.1	4.9	-	2.6	10.7	8.8	3.1
Former Socialist Countries									
Czech Republic	3,575	52.7	44.2	12.2	12.2	11.8	7.7	11.3	0.4
Hungary	5,260	51.2	41.3	15.7	7.6	8.0	2.0	13.5	-
Slovak Republic	2,705	49.4	44.7	16.2	9.1	9.6	3.0	15.1	0.8
Slovenia b/	6,018	47.8	47.8	14.2	-	0.6	4.2	2.0	-
POLAND	4,720	46.0	42.5	12.7	-	5.3	9.1	8.4	0.9
Ukraine b/	1,830	44.4	36.0	11.6	-	5.8	2.8	..	0.4
Belarus b/	2,880	38.2	35.2	18.5	-	9.7	2.8	..	0.4
Russia b/	2,680	33.6	33.6	19.0	-	10.2	2.8	..	..
Lithuania b/	1,280	33.1	31.3	11.5	-	6.5	5.0	..	0.1
Middle-Income Countries									
Korea	10,070	18.5	18.2	7.2	5.0	2.7	3.9	1.3	0.2
Argentina	5,840	25.0	23.8	12.6	8.6	1.8	..	5.6	0.2
Chile	5,380	23.4	26.3	14.3	11.6	2.7	0.5	2.3	-
POLAND	4,720	46.0	42.5	12.7	-	5.3	9.1	8.4	0.9
Tunisia	3,780	28.4	26.5	7.7	2.9	1.6	1.9	4.0	0.5
Morocco	2,800	26.5	20.2	8.8	4.9	2.3	2.3	0.9	0.5
Philippines	2,900	17.9	16.8	5.1	1.9	2.5	1.9	-	0
Unweighted Average									
OECD total		44.5	38.4	11.7	5.5	2.9	11.4	9.0	2.1
OECD Europe		50.5	39.7	12.7	6.5	2.6	11.1	10.3	1.8
EEC		50.7	39.9	12.6	7.0	3.0	10.4	11.3	1.9
Former soc. countries		43.6	39.7	14.7	11.3	6.9	4.8	10.9	1.3
Middle-income countries		26.5	24.9	9.7	5.9	2.7	2.5	2.9	0.4

a. Purchasing power of currencies (PPC) of GDP per capita (current international dollars) involves deriving implicit quantities from national accounts expenditure data and reevaluating the quantities in each country at a single set of average prices.
b. PPC unavailable; country with observed value of GDP per capita.

Sources: Multiquery Database The World Bank, 1993, Government Finance Statistics, IMF, 1993.

Box 2.2: Poland- Structure of Tax Administration

Tax administration in Poland used to be an SOE-based system, which combined decentralized control over the finances of state-owned enterprises with control over money flows. At present, the structure of administration is in a state of flux, and there appears to be no articulate approach to organization. Within the Ministry of Finance, the tax function is split between three under-secretariats and the computer center. One under-secretariat deals with tax policy and legislation, a second with tax collection operations, and a third with fiscal control. Customs administration, formerly attached to the Ministry of Foreign Trade, is now a semi-autonomous body.

One Deputy Minister oversees headquarters staff and the work organization of the Treasury Chambers. The Inspector General for Fiscal Control oversees the recently created Tax Audit offices. A second Deputy Minister oversees tax collection operations and fiscal control; they both have independent regional operations. The regional office, the Treasury Chamber, coincides with the voivodships and subsumes both second-instance collection operations and fiscal control. Hence, taxpayer appeals on tax audits go to the Treasury Chambers. The Treasury Chamber is also the general administrative unit for all tax agencies under its jurisdiction. Payment of taxes (the collection function) is organized with the local office — tax agency — as the basic operational unit. Taxpayer audits and inspections operate on two different levels, national and local. The function of performance evaluation still very low despite some efforts to improve it in fiscal control. There is no conscious organizational design to provide taxpayer services.

Collection and tax arrears enforcement. About 33,400 people work in tax collection, most of them (30,000) in 327 local tax agencies. Audit staffing is around 7000. The initial focus on revenue collection has resulted in the neglect of such compliance-enhancing activities as the audit. Division of work for regional inspectors is by type of tax, which may not be the most efficient approach. Nationally, tax audits are only part of the auditing work of the Inspectors General Office. Financial investigations also include audits of spending.

Customs administration. Customs is an independent agency. There is a central customs office plus 15 regional offices, 300 customs points, and three free trade zones. Total of staff is about 12,000.

Completing Tax Reform

In increasing public revenues, Poland's challenges will be to maintain revenue buoyancy as privatization shifts the tax base, to adjust taxes to minimize economic costs and improve equity, and to tackle the revenue implications of funding pension and possibly health care reform.

Maintaining revenue buoyancy will be complicated by many factors, some deriving from government policy. For one thing, in 1994-95, in implementing the State Enterprises Pact and preparing to join the GATT, Poland will abolish taxes (the *popiwek*, the dividend tax, and the 6-percent import tax[2]) that as recently as 1993 yielded more than 2 percent of GDP. There is constant pressure to use the tax system to stimulate a variety of behaviors, always involving some kind of foregone tax revenue. And, continued expansion of the private sector is progressively making taxpayers less willing to comply with tax legislation, a phenomenon likely to increase if not checked at an early stage.

Two temptations must be avoided. The first is to react to the lost revenue by increasing tax rates — that is, extracting more from those already in the tax net. The economic costs of high, punitive rates are well documented. The second temptation to resist is the multiplication of taxes, a common response among panicked legislators in countries whose tax system is disintegrating. Introducing "tax handles"(ad hoc, often highly distorted taxes that may initially bring in large revenues) is ultimately self-defeating: it makes administration of the formal system more difficult and generates outright hostility in taxpayers.

---

2 The import tax will be abolished on January 1, 1997. Its rate will be reduced to 5 percent in 1995 and to 3 percent in 1996.

The strategy for safeguarding public revenues should instead involve both *broadening the tax base* and *strengthening the tax administration's ability to enforce rules*. Broadening the tax base will yield increased revenues, improve the perceived equity of the system, and make the job of tax administration easier. It will not be possible, however, without decisive administrative reform.

The Polish government's strategy addresses many of the right objectives. By phasing out state enterprise-specific taxation, it aims to broaden the tax base by bringing into the formal tax system many activities and taxpayers — especially in the private sector — not presently captured. But the implementation of some objectives appears to be counterproductive. The 1994 budget introduced a form of presumptive income tax for some hard-to-tax sectors, for example; at the same time it increased marginal tax rates on personal income, apparently unconcerned that high taxes on savings could discourage the very thing Poland needs for investment.

Some good measures need administrative follow-up: for example, lowering the threshold for including taxpayers in the formal tax system and establishing incentives to discourage the underreporting of investment spending (investments are often called current costs), the overreporting of costs, and the resulting underreporting of profits. New tax incentives for investment were proposed in the reforms of 1993/94: tax breaks of 25 percent on annual pre-profit tax and up to 50 percent for certain categories of production (e.g, a high share of exports in total sold). The new incentives are available only to taxpayers who exceed some levels of profitability (up to 8 percent depending on the branch). The presumptive tax schemes aim to ensure a minimum tax payment by certain categories of taxpayers among whom evasion is thought to be high.[3]

More can be done to broaden the tax base by simply re-examining the rationale for tax exemptions, many of which lead to revenue loss and abuse. Exempt from the VAT, for example, are some meat industry products and by-products, fish and processed fish, raw materials for the dairy industry, and milk, eggs, and poultry (except when canned). Also exempt are some handicrafts and artisan products, horticultural products (except for tropical fruit), animal breeding products, and products of forestry and hunting. Exempt services include typical state and local government services (except gas, heat, and electricity, and legal and notary services) and financial services (except leasing and foreign exchange trade). From an administrative perspective, some of these exemptions appear risky. The definition of handicrafts and artisan production, for example, may open loopholes for businesses to define themselves as artisans and makers of handicrafts. The rationale for some exemptions is unclear, and the net effect appears to be administrative complexity and more avenues for tax evasion.

A number of structural issues about government revenues must be addressed in the next few years. The proposed *reform of the pension system*, for instance, could be an opportunity to increase general revenues contribution to social funds, thereby reducing the distorting effect of high payroll taxes. Similar decisions must be faced about the financing of *health care costs.*

Reinventing Tax Administration

The task of the Polish tax administration in the last four years has been arduous. It has tried to reinvent itself, to convert an old, state enterprise-based arm of the central administration into an agency capable of handling volumes of tax returns, issuing refunds, and ensuring compliance from an increasingly uncooperative taxpayer community (box 2.1). Still, the tax administration completed the first steps in establishing a compliance-based system for both income tax and VAT for 21.5 million registered taxpayers. In 1993, it issued the forms taxpayers need, received the forms together with payment of the income taxes, and also registered taxpayers, payments, and returns for VAT. Its

---

3 The *small taxpayers regime*, introduced in 1993, imposes a minimum payment from some hard-to-tax group, on the basis of assumed income/sales ratios (2.5 percent for trade, 7.5 percent for services and 5 percent for production).

awareness campaign to prepare taxpayers for the VAT obligation helped create a sense of the tax's legitimacy. The result was high compliance levels; collection was better than expected.

VAT payers responded positively in the first semester of implementation. The transition from a turnover tax to a VAT was not difficult for turnover taxpayers, including importers. But the honeymoon between taxpayers and authorities may come to an abrupt end if taxpayers detect administrative inability to monitor them or begin to feel that evading taxes gives them a competitive edge. Taxpayers will reduce compliance if they are allowed to. Currently, about 20 percent of gross VAT collections are being rebated, which seems high, considering that the VAT is relatively broad-based and that a wide range of services do not qualify for rebate rights. This high rebate rate may reflect loopholes in the law, or poor administrative controls, or both.

To prevent a deteriorating tax base, it is essential to develop a credible tax auditing capability. Systems (including adequate technical equipment) must be put in place to monitor compliance, detect evasion, and prevent noncompliance. The institution charged with this function — the Inspection General or Fiscal Control Unit — was created in 1993, but development of the audit/inspection function needs improvement and audit coverage is inadequate.[4] Few organized efforts have been made to ascertain or even estimate underreporting or to gauge the number of unregistered taxpayers. Nor is anybody trying to understand the economics of hard-to-tax sectors. Audit plans are based on consultations within the Ministry as to what the audit program should be for a given period, and consultations involve audits outside the scope of taxation.

There has been considerable progress, however, in customs operations, although most operations are manual, and there is ample scope for improving revenue collection and shortening processing time. Control of contraband, especially spirits, was recently addressed by establishing bands to be applied to all liquor bottles sold in Poland as proof of duty payments.

The Inadequacy of Automation. The task of tax administration is defined by formal tax laws, with procedural rules defining how tax administration is to be carried out. The structure of tax administration is a tool for ensuring taxpayer compliance. The tax system has lagged in reform, with progress uneven to date. As each tax was defined, procedures were introduced for it. By contrast, in Hungary, a common procedural code was enacted for all taxes. A common procedural framework for all taxes creates fewer problems for both the tax administrator and the taxpayer. With different procedures for each tax, inconsistencies can emerge among tax forms and collection procedures. Meeting different information requirements requires a duplication of effort and hence increases the taxpayers' compliance costs. It is also more difficult to cross-check taxpayers' position on different tax obligations. As things stand, a taxpayer in arrears on income tax could request and get refunds under the VAT.

The strategy for automating tax administration was to sign a contract with a hardware producer, which also covered the development of application software for tax administration. Judged by the cost of hardware — about US$80 million — automation was a clear investment priority from

---

4 The selection of taxpayers to audit is normally at the discretion of the inspector. Local audit staff are currently trying to establish audit methods at voivod offices. Each voivod group has wide latitude in deciding whom to audit within the guidelines provided by the Ministry of Finance. Collection biased data capture will not allow the provision of good information for structured checks of VAT: at present the only possible check is the VAT/Turnover Ratio. Returns to be audited are selected subjectively; there is no ex ante hypothesis for selecting audit subjects. And the administration is incapable of gathering and analyzing information on revenues from private sector activity, despite public indignation about the private sector's failure to comply.

the beginning. But development of those computer programs in accordance to the recently enacted tax law was less than satisfactory. Which hardware to buy should probably have been the last decision.

Computers were delivered to local tax chambers and to the Ministry of Finance before the applications designed to computerize tax administration processes were ready, so they remained idle for a long time. Local initiative produced "applications" that were not so much defining a system as accommodating computers to the existing manual procedures and division of work. Still, these applications are an important part of tax administration's so-called automation. Software development at central headquarters focused on relatively narrow functions (registration, declaration, and payment); the computers' capacity as process organizers and integrators is not being tapped. The distribution and configuration of computer equipment does not allow the interregional cross-checking of taxpayers. Most tax offices received one or two mid-size machines and several PCs. Networking capacity is nil.

Automation has been more complete for VAT, which was introduced in early 1993. Under pressure from a deadline that could not have been missed without damaging credibility, the Ministry of Finance's automation department prepared a development plan that combined the existing strategy with a directive aimed to unify, nationwide, computerized procedures for dealing with VAT payers. This operation undergoes constant improvement as upgraded versions of the collection cycle are distributed, to be managed by PCs in the regional offices. By contrast, the development of systems to administer income tax collection was left to the agencies' discretion so there is no uniformity between offices. Not surprisingly, results vary from office to office.

Completing Administrative Reform. Despite enormous efforts to implement new legislation, the operations of tax agencies and chambers and fiscal control offices leave much to be desired. What is needed is a uniform strategy for the next stage of reform: improving the capacity to enforce compliance. The goal of all compliance activities (auditing, compliance reporting guidelines, short- and long-form audits, public relations, and possibly criminal prosecutions) should be to encourage the desired taxpayer behavior. The next steps in reform should be to formulate a strategy to increase taxpayer compliance, improve automation, train tax administrators, and develop taxpayer relations and services.

A strategy for increased compliance. This strategy must encompass procedural rules, administrative functions, and organizational changes that facilitate tax auditing. The current division of labor does not allow either the specialization needed to develop a sound tax audit and inspection function or the consolidation needed for a managerial overview of the process as a whole. The tax administration law now in preparation could provide an opportunity to analyze the current tax administration and see what needs changing. Certainly procedural rules and organizational changes are needed to consolidate the tasks of auditors as a team responsible for implementing uniform compliance strategies. The administration should not only develop computer applications for auditing, but should study the workings of key economic sectors, especially such traditionally hard-to-tax sectors as construction, transport, agriculture, and independent professionals. Understanding how hard-to-tax groups of taxpayers operate is essential for specifying which automated strategy to implement to enforce their compliance. Particular attention should be paid to getting the informal sector into the tax system.

Improved automation. Increased automation is a necessity given the high volume of tax documents needed under current tax rules and the complexity of tax administration. Automation strategy must follow the conceptual definitions and policies outlined by law, but should focus on enforcement. There are signs of tax evasion, which must be detected and proven within 3 years of a tax return deadline. Computer software should be developed to support audits and inspections.

Systems are needed to identify and quantify possible evasion cases and to support field inspections in the quickly changing Polish environment. It is important to (a) create a data base for an audit selection and operation system; (b) establish a follow-up system to ensure that taxpayers identified as noncompliers are pursued until they comply; (c) develop sector models that allow tax offices to compare filed returns with theoretical models to identify likely candidates for auditing; (d) define a strategy to publicly advertise auditing results for different sectors; and (e) prepare information about sectors to support the audit process.

The authorities could consider dividing tax processing into two parts. One part could consolidate all tax payments by type of tax onto one payment coupon for each taxpayer. The other part could consolidate all tax declaration documents and activities. The information captured by both activities could be consolidated in regional and national master files to support all tax administration activities. This reorganization may be the best alternative to a comprehensive audit and inspection program.

Training tax administrators. Training is essential in tax administration. Taxpayers have problems and questions the tax administration staff must be trained to deal with, just as it must be trained to handle automation. There should be management training, training in tax technicalities and operations, and training in computer applications. Top and middle managers need management skills, and in-house expertise is needed to deal with the day-to-day problems of taxpayer compliance and planning enforcement. (State-of-the-art developments include tax evasion analysis and modeling, audit planning and management, and the identification and management of external source information). As automation takes root, more and more staff should be able to handle automated processes.

Developing taxpayer relations and services. Finally, communicating well with the tax community is essential for establishing the legitimacy of the tax system and making the tax system sustainable. Day-to-day management of the tax system should encourage the public to comply fully with tax laws. Tax forms should be designed so it is easy for taxpayers to fill them out and calculate what they owe; publications, seminars, educational campaigns, and so forth should be developed for taxpayer assistance and education; priority should be given to developing fast, smooth processing of forms; a group in tax administration should be prepared to get close to and monitor the emerging informal sector; and information should be gathered about different economic sectors; with an eye to developing sector models against which auditors can select returns (or nonreturns) for auditing.

Reform of Spending Programs

Total public spending has remained roughly constant as a proportion (about half) of GDP but the structure of public spending has changed substantially with the economic transformation (figure 2.2). The drop in subsidies (especially to state enterprises) has matched a jump in cash benefits, especially unemployment benefits and other recession-related outlays, and bigger pension outlays as more and more unemployed workers are absorbed into the rolls of pensioners. The decline in real investment outlays has given the government some room for maneuver.

These shifts in the composition of spending have not been painless. The reallocation of expenditures has taken place in a context of restraint, with continuous struggles for increased allocations to specific programs or sectors. Success in budget consolidation and the avoidance of explosive growth has been due largely to ad hoc measures to prevent existing programs from overrunning the deficit. Short-term measures have included severe across-the-board cuts in programs, and the use of indexing (at the expense of more rational policies) to achieve savings in pension and wage payments.

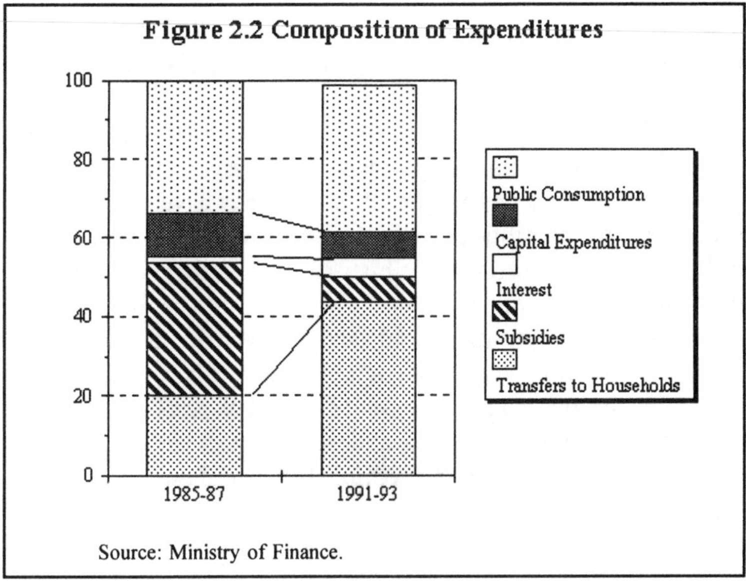

Source: Ministry of Finance.

An ad hoc approach was necessary for the crisis that beset Poland's public finances in 1991-92, but a more structured approach to spending reform is needed now. Ad hoc cuts tend to create more problems than they solve, by leaving potentially explosive programs unchanged, by disappointing the expectations of those (such as pensioners) who feel entitled to what the law says, and by spreading available resources so thin that it is nearly impossible to deliver public goods.

In the next few years, spending programs will be under many pressures. Social transfers are likely to keep increasing as the population ages and pensions kick in. Payments on external debt will absorb proportionately more of expenditures after the external debt restructuring agreements are concluded; and domestic debt will increase to absorb the costs of restructuring the financial sector and financing the budget deficit. There will also be heavy pressure for more spending on health and education.

In this section we analyze the scope for reform of the social security system, of programs targeted to the poor, and of the public investment program. The decentralization of spending and the financing of infrastructure investments by local governments are dealt with in the next section.

Pension Reform

The public sector's role as provider of transfers to households has swollen with the transition. Much of the social protection implicitly performed by state enterprises before has been made explicit by the abolition of subsidies, and those burdens have shifted to public finance. Spending has substantially increased for pensions, unemployment benefits, and social assistance. Because of its size and its potential for explosive growth, the pension system is clearly the main threat to the long-term health of public finance.

As in most Central and Eastern European countries after the Second World War, Poland's early individualized pension system was slowly transformed into a pay-as-you-go defined-benefit scheme. Between 1968 and 1987, the administrative arrangements for providing pensions were progressively transferred from individual pension funds to two public agencies, the General Social Insurance Fund (FUS) for the general population and the Social Insurance Fund for Farmers (KRUS). These funds cover social insurance risks such as pensions and sick pay, as well as family allowances.[5]

The Social Security Act of 1991 began to reverse the post-war notion of entitlement to a state pension and to reestablish a relationship between a worker's contributions history and benefits paid.

---

[5] Unemployment benefits are financed through a separate payroll tax and are administered through the Labor Fund (FP). As in many CEE countries, social assistance is administered largely by local governments.

The 1991 Act also abolished some occupation-specific privileges that certain groups had gained over time (although many still remain) and limited the credit that could be obtained from noncontributory periods.

Poland's current pension system consists of a single public tier financed by employer-only payroll contributions on a pay-as-you-go basis. Transfers from the state budget cover an increasing gap between contributions and benefits. Benefits have a minimum guarantee and an upper limit. Although numerous occupation-specific privileges still exist, such as early retirement and additional benefits independent of contributions history, old-age pensions are increasingly calculated on the basis of both past income and contributions.[6] This makes the current single public tier a hybrid between a basic social assistance pension and an earnings-related, defined-benefit pension. Similar formulas are used to calculate disability and survivor pensions.

Insurance companies — PZU and WARTA being the largest — are also beginning to offer small private schemes. (ZUS and KRUS are also considering private options.) A proper regulatory framework has not yet been established for these private schemes.

Main Issues

As currently structured, the Polish social insurance system — especially pensions — increasingly strains the state budget, without consistently meeting either redistributive or social insurance objectives. Past governments have tried to address key problems, largely without success. Without significant reform, the medium-term prognosis for the pension system is grim.

Impact on the state budget. Poland has experienced an explosive increase in spending on social insurance-based cash transfers (unemployment and social insurance benefits) in the past few years. Total spending on benefits provided by FUS and KRUS increased from 8.4 percent of GDP in 1988 to a budgeted 16 percent for 1994. In the same period, benefits from the Labor Fund (FP) increased from 0.1 percent to 2.0 percent of GDP (table 2.4). The combined outlay on benefits financed through social insurance (20 percent of GDP in 1993) is higher than similar outlays in other CEE countries and in such low-income OECD countries as Portugal (8.9 percent of GDP) and Spain (12.9 percent). Even richer OECD countries, such as Italy and Germany, spend less than Poland (17.9 percent and 15.4 percent respectively). Only France (21.0 percent) and the Netherlands (24.8 percent) spend as much or more.

The fiscal crisis created by the pension system was anticipated in the mid-1980s. Initially, fundamental structural reform was avoided by systematic underindexing and by allowing inflation to erode the real value of benefits. This strategy created a highly inequitable pension system that hits long-term pensioners the hardest (they are least able to supplement their pensions with additional earnings). Subsequent cost-of-living adjustments did little to improve the equity of pensions or relieve the fiscal burden. Combined spending on pensions by FUS and KRUS increased from 7.12 percent of GDP in 1988 to 15.2 percent in 1993. Pension payments in Poland are 60 percent higher than the

---

6 $P = 0.24NW + (0.013\ N1 + 0.007\ N2)B$

Where:

P = pensions of a specific individual; NW = national average monthly wage in previous quarter; N1 = number of eligible years with contributions; N2 = number of eligible years without contributions; B = individual assessment base = best individual average monthly wage (IW); best five consecutive years during past 14 year period in 1994, increasing to best 10 consecutive years during past 20 year period in 1999. B reduced to 91 percent of IW under 1993 Budget Law; to 93 percent of IW expected under 1994 Budget Law. B also has an upper and lower limit (39% $AW \leq B \geq 250\%$ A). B rarely > 160%.

OECD average of 9.7 percent of GDP (and 85 percent higher than an OECD adjusted average of 8.1 percent of GDP, based on Poland's demographic structure). They are also among the highest in CEE countries. Only the Ukraine comes close to Poland with an expenditure of 13.9 percent of GDP in 1992.

Table 2.4: Spending on Social Insurance, 1988-94
(Percent of GDP)

	1988	1989	1990	1991	1992	1993	1994
FUS	8.4	10.4	9.1	14.0	16.8	15.8	16.0
Pensions	6.3	7.1	6.9	10.7	13.2	12.6	12.9
KRUS	0.9	1.1	1.3	1.8	2.2	2.2	2.4
Pensions	0.8	1.0	1.2	1.5	1.8	2.0	2.3
FP	0.1	0.1	0.6	1.7	2.1	2.0	2.2
TOTAL	9.4	11.5	11.0	17.4	21.1	20.0	20.6
Pensions	7.1	8.1	8.1	12.2	15.0	14.6	15.2

Sources: GUS, ZUS, Ministry of Finance.

Weaknesses in the system. The Polish pension system adds disproportionately to the fiscal burden chiefly because of:

- Liberal eligibility criteria.
- Occupation-specific privileges.
- High average replacement rates.
- Deteriorating dependency ratios.
- Poor contribution compliance.
- Weak administration.

These characteristics are discussed below.

It is generally recognized that the crisis in the Polish pension system is related to the rapid increase in the absolute number of claims for old-age pensions immediately following the transition. The current statutory retirement age is 65 for men and 60 for women; the minimum statutory contribution period is 25 years of full employment for men and 20 for women.[7] Once these conditions are met, pensioners have the right to both work and receive a pension. Liberal eligibility criteria for early retirement and disability pensions, coupled with no financial disincentives (such as reduced benefit levels), have made it much more attractive for elderly workers to apply for early retirement or a disability pension than to risk unemployment. Special legislation introduced in 1991 even encouraged early retirement for workers displaced by the liquidation or reorganization of the state enterprises.[8] As a result of all these factors, the average retirement age dropped from 59.0 years in 1989 to 56.9 years in 1992, while the average age of disability pensioners dropped from 49.0 to 45.9. The number of FUS

---

7 There are statutory provisions for early retirement for such categories as veterans, disability, harmful employment for more than 15 years, and women aged 55 after 30 years' work.

8 To qualify, men had to have a 40-year employment history; women, 35 years.

pensioners grew from 5.5 million in 1988 to 6.6 million (20.3 percent) in 1993, while the number of KRUS pensioners grew from 1.4 million to 2.0 million (43.8 percent). Among the three groups of FUS beneficiaries, the number of old-age pensioners grew much more (33.1 percent) than that of disability pensioners (14.0 percent) and survivor pensioners (8.2 percent) in the same period (table 2.5).

Table 2.5: Types of FUS Pensioners as Percentage of Total

	1988	1989	1990	1991	1992	1993
Old age	41.5	41.5	43.0	45.8	45.9	46.0
Disability	39.0	39.4	38.6	37.5	37.5	37.2
Survivors	18.1	18.3	17.6	16.3	16.3	16.3
Others	1.3	0.8	0.7	0.4	0.3	0.5
TOTAL	100.0	100.0	100.0	100.0	100.0	100.0

Source: GUS.

A number of occupation-specific privileges still distort the actuarial basis for determining both contributions and benefits. For instance, although payroll contributions for FUS were raised to 45 percent of gross wages in March 1992, they are practically zero for farmers and other occupational groups (and the military and police make no contributions at all).[9] As for benefits, occupation-specific retirement bonuses still exist despite several attempts to abolish them. These bonuses allow certain groups (miners, railway workers, teachers, and journalists) to add noncontribution years to the recognized contribution years used in the formula to calculate pensions. The bonuses weaken the link between contributions and benefits, and reinforce the connection between benefits and political connections. Occupation-specific privileges, rising unemployment, early retirement, and liberal disability classifications are among the factors that forced FUS pension dependency ratios below two in 1992.

Table 2.6: Average Pension as a Percentage of Average Wage

	1988	1989	1990	1992	1993
Old age	53.3	64.1	75.6	71.7	71.5
Disability	44.3	50.2	55.7	51.6	52.5

Source: GUS.

The average old-age and disability pensions lost less real value than wages did in the early 1990s and are among the highest in the region. The average old-age pension increased from 53.3 percent of

---

9 That 45-percent contribution also finances other nonpension benefits administered by ZUS, such as sickness pay and family allowances. Nonpension benefits account for about 8 percent of payroll, leaving a net contribution for pensions of about 37 percent of payroll.

the average wage in 1988 to 71.5 percent in 1993,[10] while the average disability pension increased from 44.3 percent to 52.5 percent.

Other factors being equal, demographic pressures could force spending on pensions up to 21.7 percent of GDP by the year 2020 and to 26.8 percent by 2050. Even if the average retirement age were raised to 65 from its low current levels (58.7 for men and 55.2 for women) and the eligibility criteria for early retirement and disability tightened, the population dependency ratios would still drop from six to below three over the next five decades, severely straining the pension system. And since not everyone participates in the labor market, the real pension dependency ratio will be even lower (below two by 2050) than the estimated dependency ratio for the population. A cumulative 79-percent increase in contributions would be needed to maintain benefits at 1992 levels until 2050, based on demographic pressures alone.

On the revenue side, payroll contributions to finance social insurance benefits have declined steadily in the 1990s because contribution compliance has deteriorated with the transition. FUS collected more than 100 percent of its contributions in 1988 (because it collected accounts in arrears) but that dropped to 92 percent by the end of 1993. Of the Zł 30.2-trillion in arrears at the beginning of 1994 (1.5 percent of GDP), Zł 26.0 trillion was attributable to state enterprises. Accounts in arrears and bankruptcies account for most of the official debt, but legal avoidance (exploiting loopholes) and illegal evasion also probably cause significant losses for FUS and KRUS.

Finally, FUS has a weak administration with inefficient management practices and antiquated infrastructure.[11] Significant administrative reform is long overdue. The three main management issues in social insurance are the process for determining eligibility and collecting contributions; the contractual relationship between the Ministry of Labor and Social Policy (MOLSP) and the General Social Insurance Administration (ZUS); and the organization and management of ZUS, which has no clear business plan.

Increasing state subsidies. As a result of the factors just described, transfers from the state budget to cover the increasing budget shortfall of FUS, KRUS and FP have increased dramatically, from 1.5 percent of GDP in 1988 to 7.6 percent in 1993. These programs consumed only 4.2 percent of the state budget in 1988, and five years later they consume more than a quarter of budgetary resources. Payroll contributions play a dwindling role in the financing of Poland's social insurance benefits.

Policy Options for Pension Reform

The government has established a Social Insurance Reform Commission (SIRC) to examine policy options that would reach beyond "quick fixes" into the next century. The Commission comprises representatives from Parliament, the Senate, Judges of the Constitutional Court, trade unions, academics, employers, and pensioners. It is mandated to submit its report by June 1994. In conducting its enquiry and formulating its reform proposals, the Social Insurance Reform Commission is trying to address the main problems with the system by drawing on as broad a nonpartisan base as possible, without compromising the underlying objectives of reform: to reduce the impact of pensions and other

---

[10] In Hungary and the Czech republic the average old-age pension was 49.0 percent of the average wage in 1992, while in Romania it was 43 percent and in Bulgaria 34 percent.

[11] KRUS, which has recently undergone management reform and has a modern, computerized infrastructure, is in a much better position than FUS.

cash transfers on the state budget; to minimize the impact of high payroll taxes on labor incentives, international competitiveness, and contribution compliance; and to provide both income security and protection against poverty during old age, survivorship, or disability.

The major policy alternatives the SIRC is examining include:

- Pay-as-you-go versus funded pension systems.
- Public versus private schemes.
- Mandatory versus voluntary membership.

In practice, most Western countries have combined theoretical models rather than rely on any one. The resulting pension systems usually include several of the following elements:

- Basic flat-rate social assistance to protect low-income groups from poverty in old age (mandatory, public, and pay-as-you-go).
- An income-related but capped defined-benefit program to provide income smoothing (mandatory, public and pay-as-you-go).
- Contributions-related contractual savings programs to provide income smoothing (mandatory, public/private, and funded).
- Voluntary supplementary private insurance to provide both income smoothing and a vehicle for personal savings (voluntary, private, and funded).

In examining the policy options for funded systems, it is important to remember that Poland is in a very different position from Chile, which introduced its funded pension scheme during a period of economic growth, when it had established capital and financial markets, and did not need to do consensus-building for reform. By contrast, Polish policymakers faced a fragile economic recovery and immature capital and financial markets, and reform of the Polish pension system must accommodate diverse interests. Success is most likely with a two-pronged strategy: (a) adjusting the public pay-as-you-go pension system to provide adequate, equitable protection against poverty in old age, survivorship, and disability; and (b) adding one or more additional public and/or private tiers that affordably provide income smoothing.

The strategy proposed here is to simultaneously reform the existing system and introduce a new, multi-tier system, to be phased in over the next 15 to 20 years. Eligible workers close to retirement and pensioners currently receiving benefits would retain a right to the present structure of pensions, with the modifications discussed below. The new, multi-tiered system would become operational around the year 2010, and would completely replace the old system by the year 2030. Immediate, substantial cost savings can be achieved with this strategy.

Adjusting the Public Pay-As-You-Go Pension System

The agenda for reform of the existing pay-as-you-go system must act on five related fronts: (1) enforcing contribution compliance; (2) raising the average age of retirement and tightening eligibility requirements for disability pensions; (3) replacing indexation to wages with indexation to the consumer price index (CPI); (4) removing noninsurable risks; and (5) modernizing pension administration.

As a starting point for strengthening the current public pay-as-you-go pension system, the government intends to *improve contribution collection*. Although the increases in social insurance spending that occurred immediately after the transition appear to have leveled off in the past two years, the accumulated debt to FUS and KRUS is increasing at an unsustainable annual rate (Zł 30.3 trillion or 1.5 percent of GDP by the end of 1993). Increases in debt to FUS alone in 1993 were Zł 15.6 trillion or nearly 5 percent of projected revenues. Since over 85 percent of this cumulative debt is attributable to the state enterprises (especially coal mines and steel mills), a solution to the problem must be found in the measures proposed in Chapter 3.

The second set of policy reforms needed to improve the public pay-as-you-go pension system is to *increase the average age of retirement* both for old-age and disability pensions. Several measures could still be taken to achieve this goal. First, the statutory age of retirement for women could be raised to 65, the age for men, for equity and because of their longer life expectancy. Second (because so much of the increased spending on pensions since 1988 is for massive early retirement), while early retirement could remain open to any participant in a pension scheme, it should be subject to a strict earnings test and to an appropriate reduction in benefits if the person continues to work. Third, all occupation-specific retirement and disability privileges should be abolished from the basic public pay-as-you-go pensions system. Special privileges for groups of workers such as farmers (who pay a reduced premium) or the military and police (who make no contributions) should be reserved for other tiers of the system where contributions and payment periods can be adjusted to shoulder the cost. The number of disability pensions could be greatly reduced by withdrawing benefits from individuals capable of working. For those with a reduced-earnings capacity or ability to work only under special conditions, incentives could be introduced to resume or continue work. Permanent loss of a faculty that does not reduce earning capacity would best be handled through a lump-sum payment through private insurance. In all cases, certification of disability should be subject to systematic medical review by qualified examiners. It is important to *avoid creating legal loopholes*, for example, requiring contributions only on work contracts exceeding six months — which are vulnerable to abuse (this case by employers who give repeated short-term contracts). Most Western social security administrations have special departments that deal with abuse and fraud full-time and have considerable enforcement authority and capacity. This is not yet common practice in Poland and other CEE countries but must become a critical part of the business function of ZUS and KRUS.

A third set of reforms in the public pay-as-you-go pension system is to *change the indexation mechanism*. Presently, pensions are adjusted quarterly or semiannually by 93 percent of the growth of average wages for the previous period, provided growth was at least 10 percent. The rationale for indexing wages rather than to prices is not strong, and as real wages tend to increase over time, wage indexation is potentially explosive. Both for fairness and fiscal sustainability, indexing pay-as-you-go benefits to the CPI seems appropriate.

Finally, *modernizing administration* is a prerequisite for many other cost-saving policy options and for introducing additional income-related tiers to the current public pay-as-you-go system. The administrative infrastructure of the social insurance system is antiquated and inefficient and provides poor client services: Records are entered and retrieved manually, office equipment (telecommunications systems, photocopiers, facsimile machines, and word processors) is inadequate, and the accountants still use single-entry cash accounting. The administration has no management information system to assist it in day-to-day tasks. Information technology initiatives at the local level, with little central coordination, will soon produce major problems of data compatibility and capacity. No central master file of customer or operational data is available to the regions. There are no reliable individual contribution records and there is no efficient way to identify individuals, making it impossible to rationally link individual eligibility and cash benefits.

Creating a Multi-Tier System

There are several compelling arguments why a funded component of a multi-tier system would be appropriate in Poland. It would (a) increase personal incentives, (b) control public spending, (c) support capital and financial markets, (d) reduce inflationary pressures by increasing personal savings, and (e) increase public resources available for poverty relief. In Poland, there has already been considerable debate about moving toward a multi-tier system with a funded component. The idea is not as radical as it may appear. Elements of the first and second tiers already exist under the current hybrid public pay-as-you-go system, and early elements of the third tier exist in the largely unregulated private insurance schemes.

The aim would be to separate the distinct elements of the first and second tiers into two transparent sub-systems and to create a proper regulatory framework for the third (mandatory funded) and eventual fourth (supplemental voluntary) tiers. The new multi-tier system could have a basic flat-rate social assistance tier, an income-related defined benefit tier, and a contributions-related contractual savings tier.

Basic flat-rate social assistance tier. In designing a multi-tier pension system, several important policy options should be considered for each element. The basic flat-rate social assistance component (to protect low-income groups from poverty in old age) could be either universal or means-tested. Means-testing would allow a bigger benefit for those who really need it, but would currently be difficult to implement because data on income is still not reliable in Poland. Moreover, means-testing with a sharp cut-off would create a poverty trap for those passing from the social assistance tier to the next tier. In the near future, Poland must continue its universal provision of flat-rate social assistance in old age. When income data becomes more reliable, the social assistance component could be considerably improved by: (a) restricting benefits to a means-tested group of pensioners; (b) setting the benefit below the minimum wage and just above the subsistence level instead of as close to the average wage as it is currently; and (c) financing the benefits from general budgetary funds, possibly through a flat-rate surcharge on income tax or a surcharge on VAT or both.

Income-related defined benefit tier. A second tier, which would also be financed on a pay-as-you-go basis, could cover those pensioners who have already retired or who will retire in the next 20 years. The basic policy options for this involve: (a) a connection between contributions history and benefits; (b) mechanisms for indexation; and (c) a decision about whether or not there is a cut-off for contributions and benefits. This tier could be phased out as the third tier becomes operational or could run parallel to the third tier, to cover population groups that would be inappropriate candidates for a fully funded scheme.

A reform of these two programs could be simply achieved by splitting the current benefit formula (P = 0.24NW + (0.013 N1 + 0.007 N2)B) into its two components:[12] (a) the first component (0.24NW) would provide basic flat-rate social assistance on a universal basis as a protection against poverty; (b) the second component (0.013 N1 + 0.007 N2)B) would provide an income-related pension for income smoothing. The current formula for the basic flat-rate social assistance benefit (0.24NW) could then be substituted for a new formula tied to the subsistence level rather than to the average wage.

The current formula for the income-based defined benefit (0.013 N1 + 0.007 N2)B) could be modified to: (a) remove the noncontributory component (0.007N2); (b) strengthen the relationship between contribution history and benefits by increasing the number of years counted under N1 (this

12 For a discussion of the formula, see note 6.

reform has already been started and will continue until 1999); (c) reduce the coefficient on N1; and (d) lower the cap on monthly benefits (currently 250 percent of the average weekly wage) and introduce a cap on contributions. Employers and employees should contribute to both programs. These reforms could result in a lower marginal tax than is currently necessary, thereby freeing up resources for adding the additional tiers.

Contributions-related contractual savings tier. A third tier could provide income smoothing on a funded basis. In moving from a purely public pay-as-you-go pension system to a multi-tier system with a funded component, few countries have tried to pass directly from one to the other. Certain policy options must be examined as the funded tier is phased in. These are: (a) whether the program is public or private; (b) whether it is mandatory or voluntary; (c) whether or not to include contributions from workers with less than 20 years of labor force participation; (d) how to phase in contributions under the new scheme; (e) how to pay out the benefits after retirement; and (f) how to get effective, efficient portfolio management.

Creating a funded third tier requires establishing historical records of personal contributions. The administrative framework could be a simple extension of the banking system, and could be either public or private. What's important is that it be operated independently of the public social assistance defined-benefit programs so there is no cross-subsidization and no temptation to use the cumulative funds to finance debt servicing obligations. The public track record on managed funds is poor. It has been difficult for Government not to "dip into the till" and "borrow" against accumulated assets. This creates a contingent liability that is no better than under a pay-as-you-go system. A clear legal framework must be established to prohibit such action with publicly managed funds. The alternative would be to have the fund managed by "private carriers," but poor portfolio management or fraud could bankrupt the fund. Strict regulation is essential for privately managed funds.

The funded tier should be mandatory, not voluntary. A voluntary system will always encourage moral hazard, adverse selection, and free riders. The simplest administrative solution is for contributions to be deducted by employers and deposited in designated personal retirement accounts of a National Pensions Fund or National Savings Bank. To ensure transparency, annual statements should be given, clearly indicating the growth of accumulated capital. Making the funded tier mandatory, and issuing annual statements will increase contributors' acceptance of the scheme.

Workers with fewer than 20 years of future labor force participation are unlikely to accumulate enough retirement savings for full pensions, so it is inadvisable to force them to participate in such a plan (their limited benefit levels on retirement could discredit the program). A compromise would be to allow them to participate on a voluntary basis with no reduction in their contributions liability or in the benefits gained from the public pay-as-you-go defined benefit tier that would be maintained for this time period. One objective of establishing a funded scheme is to boost savings available for investment in domestic capital and financial markets, so the longer the time lag between the first contribution and the first payment — say, 20 years — the better. It would be good policy not to allow individuals to cash in their benefits before retirement or to use them as collateral against other financial transactions (such as the purchase of a home).

Both employers and employees should contribute to the scheme's financing. A contribution of 15 to 20 percent of annual earnings will be necessary if sufficient individual savings are to accumulate to provide adequate income smoothing in retirement. But it would not be reasonable to start the scheme at this level because of: (a) the low level of income during the transition; (b) the already high tax burden needed to maintain social assistance payments; (c) the new fund's low institutional capacity; and (d) the lack of available capital and financial markets to invest the funds. A reasonable approach must be to start with a 5-percent contribution and increase it 1 percent a year over a decade while slowly reducing other social insurance commitments. The additional contributions needed to fund the third tier would be fully offset by the savings shown to be possible through the actuarial calculations of both ZUS and the MOLSP. In the second decade, when disposable income should have improved and economic growth fully resumed, and when the first cohorts under the program were ready to retire, the contribution rate would be 15 percent. This gradual approach would keep the double burden (inevitable in a gradual move from a pure pay-as-you-go scheme to a funded scheme) low for at least the first decade.

Payments to retirees could be made either through a regulated spend-down or through actuarially adjusted annuities. The risk of the first method is that some pensioners will live longer than expected, will run out of resources in the later years of retirement, and will end up on basic flat-rate social assistance. The alternative would be to develop a mechanism for underwriting an annuity program. This has not yet been tested in the transitional economies.

To avoid the risks of inflation and immature capital/financial markets there must be tight control over the pension fund and substantial external guarantees for any investments made in the early years of the program. In the first decade, pension fund investments could be made in collaboration with external commercial investors who undertake much of the risk assessment. Once the system matures, responsibility could be transferred fully to domestic investors. Meanwhile, an appropriate legal and regulatory framework for capital markets will be developed (see Chapter 3).

Improving the Social Safety Net

There are signs that an upturn in economic activity is beginning to reduce or at least alleviate the incidence of poverty and long-term unemployment that emerged when the transition began. As in most other countries, a medium-term strategy of growth and stable macroeconomic conditions will provide the best poverty relief.

But growth alone will not suffice. Specific, targeted government action can help alleviate the most extreme cases of poverty, safeguard human capital from waste, and support economic reform. Currently, a number of public program address poverty relief, directly or indirectly. Given tight budgetary constraints, it is important to answer two questions: How well targeted are these programs, or, to put it another way, how much "spillage" to the nonpoor could be avoided, freeing up resources for the poor? And what changes could be made in the present programs to efficiently reduce poverty? Here we discuss two broad alternatives: a guaranteed minimum to all, which would eliminate poverty; and policy reform that could substantially reduce poverty at the same time that they produce gains for the budget. We do not discuss the poverty-reducing aspects of pensions. The pension reform proposed in the previous section would clearly help separate poverty relief from income maintenance.

Resources devoted to social protection (other than pension payments) amounted to about Zł 40 trillion in 1993 (8 percent of total public expenditures and 4 percent of GDP). The most important programs funded are unemployment benefits (administered through the Labor Fund), social assistance (centrally funded and administered at the *gmina*, or municipality, level), and family allowances and sickness and maternity leave (administered through FUS). How effectively these payments reach the intended poor varies.

Unemployment benefits are received by 9.3 percent of households, fairly evenly distributed over the main socioeconomic groups. But 56.6 percent of social income recipients received unemployment benefits. Since more than 70 percent of households receiving social income contain an unemployed person, many of the unemployed no longer receive benefits. *Social assistance* is received by 3.6 percent of all households, fairly equally distributed among different socioeconomic groups (except for the two post-transition groups). Less than 1 percent of self-employed households benefit from social assistance but 29 percent of social-income recipient households receive it. There are virtually no differences by city size and only minor regional differences.

The extent to which components of the social safety net are targeted toward the poor differs significantly. Only 41 percent of households below the minimum wage receive a *pension*, against 55 percent of households above minimum wage. The average pension received by poor households is Zł 1,851,900 a month, which is well above both the minimum pension and the minimum wage (but contributes of course to the whole household).

Unemployment benefits are targeted much more to the poor: 19.2 percent of poor households receive them, compared with only 7.2 percent of non-poor households. *Family allowances* are also received proportionately more by poor households, although to a lesser degree than unemployment benefits: 64.1 percent of poor households receive family allowances, and only 46.6 percent of the nonpoor. The amount received by poor households (Zł 498,300 a month) is also 40 percent higher than the exact amount received by non-poor households (because poor households have more children). *Other social insurance*, received by relatively few households, is received three times more frequently by poor than non-poor households.

Social assistance is well targeted toward the poor: 9.6 percent of households below minimum pension get social assistance, but only 2.5 percent of households above minimum wage. This ratio of almost 4:1 is the best of any component of the social safety net; it stands to reason that income-testing for social assistance is the reason. The amounts received by nonpoor recipients are slightly higher, however. On average, farmer households receive the least social assistance and social-income recipient households the most.

Assistance from Poland's social safety net accounts for 44.9 percent of spending in an average household. Pensions provide the lion's share of funds, contributing 36.5 percent of the household budget. Unemployment benefits cover 3 percent of household expenditures and all other nonpension benefits, 5.5 percent.

The social safety net is mildly progressive, providing funds for 55.1 percent of average spending in households below the minimum pension and 42.7 percent of spending of households above the minimum wage. This is the sum, however, of two very different effects, from pensions and from other transfers. The share of household spending covered by pensions is actually lower for the poor than for the nonpoor. By contrast, unemployment benefits cover 9.2 percent of spending by the poor and only 1.8 percent of spending by the nonpoor (a ratio of 5:1). The remaining social transfers cover 15.6 percent of the expenditures of the poor, but only 3.7 percent of those of the nonpoor (a ratio of 4:1). If Poland's social safety net is progressive, it is entirely because of the nonpension components, especially unemployment benefits and the family allowance.

The success of a social transfer system is measured not only by the degree to which benefits are received by the poor, but also by the extent to which it helps to *close the poverty gap*. Total social transfers received by the poor are more than twice the size (215 percent) of the remaining poverty gap — that is, without the transfers, the poverty gap would be about 3.2 times larger. But there is significant leakage from social transfers. More than one-third of recipients of non-pension benefits, and two-thirds of those receiving the family allowance, are not poor even before receiving the transfer. This means the resource base of the safety net could be reoriented to shift funds toward the poor. Even after receiving transfers, 13 percent of recipients of family allowances remain poor and more than 20 percent of the recipients of other transfers (except pensions). The social safety net must be redirected, aimed at those people.

What resources would be needed to close the poverty gap? People are considered poor if their expenditures fall below the equivalent of the minimum wage (some US$3 per day, calculated at purchasing power parity). The poverty gap — the absolute value of income needed — is calculated at

13.2 percent of the poverty line. Roughly 5.5 million people fall into this category. For the whole country, the annual poverty gap corresponds to about US$612 million a year, or roughly 0.8 percent of GDP. That is not the amount of resources needed to eliminate poverty. Allowing for a standard "spillage ratio" from transfer programs (the extent to which they benefit the nonpoor), the amount of resources needed to close the gap more than doubles, to more than 1.7 percent of GDP.

A program to provide everybody with a guaranteed "social minimum," besides being very costly, would be extremely difficult to monitor. Income testing, as Polish workers know, is difficult and abuse would be massive. A strategy for poverty relief should capitalize on the strengths of existing programs, and ascertain how they can be modified to achieve better targeting and minimal negative side-effects.

Children in large families are overrepresented in the poor population. Targeting could be improved by wisely increasing resources devoted to these families, providing leakage is minimized. One proposal would be to target family allowances only to poor families.

We propose that income-testing be adopted, and that the resources saved be targeted to the truly poor. To minimize leakage, we propose that family allowances be doubled (per child) for families with four or more children; and that day care vouchers worth about US$20 be distributed to poor families, to encourage and facilitate work by single mothers. A program of school meals would, at limited cost to the budget, provide additional poverty relief. We estimate that these changes would result in budgetary savings (of some 0.4 percent of GDP), while reducing the overall poverty incidence by 3.3 percent of total population, or *one quarter of all currently poor.*

The resources to fund benefit increases would come from limiting entitlements. There is obvious room for improvement here; three-fourths of all family allowances are received by households that are not poor. Two possibilities for reducing leakage are to make family allowances taxable, or to subject the entitlement to an income test, based on the income tax declaration. Families would be entitled to allowances only if their income were to fall below a certain threshold — say, 50 percent of the average wage. Including family allowances in taxable income would progressively reduce the value of the family allowance for better-off families, some of which might drop out of the system, but would also slightly affect poor families whose incomes do not fall entirely below the minimum threshold. But subjecting the entitlement to income verification, while cumbersome administratively, would produce more savings, depending on the income threshold chosen. Simulations based on the current structure of income and expenditures indicate that, at a threshold of 50 percent of the average wage, income verification would reduce expenditures on family allowances by one-third, or about 0.6 percent of GDP, *without adverse effects on the incidence of poverty.* Including family allowances in the taxable base would produce savings of only half that much, while slightly increasing the incidence of poverty.

Options for Health Care Reform

After the Second World War, the sickness funds in Poland (as in most CEE countries) were slowly replaced by a National Health Service (NHS) financed by general revenues similar to that found in such OECD countries as Italy, New Zealand, Sweden, Spain, and the U.K.[13] By the early 1970s, the Polish health sector had basic physical infrastructure, trained staff, and education programs comparable to those in developing countries with similar per capita GDP, and even comparable to the OECD. A comprehensive, integrated network of hospitals, clinics, and other clinical facilities provided universal

---

13 Austria, Germany, and Switzerland maintained sickness funds as the main source of health care financing.

access to health care. The average population per doctor dropped from 700 in 1970 to less than 490 in the early 1990s, while the average population per nurse dropped from 250 to less than 190. Health care spending increased from below 3 percent of GDP in 1970 to over 5 percent of GDP in the early 1990s.

The single strongest predictor of a nation's health status is its per capita GDP, not the character of its health services. Among countries at a similar stage of economic development, equity in access to affordable health services appears to be one of the most important determinants of good health. Extending entitlement to a full range of health services to the entire population was one of the most important achievements in the Polish health sector in the previous era. Combined with rapid economic growth, more readily available food, shelter, and employment, expanded social benefits and education, universal access to health care significantly improved health status.[14]

Disturbing Trends

Still, disturbing trends began after the mid-1960s, and some of them intensified in the 1990s because of resource shortages, high unemployment, and other social adjustments associated with the transition: a widening gap between Poland's health status and Western Europe's; imbalances in allocations between health and other sectors; inequities in health services delivery; inequities in health care financing; and widespread inefficiency and poor value for money.

Widening gap in health status. Deaths from infectious diseases dropped 80 percent between 1960 and the early 1990s, but the incidence and death rate from adult diseases increased significantly: the death rate increased fivefold from diabetes, tripled for cardio-cerebrovascular diseases and cirrhosis, doubled for cancer, and increased 50 percent from accidents. These trends appear to have stabilized in the early 1990, but there is now a wide gap in life expectancy and mortality between Poland and Western Europe. Much of this divergence is attributable to an epidemic of cardiovascular disease and ischemic heart disease in middle-aged men. Health status (in terms of standardized mortality rates and infant mortality rates) also varies significantly from one part of the country to another. These variations reflect differences in socioeconomic status among various voivodships as well as differences in budget allocations and the availability of quality of health services.

The health gap places a heavy burden on Poland's economy, putting it at a competitive disadvantage with its healthier neighbors. The economy suffers from lost productivity because of high sickness rates; the opportunity cost of lost investments in human capital (because those who die in middle age have received publicly funded education and other services but haven't contributed their full share to economic growth); and heavy social expenditures on disability pensions and care for the chronically ill.

Imbalances in allocations. There is good evidence that the health sector (one of the so-called nonproductive sectors) has been accorded a lower priority than the industrial sectors. Wages for Polish health care workers have remained at the bottom of the relative wage scale since the 1980s. Health

---

[14] The crude birth rate dropped from 1.7 percent in 1970 to 1.6 percent in the early 1990s; the infant mortality rate dropped from 3.3 percent to less than 1.6 percent; child mortality dropped from 7.0 percent to less than 2.0 percent; and average life expectancy at birth increased from 65 to 71 years. Immunization rates are almost 100 percent. Diseases and death from such illness as pertussis, measles, and polio have been all but eliminated. Many of these key health indicators have not changed during the transition.

workers' educational attainment is also lower than norms observed in Western countries; more than 80 percent of the health sector employees have only secondary vocational education or lower and less than 10 percent have higher education. These trends, which have not changed significantly during the transition, have significantly reduced the quality of the health sector workforce.

Inequity in health service delivery. Within the health sector, serious vertical inequities emerged despite the potential for an intersectoral approach to health and health services planning under the five-year plans. An overcentralized health sector suffers from both overlaps and gaps because different ministries all try to provide services for their own enterprise-based workers. By the early 1970s, there was a massive, lopsided build-up in acute care hospitals, and overspecialization at the expense of basic health services, health promotion, and disease prevention. By the 1990s, more than 75 percent of the health care budget was spent on institutional care and more than 75 percent of medical doctors were specialists (and over 50 percent of these, subspecialists).

Because low-income and other vulnerable populations are even more vulnerable when primary health care is unavailable, these trends impose inequities in health care. Inadequate housing for the elderly and insufficient chronic care facilities have led to the widespread use of hospitals for residential care. Not only is this expensive, but it leads to poor care as most acute-care institutions are not designed to treat many of the non-acute problems geriatric patients have. It will take years to correct the distortions that emerged in the communist era and that persist today, to catch up with needed investments, and to retrain staff.

Inequity in health care financing. Inequity has emerged in other ways in the health sector: (a) in the use of informal gratuities as a form of co-payment; (b) in unbalanced regional budget allocations; (c) in uneven access to health sector services; and (d) in distortions in service utilization.

There is little reliable information on out-of-pocket private spending on health care in Poland, but episodic surveys and special studies suggest that it may be as high as 10 to 15 percent of total health care expenditures. Out-of-pocket spending includes legal payments to private doctors and informal "tips" or "gifts" to public sector personnel for better services. The value of food, linen, and other items families provide for hospitalized relatives is poorly documented but it is substantial, according to anecdotal evidence. Since user fees are usually flat, they are regressive in nature and affect low-income families the most in terms of both ability to pay extra and quality of services when unable to do so.

Despite centralized planning, significant variations emerged from one voivodship to another in the number of doctors, nurses, and beds per 10,000 people (see annex table 4.10). Significant surpluses and shortages developed because of variations in political patronage and local patterns of utilization.

Inefficient use of scarce resources. Access to health care is also inequitable because of the inefficient management of scarce resources. Patients who visit doctors in primary care feel they are wasting their time waiting in line to be told that the services they need are not available. Not surprisingly, they are willing to pay substantial gratuities to be referred quickly up the line, or to use services outside their official catchment area. The reduced disposable income of low wage earners and the unemployed during the transition has aggravated the inequity created by such practices.

Government Proposal

On January 29, 1994, the Presidium of Health Care Committee of the Senate and the Minister of Health invited various parliamentary and nonparliamentary groups, trade unions, and experts to a meeting on health care reform. At this meeting, it was decided that the strategic goals of changes being introduced in the health sector should be to: (a) halt and reverse the recent unfavorable trends in health status; (b) stop the recent deterioration in the quality of health services due to resource shortages; and (c) improve efficiency in the use of scarce resources.[15]

These objectives would be achieved through a new National Health Program, with changes in both the organization and financing of health services. The program would fundamentally redefine the state's role in the health sector by: (a) shifting the emphasis from a centrally planned institutional care model to a more cost-effective decentralized primary health care model; (b) supplementing the state financing of health services with resources collected through a contributory health insurance scheme; and (c) using market mechanisms to allocate scarce resources by reimbursing health care providers for performance rather through global budgets and salaries.

These reform proposals carry special opportunities and risks. There is an opportunity to improve health care financing and delivery by drawing on the best experiences elsewhere in the world, while avoiding known pitfalls. There is a risk that institutional changes will take longer than expected, so services will deteriorate further.[16] There is also a risk that shifting the responsibility for health care financing from the state budget to contributory health insurance will lessen the public sector's commitment to maintaining essential health services. The feeling may be that health costs will be taken care of through insurance and only later, if insurance premiums are sufficient, will the state need to finance the shortfall — which, in effect, has always had contingent liability. If in the meantime the costs have skyrocketed (partly because the state was not directly involved), readjustment will be even more difficult. Finally, there is a risk that the ill-conceived introduction of market mechanisms into the health sector will lead to uncontrollable market failure, the loss of cost control, a further deterioration in equity, and a general weakening of the sector's critical role in the safety net.

Finding ways to attack the already high and rising rates of cardio-cerebrovascular disease among adults, especially men, will be central to improving equity in health in Poland. The main risk factors are well known: smoking, obesity, poor diet (high in animal fat and salt, low in fruits and fresh vegetables), high cholesterol, and lack of exercise. Surprisingly, although cost-effective interventions are well known, Poland has not yet introduced policies such as: (a) tax-based disincentives to consume tobacco and unhealthy foods; (b) legislation banning smoking in public places as well as tobacco advertising and requiring food labeling; and (c) widespread public education programs to sensitize the population (especially children) about diets, physical exercise, and dangerous behavior (smoking, substance abuse, and unprotected sex). Without such intersectoral policies, reform of only the health sector is unlikely to have a long-term effect on health status.

Policy Options

Improving equity in access to cost-effective health services will ultimately depend on restoring the macroeconomic balance so financial resources for the health sector will eventually increase in line with GDP growth; securing stable, adequate health care financing for essential health services; and reducing disparities in the allocation of scarce resources among various social groups and regions.

Restoring the macroeconomic balance. From the late 1970s to the mid-1980s, total spending on health services by the Ministry of Health increased in real terms and relative to GDP and general

---

15 The Health Services Development Project (Loan 9816-POL), which focuses on primary care and management development, is consistent with the government's health sector strategy.

16 Both the World Bank and the European Community have made substantial resources available for the development of a primary care network in Poland, but the Ministry of Health is finding that resource shortages are not the only constraint on introducing an effective primary care network.

government spending. This growth slowed precipitously in 1989, and spending on health care (recurrent and capital) has since remained relatively stable in real terms.[17] Central to Poland's success in controlling health care spending during the transition has been its continued use of general revenue to finance health services; it imposes a hard budget cap. This successful cost control is noteworthy, considering marked increases in the price of fuel, pharmaceuticals, imported equipment, and specialized goods and services, and the strong demand by doctors and other health care personnel that their salaries catch up with those of industrial workers. Inflationary tendencies during the transition have been much greater among those CEE countries that have experimented with payroll levies to finance the health sector and with performance-based reimbursement for heath care providers.

Securing stable and adequate financing. In the early stages of the transition, Poland's health sector had enough internal reserves to withstand significant budget cuts without seriously compromising the quality of care provided. With tight budget constraints and explosive increases in prices (especially of imported pharmaceuticals and equipment), this is no longer true. Like most other CEE countries, and many of the former Soviet Republics, the government in Poland is now looking at social insurance and direct user charges as ways to mobilize more resources for the health sector. Four proposals that have recently been tabled cover most policy options for mobilizing additional resources for the sector.[18]

Proposal "A" (from table 2.7) would maintain the financing of health care from general government revenues but would increase the health sector's share of the state budget. This is the system used in the United Kingdom. The advantages of proposal A are that: (a) general revenues provide more equitable health care financing when based on progressive taxation; (b) the tax system is an efficient method for collecting revenues because of low administrative overhead and strong enforcement of tax compliance; and (c) a centralized system of financing ensures continuity in fiscal control over health care spending. The main disadvantages of continuing to use general revenues for financing health services include: (a) the vulnerability of a single source of health care financing to shifts in public spending priorities at times of political volatility;[19] (b) the weak signal sent to the population that health care is expensive and not free even if it provided at no "direct charge"; and (c) the historical association between general revenue financing and inefficient use of scarce resources.

Table 2.7: Recent Reform Proposals for Health Care Financing

Administrative arrangement	Source of financing	
	General revenues	*Social insurance*
Centralized	A	C
Decentralized	B	D
Occupational	Nil	E

Source: Governmet Authorities.

17 The 1994 budget for the health sector is Zł 84.2 trillion or 4.0 percent of GDP. In absolute terms, Poland spends much less on health care than most Western countries (US$107 per capita at current exchange rates); it spends about the same as many other countries at its level of economic development.

18 Competitive private health insurance is not considered a viable option anywhere outside of the United States, where it is being challenged by the health care reform movement.

19 As has happened in Albania, Slovakia, and the many republics of the former Soviet Union, with the result of underfunding and a drop in health care resources.

Proposal "B" would shift financing from general revenues to local taxation plus equalization transfers. This is the system used to finance health services in Sweden and proposed for Poland by *Solidarity* in the past. The advantages are similar to those for proposal "A" in that: (a) local taxation, when progressive, still provides equity, especially countered with equalization transfers from richer to poorer regions of the country; (b) administrative overhead remains low and enforcement of tax compliance strong; and (c) fiscal control over health care spending is maintained. The main disadvantages of proposal B include: (a) the vulnerability of local taxation to regional disparities in income, which may not be fully offset by equalization transfers; (b) the lack of a tradition of local taxation (which may change with proposed local government reform); and (c) few improvements in efficiency unless associated with changes in provider reimbursements.

Proposal "C" would shift from general revenues to national contributory social insurance (or an earmarked payroll levy) for financing health care. This is the system used in Australia and proposed by the previous Interministerial Committee on Health Insurance (Ministry of Health, Ministry of Labor and Social Policy, and Ministry of Finance). The advantages of this proposal are that: (a) national social insurance still provides an acceptable degree of equity when based on a progressive contribution schedule, but less so than general revenue since the tax base is narrower and there is usually a ceiling on contributions; (b) administrative overhead can remain low and enforcement of tax compliance strong if performed through a central health insurance agency; and (c) it provides an indirect signal to the population that health care is not free. The main disadvantages of introducing this system include: (a) dwindling financial resources during periods of recession because of rising unemployment and contribution evasion; (b) the need to increase social insurance contributions at a time when people and enterprises are already heavily "taxed" by other social insurance charges (over half of the gross wage bill;[20] (c) the need to establish new administrative infrastructure and enforcement mechanisms and hence increased administrative overhead initially; and (d) few improvements in efficiency unless associated with changes in provider reimbursements.

Proposal "D" would shift from general revenue to a decentralized contributory social insurance (or an earmarked payroll levy) for financing health care. This proposal is similar to variant "C," except that the collection of contributions and the administration of benefits would be decentralized. This proposal could be viewed as a variant of the Canadian system for financing health services, but with territories serving roughly 300,000 people rather than 500,000 to 8 million people as in Canada. This is the proposal previously supported by the social policy advisor to the President. The advantages of this system are similar to those for proposal "C." The main disadvantages, in addition to those for proposal "C," are much greater difficulties in maintaining equity through equalization transfers, and much more expensive administration because of local duplication of effort.

A fifth option, variant "E," which the Polish government is not seriously considering, is based on the German employment-based sickness funds. This model has few advantages over other forms of health care financing and several serious disadvantages. The main disadvantages, in addition to those given for variants "C" and "D," include: (a) an extremely complex and expensive administrative infrastructure; (b) a significant loss in cost control because supplier-induced demand neutralizes any advantage gained by sending a signal to the population that health care is not free; and (c) potentially reduced labor mobility unless it is associated with a (surely complex) system for ensuring transferability among employment-based funds. The German sickness funds usually pay doctors a fee-for-service,

---

20 Passing health care financing from the state budget to contributory social insurance is, therefore, also associated with a number of adverse labor incentives at a time that this may be least desirable from the point of view of supporting growth of the private sector. It adds to the cost of labor and hurts international competitiveness.

although there is no reason other forms of health care reimbursement such as capitation payments (payment according to the number of patients on a doctor's list rather than according to each visit or activity performed), could not be used instead.

Using scarce resources more equitably. Few improvements should be expected in the cost-effectiveness of interventions or the efficiency of service delivery by merely shifting from general revenues to social insurance for health care financing. Improving effectiveness and efficiency requires changing the incentive structure for health care providers, the organization of the health care delivery system, and the culture of clinical and health management practices. Any of the above five options could be combined with any number of provider reimbursement systems; and new incentives in provider reimbursements can be introduced with or without global changes in health care financing.

The main implications for equity are twofold. First, a switch to user fees or co-payments has obvious implications for low-income groups despite arguments about efficiency and the signals it may send. Such co-payments are already widespread in Poland in the form of gratuities. Equity would probably improve rather than worsen by formalizing these payments and establishing an official fee schedule. Second, introducing more complex performance-based reimbursements for health care providers will make cost containment more difficult because such payment mechanisms, by their nature, are incentives for health care providers to produce more services. If well designed, such incentives can improve equity by directing health care providers into desired areas of activity. If poorly designed, they can have a negative impact on equity, as health care providers increase activities in areas that are neither cost-effective nor efficient.

Recommendations for Health Care Reform

Health sector reforms that do not improve health and make access to health care more equitable are largely a waste. Many health reform proposals for Poland, particularly for financing, have not passed this acid test.

In choosing among policy options, it is important to remember that there is no magic pill to cure health care financing. The money has to come out of someone's pocket. Switching from general revenues to social insurance, or vice versa, will not increase the available pool of resources, but it will determine who pays and how much is allocated to the health sector rather than to competing demands. The mechanism chosen to finance health services has significant implications for equity and health status but not for efficiency in service delivery, which depends much more on the nature of provider reimbursements.

If the objectives are cost control, broad-based equity in financing health services, and administrative efficiency in collecting resources, the best choice would be proposals A or B, general government revenues and/or local taxation. But if the main concern is the size of the state budget and excessive central government control, general government revenues are a bad choice. If the main objective is sending a strong signal to the population that health care is expensive, then some sort of national social insurance (proposal "C") may be a better choice. But if a main concern is labor costs and incentives that encourage the private sector to grow, contributory social insurance is a bad choice.

In each case, there are important trade-offs, which is why most Western counties use a mixture of general revenues and social insurance to finance health services rather than rely on any one source of financing. Policymakers in Poland and other CEE countries are faced with difficult dilemmas in this respect. They may be tempted to reduce the fiscal deficit by transferring responsibility for health care financing to contributory social insurance, but this not only reduces the state budget but also reduces government control over health care costs. The medical profession and other interest groups, who are more preoccupied with resource mobilization than fiscal control, often support such proposals, seeing them as an opportunity to remove health care financing from the clutches of the government and to close the gap in income between them and their richer Western European counterparts. In the end, the contingent liability ultimately rests with the government, which may find itself in too weak a position to control costs or ensure an equitable redistribution of resources once responsibility for health care financing has been transferred to a semi-autonomous health insurance fund.

So far, health insurance has not led to the expected mobilization of financial resources in CEE countries that have introduced it for two reasons: (a) health insurance contributions were usually introduced to replace rather than to supplement budgetary sources of health care financing; and (b) rising unemployment, combined with less contribution compliance (from a growing informal sector), slowly erodes the contributions base. If the political imperative to move away from general financing of health care is so strong that it overrides considerations of equity, administrative efficiency, and cost containment (strong points of model "A"), the next best choice is national health insurance (model "C"). Both of the decentralized models, "B" and "D," are likely to be associated with enough loss of equity and efficiency to make them distant third and fourth choices.

Reforming Public Investment

The medium-term economic scenario described in Chapter 1 assigns public investment a crucial role in improving capital formation. Providing adequate human and physical infrastructure is essential for private sector development, and public investment resources can complement private resources in crucial areas. Public investment in Poland is in a state of transition. Capital spending has been curtailed because social expenditures were rapidly overtaking revenues, but also because the state's role was changing. Under communism, it was natural for the state to direct investment and contribute funds in areas that are now considered part of the private sector's domain. Even in sectors where the public sector will still play an important role, it is seeking was to create partnerships with the private sector in both the funding and operations of investment projects.

To reform public sector investment, the task is both to allocate and use resources efficiently (which is not presently being done) and to redefine the role of the state, devolving to the private sector in whole or in part responsibility for investments that were formerly considered part of the public domain.

Public Investment: How Much and What Kind?

Investment allocations in central and local government budgets fell sharply in recent years. For 1993, they were an estimated 3.2 percent of GDP — well below the 1988 level (table 2.8). The suspension and cutting back of many public sector investment projects has been inevitable.

Still, the share of public resources devoted to capital formation probably compares less badly with that of other countries than the raw data would suggest. Poland's definition of public investment to some extent still reflects conventions used under the centrally planned economy and is generally narrower than that applied in many Western economies. It is limited to capital assets and does not include one-time expenditures on institution building and systems development; it has traditionally applied only to construction activities and has often excluded the costs of equipping completed facilities; and it has been limited to new capital items, with rehabilitation and modernization expenditures classified as recurrent expenditures, even when they have substantially increased asset values. Also, the state budget does not give a complete picture of public investment financing because it includes neither the significant share of state enterprise investment being financed by government guaranteed credit, nor funding from external financing agencies, when it is provided directly to budgetary units. Financing from these sources is reflected in an appendix to the budget that details the financing requirements for the larger central investment projects, but these projects account for only about one-third of the total investment allocations in the 1994 budget.

Table 2.8: Public Investment, 1988-93						
	1988	1989	1990	1991	1992	1993
			(percent of GDP)			
Total public investment	5.3	3.4	3.7	3.2	3.0	3.2
Central government	5.3	3.4	3.7	2.0	1.6	1.6
Local government	..	..	..	1.2	1.4	1.6
			(real percentage change)			
Total public investment 1/	..	-12.7	-20.8	-13.7	11.0	11.6
Central government	..	..	..	-46.1	-5.6	2.2
Local government	..	..	..	..	38.4	13.7
Memo						
Total investment (US$ Mln)	3670	2828	2277	2469	2545	2808

1/ Deflated by gross domestic investment deflation.

Source: World Bank.

Too many projects. Was public investment money wisely allocated? The answer to that question is not easy, and this itself is a major problem for Poland's public investment program (PIP). Investment allocations in the draft 1994 budget total Zł 28.9 trillion, or 4.2 percent of the total expenditure budget. (The education and health sectors together account for about 40 percent of that budget). It is difficult to gauge the quality of the investment program because — except for 165 of the largest projects, termed *central investments* and defined as having a lifetime cost exceeding Zł 100 billion — the budget does not identify individual projects.[21] For the central investment projects, which account for only one-third of investment allocation, over 75 percent of 1994 financing allocations (from all sources) are directed to the industry, transport, telecommunications, and health sectors, with 65 percent of allocations from the state budget allocated to the last three of those sectors. The sectoral allocation of investment (both for central investments and for all investment projects in the central budget) does not differ substantially from that of other market-oriented economies.[22]

Except for three projects, all central investments are continuations of existing projects. In considering the 1994 draft budget, the Budget Commission of the Sejm expressed concern that there were no new projects and that most investments were actually projects started under the centrally planned economy. The government is right to give priority to completing projects, but there is a legitimate concern that little attempt has been made to review the economic and financial viability of the portfolio of central investments or to set priorities in a program that is still too large for available financing.

Inadequate allocation of funds. Not surprisingly, because of the sheer number of projects being financed and the apparent lack of a vetting mechanism, the balance of financing needed after 1994 to complete the projects is great. Total project financing requirements amount to Zł 81.3 trillion, almost

21 Financing allocations for the central investments of ministries and voivodships are detailed for each project in a separate appendix to the budget. This provides an updated estimate of lifetime project costs and identifies the major sources of project financing. The program includes 165 central government and voivod projects, which are divided between projects of budgetary units and budgetary entities. The appendix also includes 18 municipal projects which, although not included in the central government budget, exceed the ZŁ 100 billion threshold of the central investment classification.

22 See World Bank (1992): *Poland - Strategic Investment Review*, Report No. 10321-POL.

five times the 1994 allocation. The balance for the component of project costs financed from the budget is nearly seven times the 1994 budget allocation. In other words, if financing of central investments were sustained at present levels, it would take an average 5 to 7 years to complete projects in the current program, with extremely long delays for municipal economy (water, sewerage, streets, etc.) and environmentally related projects (see figure 2.3).

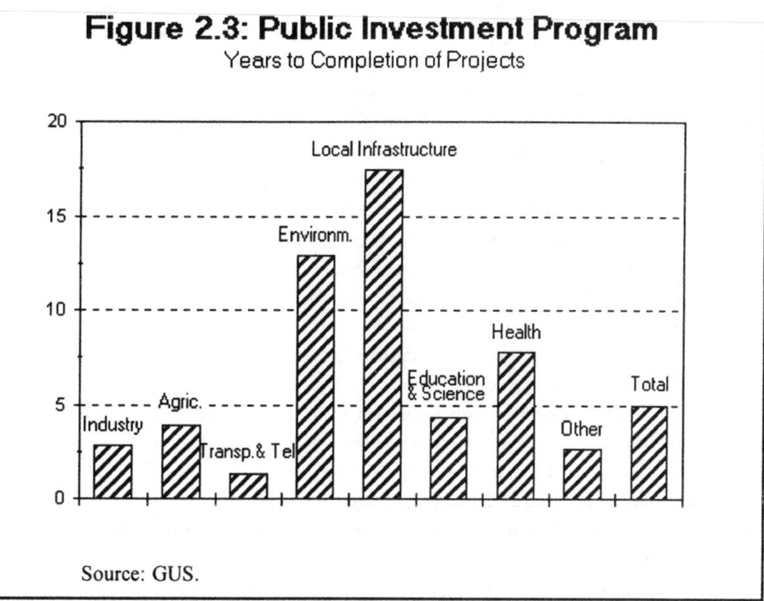

Since most capital investment projects probably have an optimum implementation period of 3 to 5 years, the present program clearly has too many projects for available funding. Rationing funds between too many projects rather than focusing resources on a smaller group of high-priority investments is inefficient because the benefit stream for all projects is delayed.

The same failure to assign priorities probably also obtains for most projects that are not central investments, which account for 71 percent of 1994 investment allocations. But little information is provided to the Ministry of Finance on the projects for which funds are to be allocated. Similarly, the Central Office of Planning does not review and monitor investments outside of the central investment program. No details are provided on non-budget sources of financing for these investments, even when such financing is provided to budgetary units under agreements external financing agencies.

Public Investment Management

Considerable progress has been made in improving budget procedures and presentations in the past four years. Expenditures are now broken down into seven categories, with subventions, wages and salaries, other recurrent costs, and investment allocations all separately identified. Introducing budget ceilings for preparation of the 1994 budget streamlined the budget process and added greater realism. But relatively little progress has been made in strengthening the coordination and management of public sector investment. Responsibility is presently divided between the Ministry of Finance for the investment budget as a whole and the Central Office of Planning, which handles central investments. The Central Office of Planning is also responsible for requests for foreign loan financing of public sector investments. But, the Central Office of Planning has limited capacity for economic and financial analysis of investment projects and the Ministry of Finance, who is primarily concerned with preparing the annual budget, presently has no capacity for reviewing the content and quality of the public investment program. The information the Central Office of Planning has on the investment program is generally limited to that provided for central investment projects: feasibility studies (most of which date from the 1970s and 1980s) and information provided annually for central investments.

The line ministries have limited ability to analyze public investment and there has been little follow-up on earlier recommendations to establish pre-investment units in these agencies. Recent decentralization measures mean that the voivod administrations now have a much more important role in allocating investment resources locally.

Box 2.3: Experience with Private Participation in Infrastructure

Countries that have experimented with private participation in infrastructure have tried options ranging from limited participation (involving "leasing" and "affermage" type arrangements) to large-scale "BOT" (involving significant amounts of capital and risk). Such arrangements cover different sectors of the economy, including power, roads, telecommunications, and water and wastewater management.

There are several innovative ways to involve the private sector in the power sector. Pakistan, to satisfy the major capital needs of the power sector, set up a Private Sector Energy Development Fund (PSEDF), funded by multilateral and bilateral sources. The PSEDF makes long-term, subordinated loans at commercial interest rates to private power projects. In Argentina there has been large-scale privatization in the power sector, using of a variety of mechanisms.

In telecommunications, significant efforts are under way to involve the private sector. Common approaches elsewhere include privatizing the dominant carrier and granting franchises to independent telephone companies in designated areas. There are also various ways for sequencing private sector participation. The internal organization of the company can be left to the new investors, for example, as was done in Argentina and Venezuela, or it can be set up beforehand, as was done in Mexico. Mexico's approach has the advantage of increasing the firm's value before sale. In Hungary 30 percent of the Telecom sector has already been privatized. In Poland, the awarding of concession contracts for local area networks has begun. It envisages both the operation of existing facilities and possibly new investments in a build-transfer framework.

The water and wastewater sectors have seen major private sector involvement around the world. In Buenos Aires, 10 million people get water and sewerage services from a consortium operating as a concession. The concession will last 30 years, with the contractor assuming full commercial risk. The contractor is responsible for operation and maintenance of the existing system as well as new investments. Mexico City has adopted a phased program of limited private sector participation to reduce physical leakage and improve cost recovery. Similar models are increasingly being adopted in other Latin American nations. In Africa, (Guinea, Ghana and Cote d'Ivoire) the private sector has been involved in providing water services. In Guinea, this participation has taken the form of a 10-year lease awarded after competitive bidding.

Eastern and Central Europe have also seen more limited private sector initiatives in the water sector. Concession-type arrangements have been made for water treatment plants in Gdansk and similar efforts are under negotiation in Hungary and the Czech republic. The main concerns of private sector participants are the absence of a regulatory framework and of mechanisms for arbitration or judicial conflict resolution and little confidence that local governments will be willing and able to link tariffs to cost increases and inflation. Municipal governments also need to develop institutional capacity to negotiate concessions, manage financial affairs, and regulate the quantity and quality of service provided by private participants. Clarity and predictability must be established in intergovernmental financial relations. While these issues are being addressed, privatization of services such as meter reading, billing, and vehicle leasing can be easily contracted out. Chile tried this successfully with a public water service company serving Santiago, and other nations have done similar things.

Responsibilities for public investment management remain fragmented and there is little concept of a wider program planned within a medium-term framework, including both budgetary and extra-budgetary sources of financing. There is a need to broaden current procedures for handling central investments to include all public investment projects, and to systematically review the entire investment program to weed out projects that either are no longer appropriate or cannot be adequately financed. The ineffectiveness of the present system is epitomized by a 1993 survey of all investment projects that identified and provided summary information on 1,165 projects with a lifetime cost exceeding Zł 20 billion. The goal of this exercise was to get line ministries and voivods to rationalize their portfolios of investment projects. Budgetary units were asked to classify projects in order of importance, and to indicate which could be discarded. Not surprisingly, *only 80* of 1200 projects were recommended for closure.

Rationalizing public investments will require refining the budget reform strategy and assigning responsibilities to, and strengthening, key government agencies. The information available in the Central Office of Planning on public investment projects and the rudimentary database on central investments is inadequate for coordinating and managing a broad multiannual public investment program (PIP). The first order of business is to ensure that information on all aspects of the PIP is routinely provided to the Central Office of Planning. The Central Office of Planning should receive information on medium-term resources, the financing intentions of external financing agencies, applications for government-guaranteed credits, sector policy studies, and sectoral public investment strategies. The Central Office of Planning should receive and maintain summary profiles for all PIP projects, project expenditure statements, and project monitoring and review reports. A database should be established for each PIP project, including past and projected expenditures and financing and a brief summary description and justification.

By the 1996 budget, all investment allocations should be brought under identifiable PIP projects. Allocations should be justified against clearly defined project objectives, project components, expected benefits, project lifetime costs, and implications for the recurrent budget. Allocations for infrastructure rehabilitation and modernization, when classified as maintenance expenditures, should be brought within the investment budget. Extra-budgetary financing of PIP projects in the form of funding from external financing agencies (World Bank, EBRD, EIB, EU, and so forth) should be identified for all PIP projects, and taken into account in the budget itself and in setting sectoral PIP resource ceilings.

The format presently used in the Budget Annex for detailing the financing of central investment projects should be modified and applied to all PIP projects. When the investment subcommittee of the parliamentary Budget Commission considers PIP projects, it should focus on including *new projects.* Once individual projects are in the PIP, annual financing allocations should reflect tactical and operational considerations and should involve minimal parliamentary scrutiny.

The PIP should be prepared within a medium-term (three-year) resource framework with provisional financing allocations shown for every PIP project for each of the three years. It should be revised and rolled forward annually to maintain the three-year time horizon and permit the revision and updating of project financing allocations. The first three-year PIP should be introduced for FY96.

Establishing a public investment management process. Improvements needed in PIP management include setting medium-term resource ceilings, establishing a process to review and rationalize sectoral investment programs, introducing procedures for the identification, preparation, and appraisal of new projects and their screening for the PIP, and strengthening the database on PIP projects.

The task of estimating medium-term PIP resources can be facilitated by looking at each major source of PIP financing from the starting point of the current year's allocations. Investment budget allocations can be projected on the basis of their current share of GDP, factoring in any projected increases, and adjusting for the inclusion of rehabilitation and modernization expenditures from the recurrent budget. Similarly, government-guaranteed credits can be estimated from current levels adjusted to reflect the government's future intentions; financing from external financing agencies can be projected by examining the forward programs of the main agencies operating in Poland. To set sectoral ceilings within this framework, current year allocations are simply adjusted to reflect government strategies to increase or decrease public investment in different sectors.

Sectoral reviews should be undertaken in 1994 and 1995 with the objective of refocusing public investment on high priority areas, matching the portfolio of investment projects with available financing, and regrouping small site-specific investments into major projects and subsectoral programs.

For some major sectors, technical assistance is likely to be needed for sectoral review and PIP rationalization. Thereafter, sector investment programs should be routinely reviewed as part of annual updating.

Line ministries should have primary responsibility for identifying, designing, and appraising PIP projects, while voivods should carry out the planning and execution of specific investments that are components of wider PIP projects. Capabilities must be built, and procedures outlined, for investment identification, preparation, and appraisal for both projects and subprojects. After the line ministries' detailed appraisal of new projects, they should be screened by the central agencies before being introduced into the PIP. A similar process should apply for reviewing individual investments that are components of larger PIP projects for which financing has already been secured.

Institutional framework. There is an urgent need to clarify the institutional framework for PIP coordination and management among the central economic management agencies. We recommend that this function be located either within a restructured and strengthened Central Office of Planning or in a separate unit established within the Ministry of Finance. In either case, responsibility for the PIP should be integrated into sectoral policy and program development. Such a unit would coordinate sectoral policy development and implementation by line ministries and agencies; determine the scope and size of the government's program in each sector; plan and manage the PIP; and develop cross-sectoral policies and programs. To be effective, the unit must have close links with both the line ministries and the Minister of Finance's budget department.

The principal line ministries need to develop sectorwide policy and programming capabilities to ensure consistency between projects and programs in different subsectors. We recommend that sectoral units be established to coordinate the development of sectoral policies and programs, determine the appropriate allocation of public sector resources within the sector, and coordinate the preparation and implementation of sectoral PIPs.

The voivods would be responsible for planning and implementation of investments that are components of larger PIP projects. This will require an investment programming function at the voivod level to coordinate sector programs operating in that voivod and to allocate investment resources between them; and a sectoral investment planning and management function in which sector departments in the voivod are advised by their line ministries.

Strengthening the decision-making process for public investments will require considerable technical assistance and training support. The government must identify the extent to which these requirements can be met by local consultants and training institutes and where it will be necessary to engage the services of external organizations.

Stimulating Private Sector Participation in Infrastructure

Better management of the public investment program will free up resources to finance new projects; indeed, it may be desirable to expand increase the envelope of public investment funds. But how big are Poland's public investment needs, and by how much should capital expenditures be increased? In many respects, Poland's infrastructure is overcapitalized in some areas, as a legacy of the communist past. Maintenance rather than expansion should be the priority in many areas. But the need to modernize and upgrade key infrastructure sectors, and the investment required to meet environmental standards exceed what could be directly financed largely through the use of public funds. Investment requirements for energy, ports, roads, telecommunications, water supply and sewerage, and similar key sectors have been estimated in the tens of billions of U.S. dollars in the next 7 to 15 years. Even moderate investment requirements would exceed any reasonable potential allocation from budgetary resources. Moreover, a backlog of social infrastructure needs must be accommodated.

There is no simple answer, but in some cases, public resources could be leveraged with substantially higher private investment flows. There are many options for organizing and financing the provision of essential infrastructure services, ranging from total government ownership and control at one end of the spectrum to total privatization at the other. In the middle are such forms of public-private partnership as contracting out, management contracts, and various types of private concessions.

At the public end of the spectrum, the government owns, operates, and finances all infrastructure projects. The government is also responsible for raising the financing and bears all risks, including construction risks (and the risk that the project will not be completed on time and within budget), operating risks (including the risk of breakdowns, repairs, and reduced operating efficiency), and commercial risks (including the risk that the loan will have to repaid from budgetary resources if the facility does not generate the projected revenues). At the privatization end of the spectrum, all risks and responsibilities are shifted to private investors.

At intermediate points along the spectrum, the government and private sector share the risks and responsibilities according to a mutually agreed-upon formula. With management contracts, for example, a private firm is brought in to manage certain facilities. The firm receives a fixed fee for providing its services (in which case it bears none of the operating risks), or a fee based on certain performance criteria (in which case it bears some operational risks related to the efficiencies it achieves). The government retains ownership of the assets, remains responsible for financing new investments, and bears most of the financial and construction risks.

With private concessions (also known as limited-recourse project financing), even more of the risk and responsibility are shifted to the private sector and away from the public sector. A private concession company builds, finances, owns, and operates a (electricity, water treatment, waste water treatment) facility and sells (electricity, water treatment, waste water treatment) services to the national (power, water, waste water) enterprise, as the case may be. The existing national enterprise remains in day-to-day contact with industrial and residential customers and is responsible for billing, the basic provision and service of quality, and so on. But instead of producing the service entirely by itself, as it now does, the enterprise purchases these services from the private concession company. The concession contract codifies the terms and conditions under which the enterprise purchases services from the concession company. The government continues to regulate prices paid by industrial and domestic customers, but prices paid by the enterprise to the concession company are negotiated in advance and codified in the concession contract.

Under the terms of a typical limited recourse project, the construction, operations, and commercial risks are transferred from the government to the private investors, but the government retains ownership of the stock of existing assets. By determining when to authorize new concessions, defining the specific facility to be constructed and financed by private investors, and defining the terms and conditions under which private investors are expected to operate, the government retains significant control over the pace and content of new sector investments. In other words, government can retain control over critical issues at the same time that it transfers many risks and responsibilities to the private sector.

Aspects of these approaches can be combined into hybrid varieties of public/private cooperation. For example, a private company can be given a contract to manage the existing facilities as well as a concession to build, finance, and operate new facilities. Or public ownership and control of existing assets can be combined with loans from private banks and the local bond market to finance new, publicly owned assets — a common approach in the United States that has helped develop local capital markets.

To encourage private sector participation in these sectors, institutional arrangements must be devised that release operators from unnecessary burdensome controls and regulations. At the same time there must be provisions to protect the interests of end users, and to conform with general developmental objectives. The scope and duration of monopoly privileges must be determined and clearly separated from activities where there could be competition. Wherever possible, an attempt should be made to commercialize existing operations and renegotiate labor contracts before any private participation initiatives. It is also imperative to establish regulatory systems for tariffs, interconnections, and distribution and to clarify service goals and develop cost containment targets and incentives. Finally, a regulatory capability must be created or reinforced to oversee concessions and ensure that concessionaires are fulfilling their obligations.

Decentralization of the Public Sector

Decentralization has been an important item in Poland's drive to democratization and in the economic transition. Primary responsibility for certain spending and revenue decisions has been shifted from the center to the 2500 *gminy*; plans to increase decentralized decision-making have been on the agenda for some time. In this section, we address two issues of importance to the pace of decentralization: efficiency and equity criteria, and conditions needed for the fiscal sustainability of various layers of government. We also review the scope of, and financing mechanism for, local investment.

Three Years of Decentralization

The fundamental break from the state (as implementation agent of a central plan) to the decentralized state (with autonomous local governments accountable to their constituents) began with passage of the Local Self-Government Act (LSGA) in March 1990. The LSGA, a general policy statement, is broadly consistent with the Council of Europe's European Charter of Local Self-Government. Under the Act, local governments are to be held accountable to their constituents through free elections (with provisions for recall) and local budget execution is to be audited by Regional Accounting Offices; local government is an autonomous tier of government, its autonomy protected by the courts; national laws may oblige municipalities (*gminy*) to carry out delegated responsibilities; local governments are autonomous for budget formulation and implementation, but the Ministry of Finance shall provide general subsidies allocated on the basis of "objective criteria"; and gminy may form associations to provide services or for purposes of representation.

Poland's decentralization program has had mixed results. Implementation of LSGA objectives has been hampered by central government limitations on local autonomy and accountability (for example, caps on local revenues and on pricing of services, and rigidity about expenditures), and local initiatives have been limited by ambiguities in the intergovernmental assignment of responsibilities. On the positive side, beneficiaries' participation in local decisions appears to have improved the quality of local services. Local governments have not generated deficits and thus have supported macroeconomic stabilization. In 1991-93, local expenditures represented about 5 percent of GDP, and some 12 percent of general government expenditures. Local government investments accounted for over 40 percent of total public investment, increasing from 38 percent of the total in 1991 to 48 percent in 1993.[23]

There has been considerable debate about, and some political momentum for, further decentralization of public administration. One proposal is to reform the status of voivodships. Currently 49 voivodships — geographic branches of the central administration — implement numerous central programs, some with local spending. Voivodships also have oversight responsibilities for gmina expenditure performance, especially for functions delegated to gminy. Reform proposals include reducing the number of voivodships, delegating more responsibilities to them, and perhaps transforming them into some form of regional self-government consistent with the policy thrust of the LSGA.

---

23 For a broader discussion of the decentralization program, see *Poland: Decentralization and Reform of the State*, World Bank Country Study, 1992.

Box 2.4: Launching the Powiat Pilot Program

In late 1993, negotiations with each *gmina* eligible to participate in the pilot program were held at the voivodship level. After preliminary agreements were reached, the voivod negotiated with the appropriate (health, culture, and so on) central ministries – except for secondary schools, for which the central ministry's voivod representative (*kurator*) negotiated directly with *gminy*.

A central issue was the expectation that central fiscal transfers for new powiat functions would not be sufficient to provide "desirable levels" of powiat services. It was expected that other *gmina* revenues would be used for new powiat services as well. If implemented, this is an area of considerable ambiguity with potential for conflict, under the pilot program and beyond.

How to fund the pilot program has not been clear. In January 1994, the "old" flow of funds continued. Funds for secondary education in the pilot powiats, for example, were flowing (a) directly from the Ministry of Education to each school administration or (b) to the school administration via the *kurator*. The *gmina* (powiat) budget was not in the loop. Changes in the financial arrangements for the pilot program were discussed as part of negotiations for central budget adjustments. Key issues for financing the powiat pilot program included:

- The regularity of fiscal transfers for decentralized responsibilities.
- Reform in fiscal flows, with funds flowing from central ministries to voivodship, and then to *gmina* budgets.
- How to handle the accumulated debt of transferred facilities, many of which (such as schools, hospitals, libraries) have arrears, mainly to providers of water and electricity and the like. The pilot powiats, of course, want services transferred free of payment arrears. The magnitude of arrears may be inferred from Prime Minister Suchocka's legislative proposal to transfer all primary education to *gminy* in 1994. In the proposal was a provision that about $150 million of the primary schools' accumulated debt would be paid off before any transfer, with the debt payment provided for in the 1994 central budget. This proposal was retracted by the current government, so the issue remains unresolved.

If the decision is to have all fiscal transfers for new powiat responsibilities flow to the pilot *gmina* budgets (otherwise the pilot program seems meaningless), in theory local governments would have some discretion in their allocation, consistent with the Local Self-Government Act. For example, if the fiscal transfers to a pilot *gmina*'s budget for education and health were 100 for each sector, then in theory the *gmina* could allocate, say, 90 to education and 110 to health, or vice versa, according to local priorities. The *gmina* would have to meet service standards set by each ministry, or the service would be taken over by the corresponding ministry. In practice, this type of flexibility is quite limited, partly because of the severe rigidity in labor costs for decentralized services. Suppose, for example, that a *gmina* receives 100 school administrators and 250 teachers as a result of decentralization. The *gmina* decides that the quality of education would not suffer (or would improve) if the administrative staff were reduced to 20 and the teaching staff to 200. Apparently existing labor laws would not permit this change; education staff are covered by national legislation. Nor could education staff be re-deployed to other *gmina* functions. The *gmina*'s decision to cut back could be implemented only through attrition. In short, serious issues must be faced in the powiat pilot program, and further decentralization to *gminy*.

A separate reform proposal, advanced as a legislative proposal by the Suchocka government, is to (re-)create *powiat*. *Powiat* would replace *rejony*, (about 300) geographic districts of the voivodship administrations. Presumably, the responsibilities and financing of gminy would not be affected by the change. In fact, gminy with populations greater than 100,000 would not be incorporated into powiats. Rather, they would add powiat functions to those they already have. Key elements of the powiat proposal are as follows:

- Powiat boundaries would coincide with boundaries for a group of gmina. Each powiat would contain at least five gminy, (at least one with a population of 10,000 or more), and the minimum powiat population would be 50,000.

- The main responsibilities of powiats would be secondary and vocational education, health services with inter-gmina coverage, powiat-level roads, police and fire protection, district cultural institutions, land surveys, property registration, and veterinary supervision. The list is not fixed; it could extend to responsibility for education and health. The transfer of responsibilities might be phased in gradually.
- Powiat councils would be elected in direct elections and the councils would then select the powiat executive (seven to nine professionals) including the "governor" (*starost*). The executives would be paid for their work.
- The Chair of the Council of Ministers would supervise powiats generally; but where powiats are delegated voivodship tasks, the voivod would supervise. Regional audit offices would supervise Powiat financial management as they supervise gminy.

The current administration withdrew the legislative proposal to create powaits but maintained the decision of the previous administration to move forward on a powait pilot program. The pilot program is limited to the 46 gminy with populations of nine than 100,000, which together account for about one-third of Poland's population. The powiat pilot program was launched in January 1994. At that time, agreements with 43 gminy were in force, and gminy were responsible for education (35 gminy[24]), secondary health (32), social welfare (19), and culture (30) (see box 2.5).[25]

Decentralization Issues and Options

Issues associated with the pace and scope of decentralization may be addressed by analyzing two basic policy considerations: economic efficiency and institutional capacity.[26] Economic efficiency gains, a major reason for decentralization, are often approached through subsidiarity, or the principle that public services should be provided by the lowest level of government at which public policy objectives may most effectively be achieved. Through decentralization, Poland hopes to achieve efficiency in both spending and allocations.

Spending efficiency means delivering services to beneficiaries at the lowest possible unit cost for a given level of service. Local delivery of services links service providers with consumers so that consumer status and preferences are more transparent and may be addressed most effectively. Local governments executing national policies may target beneficiaries more effectively and when economies of scale are readily achievable at the local level, national government benefits from efficiency gains but benefits also spill over to the local jurisdiction.

Poland's decentralization merits high marks for spending efficiency because decentralization has generally been restricted to services for which benefits are limited to local jurisdictions, consumers participated in the design of services, and local jurisdictions provided economies of scale. Proposals for

---

24 Including not only secondary schools (Ministry of Education) but also specialized and sectoral training facilities (linked, for example, to ministries of agriculture, health, industry, culture).

25 Only physical facilities (such as schools) and related staff and equipment were transferred. Areas in which the transfer does not involve facilities (such as roads and environmental protection) are not covered.

26 Here we do not consider other important public sector objectives: stability and equity, assuming that all decentralization options should be consistent with sound macroeconomic stability policy and equity policy is primarily the responsibility of the central government, although local governments may help implement it. For a more detailed analysis of these issues, see *Poland: Decentralization and Reform of the State*, 1992, especially Chapter 2.

further decentralization should be evaluated by the same criteria. Under the powiat reform proposal, for example, some services (such as police and fire protection, cultural facilities, land surveys, property registration, and veterinary supervision) may meet these criteria and their transfer to powiats may enhance spending efficiency. For other proposed services (especially some education and health responsibilities), it is not clear that decentralization would improve spending efficiency. The comparative advantages of levels of government should be carefully examined before such services are decentralized to more independent voivodships or powiats. Especially important are significant spillover benefits of human capital services. The powiat pilot program could help inform these decisions if the spending efficiency of decentralization is carefully monitored.

Box 2.5: A Sample Survey of Local Government Investment

In early 1994, the Council of Minister's Office of Public Administration (OPAR), with Bank assistance, launched a detailed survey of investments in 27 gminy. This sample is not statistically representative (for example, "municipal economy" accounts for a higher share of investment in the 27 towns than nationwide), but the survey results offer insights into investment patterns:

- In 1993, the bulk of capital spending in the sample gminy was on sewage treatment (17 percent), water supply (15 percent), education (14 percent), streets (8 percent), sewage collection (8 percent), land development (8 percent), housing (6 percent), heat supply (5 percent), and urban transit (4 percent). The figure for street is low; surface rehabilitation is either insufficient or is counted largely as recurrent spending.

- Sewerage, sewage treatment, and transport were growth sectors in 1991-1993. The share of heat supply, streets, and water declined. Solid waste investment has been small but some gminy expect it to pick up sharply after 1994.

- The high share of the so-called environmental services (water and sanitation) may reflect local priorities as well as the greater availability of soft loans for these sectors (and avoiding polluter charges is an additional investment incentive).

- Gmina budget funds are widely used for such revenue-earning services as water supply. This may partly reflect slow progress in incorporating utilities (some are still included in the budget) and partly the fact that these services do not yet generate enough revenues from user charges.

- Some gminy are investing in several sectors (hospitals, schools, telephone lines) for which formal responsibility has not yet devolved to them, which suggests they perceive these services to be underprovided.

Allocative efficiency accrues when a service devolved to a local government matches consumer preferences against consumer willingness to pay. It works best when service benefits restricted to the provider's jurisdiction can be produced with appropriate economies of scale. Allocative efficiency is promoted when local government services are provided to residents according to their preferences and are financed mainly by the residents to whom most of the benefits accrue. This method of financing is also a key to holding local officials accountable to local citizens for the quality, coverage, and financing of local services. Local allocative efficiency may be best achieved with full local financing, but it can also be promoted by local financial responsibility "at the margin." For example, some local investments may be financed partially through local revenues (for accountability and efficiency), with a matching grant from the center (promoting national objectives and investment criteria). Similarly, local recurrent expenditures may be financed partially by general intergovernmental fiscal transfers (promoting fiscal balance) and by local own-source revenues (promoting allocative efficiency and accountability).

How Poland's decentralization has affected allocated efficiency is not clear. Ambiguity about the responsibilities of different levels of government and central constraints on local decision-making have limited local accountability and incentives to promote allocative efficiency. Any allocative efficiency gains achieved to date appear to have resulted from incremental local own-source financing, because *gminy* depend fairly heavily (for about 50 percent of funding) on fiscal transfers from the center, mostly general-purpose block grants, so all local services may be eligible for at least partial financing from central funds. This lack of clarity is not particularly troubling, as decentralization is in a transition period and allocative efficiency may increase as the process evolves and matures.

Unfortunately, current proposals do not provide for own-source revenues for voivodships or powiats. The Powiat proposal merely calls for additional fiscal transfers from the center based on rejony expenditures. This means there would be little or no political cost to powiat officials for providing powiat services, so there would be little or no financial accountability to beneficiaries and few incentives to improve allocative efficiency.

The Powiat Pilot Program may identify alternative, own-source revenues for powiat services. For example, the lifting of central limitations on the property tax may be explored for large urban gminy/powiats. The International City/County Management Association reports (based on a simulation done for Kraków) that an ad valorem property tax could support 34 to 40 percent of that gmina's budget based on current spending responsibilities, compared with 24 percent under current property taxes based on flat rates per area, with caps imposed by the central government.[27] Such reforms could not only reduce pressure on central revenues but increase accountability and incentives for local allocative efficiency.

Alternative own-source revenues for subnational governments should also be examined. Subnational government surcharges (or "piggybacks") on national personal income tax could be explored, for example. Establishing these surcharges through local political decisions (perhaps within limits established by the center) may promote accountability and allocative efficiency. Local surcharges on centrally defined and administered taxes are being used increasingly in Western Europe and other regions, and may be implemented quickly at a low administrative cost.

Institutional capacity needs to be strengthened in both central and subnational governments. In the central government, a Municipal Development Agency (MDA) was recently established, along the lines recommended by the Bank's 1992 decentralization report. The MDA whose charter and terms of reference are now being defined, should monitor decentralization benefits and costs, propose policy changes, and supervise policy implementation. The MDA could also be the focus of policy dialogue for further decentralization proposals. If further decentralization is implemented, an expanded MDA would have an even more important role in promoting subnational government spending and allocative efficiency. The Office for Public Administration Reform and the recently constituted Committee on Intergovernmental Relations are steps in the right direction, but Poland needs a stronger institution, to handle decentralization.

Local governments also need strengthening. The MDA could be a channel for providing technical assistance to local governments, especially from international donors. The local government finance law for 1994 stipulates that the central government may guarantee loans to local governments,

---

27 Joseph Eckert, Bob West, and Roy Kelly, "A Framework for the Developing of the Legal and Administrative Structure for Implementing an Ad Valorem Property Tax in Poland", ICMA report for U.S.AID, mimeo., May 1993.

but local governments must improve their financial accounting and reporting systems so lenders can evaluate their creditworthiness and so the Ministry of Finance can decide on the merit, and cost, of central government guarantees.

Financing Municipal Investment

The Local Self-Government Act gives local government responsibility to provide a broad range of local infrastructure and services. Local governments have assumed the ownership of service assets, and the responsibility to mobilize resources for the operation, maintenance, and expansion of services. They have taken primary responsibility for formulating, funding, and implementing a relatively large investment program that was previously carried out under instructions (and funding) from the center. This devolution of expenditures has happened, however, without mechanisms for vetting projects, and in a very undeveloped financing environment.

Total gmina investment in 1993 reached Zł 15 trillion (about US$900 million, or 1.3 percent of GDP). At 47 percent, the ratio of municipal to total government capital expenditures is relatively high by OECD standards, but reflects mainly the low level of public investment in recent years. Since local government is in charge of such capital-intensive services such as streets, drainage, water, and heating utilities, Poland's municipal sector should invest much more — say, about 3 percent of GDP, with water and waste-water alone accounting for over 1 percent — especially considering the backlog of deferred maintenance accumulated from the 1980s, and the legacy of environmental neglect.

The national data should be interpreted with caution. Gmina investment is likely to be underreported. Rehabilitation or small capital expansion works by gmina construction crews may be counted as recurrent spending. The investments of incorporated utilities do not appear in the local government budget (although transfers to such utilities appear). The sectoral distribution of investments is difficult to discern as several major urban services are bundled into one broad budget item, "Municipal Economy," which accounts for almost two-thirds of all gmina investment. And budget classifications are not always consistent: similar street construction investments in different gminy can be entered as roads, as streets and bridges (part of municipal economy), or as land development for housing.

Sources of funds. The main source of funds for local government investment is current savings. Nationwide, gmina current savings amounted to 80 percent of capital expenditures.[28] Local governments and enterprises meet 70 percent to 90 percent of project costs from their own funds in all sectors except sewage treatment (33 percent) and streets (62 percent).

Other funding sources include voivodships grants (in all sectors except education), grants or soft loans from the voivodship and national environmental funds (VEF for water and NEF for sanitation), national budget grants (mainly for streets, housing, and public transport), and the Kuratoria (for schools). Data on these sources are not readily available. In 1992, the NEF spent Zł 0.46 trillion and

---

[28] Current savings are overstated. The "other revenues" item in the municipal budgets, accounted as current, includes the proceeds of asset sales, which should be reported as capital receipts Asset sales are an appropriate source of investment funds but not a basis for sustained operation or debt service commitments.

the VEFs Zł 1.63 trillion for "water protection" investments (the dollar total was up 60 percent from 1991), but that is not just municipal investment.[29]

Except for sewage treatment, the relative levels of national budget support (direct or through voivodships) for different types of investment in the sample gminy do not suggest clear sectoral priorities, so central funds are unlikely to substantially affect the allocation of municipal spending. An argument could be made for streamlining some of the capital grant programs channeled through national or regional agencies. If the objective is just to transfer resources across the board, this could be achieved more simply by topping up the block grant or the tax-sharing formula.

Lack of access to long-term credit. Commercial borrowing is a negligible source of municipal investment finance. NBP data for April 1993 show the total stock of debt owed by local governments to domestic banks with maturities over one year at US$10 million equivalent, or only 1 percent of annual sector investment, and most of that was Eco Bank loans with interest rate support from NEF. With few and minor exceptions (two towns borrowed small amounts from German Landesbanks), municipal investment takes place entirely on a pay-as-you-go basis.

In decentralized market economies, commercial debt financing (in the form of loans or securities) is an essential component of municipal investment finance. It enables local governments or service enterprises to better match the burden of "lumpy" investments with the period of their benefits. It also provides a strong incentive for sound management. U.S. bond rating agencies have a greater impact on local fiscal discipline in the United States than any federal watchdog does. The availability of credit allows viable projects to be started with a complete financing plan and to be completed on time. It also alleviates the need for central grant funding, and thus strengthens local autonomy and accountability.

But in the short term, anyway, Poland's domestic financial sector is unlikely to meet the borrowing needs of its municipal sector, even for commercially viable projects, because of weaknesses in both the financial and municipal sectors. Polish banks have not developed full loan appraisal capabilities, and are burdened with losses; their liabilities are mainly short-term and their lending capacity is absorbed largely by the central government. Municipalities and local enterprises generate a cash flow that could sustain sizeable borrowing, but they have no credit record and their financial planning and reporting systems are still rudimentary and not designed to substantiate their creditworthiness.

Impact on investment efficiency. The "cash-only" financing of capital expenditures limits the feasible pace and efficiency of local investment:

- Lack of credit seriously impairs local governments' ability to mobilize the resources they need for the timely repair, replacement, improvement, or expansion of basic infrastructure. Even financially sound and cost-effective projects must be postponed because of cash constraints. The infrastructure bottlenecks that ensue hinder economic growth and the improvement of living standards. Slow infrastructure delivery also

---

29 The NEF also invests in treatment facilities or process improvements for industrial plants, for example, and does not keep a separate account of its contributions to municipal utilities. Its statistics are organized by environmental objectives, such as air quality or water protection.

delays housing development, which limits worker mobility. Employment opportunities in construction are lost, and delays in repairing or replacing existing assets threaten the reliability of such basic services as heating, water supply, and urban transport.

- Lack of credit creates inequities between current users, who bear the full burden of investments, and future users who will benefit from services over the typically long useful life of infrastructure assets.

- It also militates against the efficient planning and implementation of projects, as the result of financing gaps is protracted completion delays, the loss of economies of scale in construction, and long idle periods for "work-in-progress" assets. Projects that could be completed in 2 to 3 years with a fully funded financing plan often have annual progress rates well below one-tenth of total cost. A sewage treatment plant in Wroclław, for instance, has been under construction for 17 years, and at the current pace of construction will need another 20 years before completion.

Policy Options for Developing a Municipal Credit Market

What are the options for improving municipal access to credit? One is to wait for the problem to solve itself. Municipal credit is likely to develop on its own when the financial sector is restructured, inflation abates, central borrowing shrinks, and municipalities advance on their learning curves. A do-nothing option would ensure that municipal credit ultimately develops strictly on market terms, and would eliminate the risk of a botched intervention creating bad credit for the central budget. However, the need for investment in local infrastructure and services may not be met during critical transition years.

The do-nothing option also presents some risks for fiscal and financial discipline. Public demand for better urban services could lead gminy to run unfinanced deficits and in turn to lobby the national government for grants or bailouts. Targeted national funds (such as the NEF and VEF) may come under pressure to fill a vacuum by stretching themselves beyond the focused programs for which they are intended. Another risky possibility which has strong support in local government circles, is that groups of gminy might create and own development banks, lending to their members. The risks involved would be insider lending and asset concentration, and serious prudential problems if they receive deposits from the public and are backed by a national deposit insurance scheme. Preventing this development may be politically less difficult if alternative credit sources are available.

The need for some degree of intervention is recognized in the recently approved Local Finance Law, which introduces the possibility of central government guarantees for gmina borrowing. But such guarantees would be more effective if they were part of a structured program with specific eligibility rules, technical assistance, and mechanisms to gradually shed the risk onto commercial lenders.

Government intervention in municipal credit must address two issues: term transformation (to compensate for the lack of long-term money in the economy); and credit risk enhancement. Term transformation alone (for example, an apex line of credit financed from long-term external borrowing and intermediated by the banking sector) would probably not work, as shown by recent experience with a credit line to supply heating, which has not moved any funds. Credit risk enhancement (a national agency assuming all or part of the risk of default by municipal borrowers) is feasible, because it is easier for the government to secure gmina collateral than for a commercial bank to do so. The government could intercept future intergovernmental transfers in the event of default, for example.

CHAPTER 3: STIMULATING THE SUPPLY RESPONSE

The supply response in Poland since 1990 is attributable largely to expansion of the private sector. With appropriate short-term macroeconomic management and the reform of public sector finances, the government can provide an environment for continued private sector development. But to sustain the momentum of the supply response, concerted action is needed in structural reform. Lack of progress in SOE privatization and financial sector reform hampers private sector growth. Big quasi-fiscal deficits from the loss-making state enterprises and important segments of the banking sector could hurt the budget for years to come, undermining macroeconomic stability and constricting public finance. Agricultural policies have stimulated change in a crucial sector, but often seem to oscillate between conflicting objectives. This chapter reviews progress in reform in critical areas of the economy.

Privatization, Governance, and the Restructuring of State Enterprises

The core problem in transforming Poland into a market-oriented economy is transforming the state enterprise sector. Privatization and the enforcement of hard budget constraints have been the mainstays of the government strategy since 1990, and tremendous progress has been achieved in a relatively short time. But the transformation is far from complete. Privatization has been slower than wished for, and much of industry is still state-owned, without effective ownership control. Enforcement of the hard budget constraint has meant that many state enterprises that were already in fairly good shape (for one reason or another) have been able to take advantage of the surge in demand, and — prodded by tighter constraints exercised by banks and fiscal authorities — have registered substantial productivity and profitability gains. Others, however, unable to overcome more unfavorable financial and economic circumstances have adopted defensive attitudes, exerting pressure on the government to help them for social reasons. Paradoxically, the improved financial condition of most state enterprises carries with it the danger of a greater downfall, should discipline fail. Critical decisions are required to prevent slippage. Strategic elements that have worked must be reaffirmed, and the problem of loss-makers must be addressed.

Progress on Privatization

Progress on privatization has been continuous, albeit below high initial expectations. By December 30, 1993 (three and a half years into implementation), the Ministry of Privatization recorded 2,097 fully privatized state enterprises or about 25 percent of the original — an increase of almost 600 over the previous year (table 3.1).[1] Proceeds from privatization for 1993 exceeded US$400 million, up from US$360 million in 1992. Another 423 enterprises have been commercialized but not yet privatized; still owned by the State Treasury, they await capital privatization or mass privatization. Some 1,595 agricultural enterprises (state farms and agroindustrial enterprises) have been transferred to the

---

[1] A "commercialized" enterprise, the shares of which are still in the hands of the State Treasury (a so-called one-person-Treasury-owned enterprise), is not considered fully privatized; only when a controlling block of shares has been transferred to a strategic investor (for example, through trade deals), or a majority of the shares are in the hands of private investors (for example, through an Initial Public Offering) can the enterprise be considered privatized. The Ministry of Privatization keeps track only of privatization of entire enterprises. It does not record the transfer of major assets (often entire production lines) of a state enterprise to a new private entity (through a sale or the creation of a private joint venture) when the original state enterprise still legally exists thereafter and the major "asset deals" (for example, when FIAT took over most FSM car manufacturing) are in this second category, controlled by technical ministries and not the Minister of Privatization. There is considerably under-reporting of privatization.

Agriculture State Property Agency, which is in the process of liquidating or privatizing them or selling or leasing their land. Another 263 state enterprises had been transferred to municipalities. The total manpower of privatized enterprises at the time of privatization is an estimated 500,000 to 600,000 employees. The remaining 5,924 state enterprises are mainly in industry (2,752) and construction (988).

Table 3.1: Privatization of State Enterprises

		Remaining enterprises	Privatized state enterprises				
			Liquidation			Capital privatization	
			Art. 19	Art. 37	Total	Total	Total
All Sectors	1990-93	5,924	1,082	917	1,999	98	2,097
	in 1993		*285*	*255*	*540*	*48*	*588*
Industry	1990-93	2,495	327	275	602	41	643
	in 1993		*68*	*106*	*174*	*23*	*197*
Construction	1990-93	1,016	273	351	624	7	631
	in 1993		*105*	*64*	*169*	*3*	*346*
Agriculture	1990-93	806	237	49	286	..	286
	in 1993		*65*	*22*	*87*	..	*87*
Other	1990-93	1,607	245	242	487	50	537
	in 1993		*47*	*63*	*110*	*22*	*132*

Source: Ministry of Privatization.

Although privatization brought more revenues in 1993, the pace of privatization (measured by the number of enterprises transformed) was slower than in 1992. The voluntary bottom-up approach (in which the enterprise proposes itself for privatization, or at a least agrees with government recommendations to do so) continues to drive the process. Privatization results have been mixed, depending on the privatization track pursued by the Ministry of Privatization: capital privatization, privatization through liquidation, restructuring privatization, or mass privatization.

The number of medium-size and large enterprises privatized through *capital privatization* (including initial public offerings and trade deals involving foreign investors) rose from 24 in 1992 to 45 in 1993 for a total of 98 since the program's inception. Capital privatization has made significant progress in some industrial subsectors. Most medium-size and large enterprises were transferred to private owners (including large multinationals) — for example, in glass, confectionery, detergent, heavy electrical equipment, car and light vehicle manufacturing, and telecommunications equipment.[2] There has been little or no progress in privatizing the *heavy chemical industry* (despite expressions of interest from well-known investors), the *oil sector* (despite the outline of a privatization plan in 1993 and foreign investor interest), or *very large concerns*, such as the Copper Kombinat Polska Miedz (blocked by employee lobbying) and the ORBIS hotel and tourism group.

---

[2] The privatization of five large enterprises generated revenues of $75 million (from the sale of shares) for the budget, with commitments for additional equity from the foreign investors amounting to $70 million and investment commitments of $160 million over six years. A key condition, however, has been a "market" guarantee for the three multinationals, who are assured of practically no outside competition on the Polish market for six years.

Liquidation remains the most popular approach — applied mostly to small and medium-size enterprises, generally through employee buyout. The rate of privatization on this track slowed down in 1993, falling to 331 (from 618 in 1992). This slowdown may be partly because the easiest transformations (attractive enterprises, or enterprises with managers and workers supportive of privatization) were completed in 1990-92. Many of the state enterprises are in less solid financial condition. Some are candidates for bankruptcy, others need debt restructuring or forgiveness or need to separate enterprise parts (a complex process) and determine which need liquidating and which can survive as privatized concerns. Another reason for the slowdown is the wait-and-see attitude of personnel in many state enterprises, who expect more favorable buyouts under the SOE Pact. The form of "liquidation" used most often (about 75 percent of enterprises) has been the leasing of assets, generally led by managers and employees.

Privatization through restructuring (management contracts with an option to purchase at preferential terms) of small to medium-size enterprises is progressing with less success than initially hoped for. Bids were received for 11 of the 15 enterprises processed with the help of consultants financed by USAID (5 enterprises) and by the World Bank's privatization and restructuring loan (10 enterprises). The first management contracts are being processed and bids for 12 more enterprises (prepared by consultants financed with French assistance) are being solicited in early 1994. Despite the limited success of the scheme, the Minister of Privatization plans to pursue it in a modified form. The advantage of this pilot project is the lessons it offers for later large-scale schemes involving management contracts plus attractive options to purchase medium-size to large enterprises.

Another attractive feature of Polish privatization has been the debt-equity swap option as a follow- up to commercial debt and debt service reductions, and the push to commercialize state enterprises as part of the innovative Bank-led conciliatory proceedings introduced under the Enterprise and Bank Restructuring Program. It is too early to know whether this will boost state enterprise transformation. But the demonstration effect, lessons from the first debt-to-equity swaps, and the proactive stance adopted by some banks and former creditors (as new shareholders in privatized state enterprises) should be used to privatize additional heavily indebted state enterprises — and to support the simultaneous restructuring of enterprises.

Measures to Accelerate Privatization

The government has reaffirmed its commitment to rapid privatization. Its *General Privatization Guidelines for 1994*, adopted as an Annex to the 1994 budget, articulate the government's intentions for the mass privatization program (MPP), and outline commendable priorities. These include:

- Linking privatization to restructuring, increased local and foreign investment, and the development of capital markets.
- Implementing the Enterprise Pact (a modified form of the 1992/93 proposals).
- Submitting to Parliament, and implementing, the Reprivatization Law.
- Improving the regulatory framework for enterprise liquidation, registration, and concessions, for the protection of creditors, and so on.
- Supporting the creation of new enterprises and the development of old private businesses by providing a stable, stimulating legal and financial environment.
- Promoting local investment (by individuals, managers, or workers) by making enterprise purchase financing schemes more accessible to them (better terms for leasing, better management contracts, installment terms).
- Developing the equity market, partly through more initial public offerings.

- Preparing laws on the State Treasury and on the management of Treasury-owned assets.

There is a particularly strong emphasis on favoring domestic investors and on recapitalizing enterprises by issuing new shares during privatization, instead of maximizing budget revenues by selling existing shares to private owners. The 1994 budget revenues from privatization are targeted at about US$500 million.

The government's policy intentions are commendable. But unless decisive steps are taken, Poland's privatization program may increasingly lag behind, and be completed later than, other countries that started later but adopted a more forceful approach. Improving current privatization methods will help, but not enough. It is time for Poland to update its privatization strategy, extend it to all remaining enterprises, and create a time-bound plan. Except for a few enterprises with special characteristics that could remain under state ownership longer, a program should be drafted with dated objectives by category and type of enterprise, so that there is a schedule under which all state enterprises will have been privatized or (for non-viable enterprises) liquidated, with assets made available for transfer to private owners. This was the approach originally envisaged in the SOE Pact. It should be revived and expanded.

The revised privatization plan should clearly spell out which enterprises will remain under full or majority state ownership for a longer time, and why. The list of exceptional enterprises should not be cast in stone but should be regularly revisited. The "strategic" classification may no longer be justified or private investors may emerge, willing to operate under a regulatory framework that protects public interests; when that happens, a significant share of equity could be privatized. Only in such "strategic" cases would individual transactions need government consultations on a higher level (with the approval of details resting with the Minister of Privatization). The strategic list should be reviewed and redefined at regular intervals by the Council of Ministers and Parliament, informed by the annual privatization guidelines.[3] A new institution in the State Treasury should be organized, a small state entity responsible for the oversight only of this limited (and shrinking) portfolio of strategic enterprises. Still, the government needs to clearly define a policy and execute a program for divestiture of its residual minority shareholdings (generally around 20 percent) in a growing number of medium-size and large enterprises privatized through initial public offerings and trade deals since 1990; it should not burden the State Treasury with the task of managing an unnecessarily big portfolio. The policy of keeping a "golden share" should be revisited and replaced by other legal and regulatory measures, and maintained only in exceptional cases. Such divestiture could be effected to the benefit of pension funds, a restitution fund with a finite life, or other institutional investors.

The existing privatization tracks are adaptable to the proposed strategy, if shortcomings are rectified. The *liquidation approach* has a credible track record; it could be applied to many viable state-owned small and medium-size enterprises and would appeal to more investors. The cash constraints and undercapitalization that often weaken employee buyouts could be alleviated in several ways. For example, the limited cash provided initially by the employees and their cash revenues in the early years would be used not to buy out the state but for a capital increase (often coupled with debt redemption).[4] Venture capital equity funds, which provide additional capital up front in the liquidation privatization of small and medium-size enterprises, should be encouraged and the tax treatment of capital gains should be compatible with international standards. The development of an active second or third

---

3 An exception would be enterprises, such as the railways, that are currently governed by a specific law.

4 New shares issued through a capital increase allowing reimbursement of debt could be issued below book value for existing capital, giving the new investor a favorable status.

market on the Warsaw stock exchange, geared to smaller and more risky enterprises with less stringent reporting requirements, would encourage employee buyouts and the participation of equity funds and other investors. The availability of *post-privatization restructuring assistance*, under attractive financial terms, could significantly encourage investors; partly funded by foreign grants, it would provide mainly technical assistance, training, and possibly one-shot financial support for laid-off workers.

Capital privatization should continue to play a major role in the new, expanded strategy, but two important problems must be addressed: the fast turnover of high-caliber Polish staff in the Ministry of Privatization and the climate of suspicion fueled by political accusations and investigations of transactions involving foreign investors. The Ministry of Privatization spent far too much time and energy responding to these investigations, had to repeatedly rebuild its Capital Privatization Department, and had great difficulty attracting good professionals. The government should give high priority to solving these two problems.

State enterprises less attractive to investors (with reasonable prospects for turnaround after managerial or "defensive" restructuring) should be put on a revamped *privatization restructuring* track, based on management contracts plus options to purchase within a specified time-frame. Successful managers would be rewarded with favorable terms for taking over ownership of the enterprises. Such formulas should be applied mainly to small and medium-size enterprises but could be proposed for large industrial enterprises, with the idea of eliciting bids from well-targeted foreign groups (with experience or interest in the specific industry) and consortia built around Polish investment institutions. A special legislative and fiscal regime (eliminating double taxation of dividends) for holding companies could be adopted to support the emergence of such groups and to encourage their involvement in restructuring-plus-privatization. Debt-equity swaps in the framework of foreign debt reduction are another tool to encourage risk-taking and investment in complex enterprise restructuring.

It is generally easier to transform or privatize small and medium-size enterprises than to do so for large state enterprises; there is better knowledge of the enterprise's situation, stronger motivation, and simpler administrative work. One sensible step might step be a blanket program for all state enterprises up to a certain size and not in total financial distress, decentralizing to voivods the administrative work (and, for a limited period, the supervision of enterprise ownership). This would leave only the 200 to 300 largest state enterprises under the purview of the ministries in Warsaw. The government would instruct voivods to transform all their enterprises within a year and to privatize most (for example, 90 percent) of them within two years, maximum.

As the mass privatization program is being implemented and its benefits appreciated by enterprises and investors, the Ministry of Privatization should organize additional waves of mass privatization with different characteristics: some focusing, for example, on medium-size enterprises and not only on the remaining large state enterprises, others (less risk-oriented funds) specializing in public utilities.

Some state enterprises have transferred many of their productive assets to other enterprises (leasing them or contributing them to joint ventures), so the original state enterprises are often little more then empty shells living off of revenues that should accrue to the state. A systematic inventory of such shell enterprises is now warranted, with the aim of selling all assets or shares to private owners, liquidating the shell, and using the proceeds to pay off unsatisfied creditors of the original state enterprise. A parallel program — based on the results of the Enterprise and Bank Restructuring program — could be funded to handle the debt of heavily indebted state enterprises, to make them more attractive for privatization.

Adoption of an ambitious final privatization program will need broad support. The benefits of privatization are often blurred, in debates focused more on ideology than on facts. Poland and other countries in the region now have enough experience with privatized enterprises and foreign investment to know first-hand the benefits of privatization. Comprehensive post-privatization analysis should be carried out under the auspices of the Ministry of Privatization and the results widely publicized. A similar campaign should be prepared for foreign investors, geared to attracting medium-size companies to invest in small and medium-size Polish enterprises, the segment of the economy that worldwide has generated the most growth and new jobs.

Governance of state enterprises. The start-up of the mass privatization program was repeatedly postponed and the Ministry of Privatization was unable to privatize more commercialized state enterprises through capital privatization, so the population of state enterprises transformed into one-person Treasury-owned joint stock companies controlled by the Ministry of Privatization increased to more than 450 by early 1994. Limited progress has been made in effectively supervising these enterprises, as everyone has been waiting for a decision about the future State Treasury. In theory, commercialization of a state enterprise should improve governance, but the limbo in which many commercialized enterprises linger has produced only minor improvements in enterprises. The enforcement of hard budget constraints and the credibility of no-bail-out policies seems to have improved the performance of some state enterprises.

Not that the role and set-up of the State Treasury is not important, but a State Treasury is not a substitute for privatization. The Ministry of Privatization intentionally proposed the State Treasury Agency (STA) for a late stage, when the full privatization of many more state enterprises would have become irreversible (to prevent STA becoming a holding company with a huge portfolio and a tendency toward self-perpetuation). The Ministry of Privatization envisages the State Treasury as a lean institution, delegating ownership functions as much as possible to the regions ("delegaturas"), using management contracts with different entities (such as banks), and retaining 10 percent of privatization proceeds to finance the minimum restructuring of enterprises. This concept should be further studied, and after harmonization with a new Privatization Law and an updated privatization strategy, formalized through a draft law.

Divestiture of social assets. There is increasing awareness of the difficulties involved in divesting state enterprises of ancillary assets. A USAID-financed study highlighted the magnitude of the problem and suggested some recipes for divestiture,[5] but no program or team has been set up to assist state enterprises on this issue, which delays and sometimes prevents privatization. It is urgent that the Ministry of Privatization develop and supervise an action program, establishing a project team to begin with, to help on the divestiture of state enterprises' ancillary assets.

Restitution and reprivatization. Poland lags behind several countries in establishing clear legislation on reprivatization, covering restitution and compensation of former owners for previously confiscated property. Although this issue has not had a major impact on the privatization of state enterprises, it could (with some 150,000 claims already filed) have a significant impact on the budget. If properly managed, on the other hand, it could become a helpful tool in privatization. Several draft laws have been prepared since 1993, but none has been enacted. The objectives and principles previously stated by MoP remain sound:

- Minimize the possible impact on the Budget.
- No compensation in cash.
- Return the property in kind, if it can be easily and clearly separated from other property -- or alternatively, return equivalent property.

---

[5] A 45-percent "gift" tax, for example, often effectively blocks proposed asset giveaways to employees or other entities.

- If this is not possible, compensate through reprivatization vouchers.[6]

Privatization has been constrained from the beginning by budget and staff limitations. Staff constraints have been acute because of the high turnover of Polish experts in the Ministry of Privatization, for which the support of foreign advisors cannot fully compensate. An increased budget, more staffing, new teams to develop and implement new privatization initiatives, policies to retain Polish professionals, better use of foreign experts and other externally funded support programs, and better coordination are needed to enhance the Ministry's capability.

Streamlining the Loss-Making Sectors

Disposition of a remaining group of nonviable enterprises through liquidation has been continuously postponed for various reasons. The size of this group is considerable, and so are its problems. Loss-making state enterprises account for perhaps 15 percent of industrial employment. They tend to involve large white-elephant factories as well as coal mining and the railways. Government strategy for this group has not been precisely formulated and problems have compounded. Restructuring plans for three large sectors (coal, steel, railways) envisage substantial downsizing, coupled with aid to displaced workers for severance, retraining, and relocation. Substantial progress has been made in some cases (box 3.1) but key decisions must still be made. Obviously, caution must be exercised in implementing plans that involve large reductions in workforce, but the focus should now shift to finding vehicles to cushion the social impact of restructuring (which could be supported by resources from international donors), so losses are gradually brought under control.

Funding for the social costs of adjustment must be clearly identified. The resources currently available in the intervention fund for the Enterprise and Bank Restructuring program are probably insufficient, and must be supplemented (particularly in the 1995 budget) for restructuring plans to be credible. Key decisions must also be made about how available funds will be used. The government has recently been discussing initiatives to develop alternative sources of employment in areas that are, or are likely to become, sources of unemployment as a result of restructuring. These plans, which call for collaboration among local authorities and increased private initiative, should be developed, to take advantage of available funding from European Union sources under the STRUDER program.

A number of state enterprises that are financially precarious do not belong to "sectors in crisis" but are in bankruptcy. The main creditors for most of these enterprises are the Treasury and ZUS, as they have substantial tax arrears. The government intends to take the lead in a bankruptcy-like procedure for these enterprises, along the lines of the Enterprise and Bank Restructuring Program. Through its Treasury chambers, the government will negotiate with enterprises plans to lead them toward becoming current in their tax obligations, and eventually catch up on arrears. Among schemes being put forward, one is to convert outstanding obligations into convertible bonds that would be exercised at the moment of privatization. This strategy is worthy of support, provided certain principles are maintained. First, restructuring plans should be time-bound, with commercialization of the enterprise up front and no new investments before privatization. Second, enterprises that are unable to come up with an acceptable plan, or are unable to enter any of the privatization tracks after a certain period, automatically end up in a streamlined-liquidation program.

---

6 Such vouchers could, among other things, be exchanged for shares of a new Fund owning packages of shares of privatized state enterprises (for example, 5 percent of the mass privatization companies) or used to purchase municipal housing.

Box 3.1: Two Restructuring Plans: Railroads and Coal

Railways

Polish Railways (PKP), which employs about 250,000 people, had losses in 1993 amounting to Zł 2 trillion, after receiving subsidies amounting to Zł 5.8 trillion, or about 0.5 percent of GDP. This understates true losses, from inadequate depreciation and inadequate repair and maintenance. Polish Railways is also one of the largest creditors of the PPWW to the Treasury. Substantial restructuring has already occurred: in the mid-1980s the company employed about 450,000 employees and was engaged in everything from meat processing to jail administration.

Under a restructuring plan that has been in the works for some time, Polish Railways would restructure its monolithic railroad system along its principal lines of business: commercial freight (primarily coal), intercity passenger, international passenger, and local and suburban passenger services. Eventually, it is expected to have an infrastructure department servicing institutionally separated lines of business - with suitable nondiscriminatory compensation for track use paid by each line of business (in line with European Union directives). Suburban passenger activities will be spun off to local agencies or covered under "contracts" with national or local governments, to provide unremunerative public services in return for adequate compensation. PKP will transfer its liabilities (mainly surplus labor) and nonrail assets (mainly urban real estate) to a new authority. It will try to transfer its nonrailway activities to the private sector.

The upshot of this reorganization will be to separate commercial services (unregulated and unsupported) from public services, such as urban and suburban passenger services, rural lines, and certain lines of strategic importance. The public services are to be planned and paid for by public authorities. About 30 percent of the employees will become redundant under the new streamlined corporations, so reorganization will not be painless. Transport patterns will also change more rapidly than under the old system. The gains to the economy will be considerable, however: a profitable, efficient railway system providing good service. The alternative, should these plans fall through, will be increasing costs of the government.

Coal

There are more than 300,000 employees in the sector. The Polish coal mining sector (once the industrial elite) registered gross losses in 1993 of Zł 10 trillion (0.6 percent of GDP). It is generally recognized that the sector needs restructuring. In 1990 the government targeted the seven biggest loss-making mines for closure, knowing that another eight to twelve mines would also have to be closed. But action came slowly: Hard coal prices were not liberalized until April 1992, when trade was liberalized and the phase-out of direct subsidies began. The full-fledged restructuring program was outlined only in early 1993. The objective of the hard-coal restructuring program is to make the sector efficient and competitive in a market economy, in environmentally and socially acceptable ways. The plan was supposed to evolve in three phases. Phase one was to include reorganization of the sector, commercialization of companies, cost-cutting measures, and the renegotiation of prices between mines and major customers. Crucial measures – such as mine closures and mergers, and rationalization of the labor force in the newly formed mining companies – could not be addressed in an election period, for lack of funding and progress on social support measures. Social support measures are projected to take place in the *second phase* (1994/95). Further rationalization is envisaged for the *third phase* (1996 to 2000), which is still being refined.

The program will entail legal severance pay, special incentive packages for early retirement or "miner's holidays," labor adjustment services, job creation programs, worker retraining programs, and so on. Closures, mergers, worker and mining company rationalization will reduce employment in the sector by an estimated 52,000. It has been agreed with the unions that there will be no forced dismissals. Only natural attrition and voluntary departures in return for incentive packages will be used to reduce jobs.

This procedure would be supported by measures to:

- Modify laws and regulations on real liquidation to simplify procedures and require liquidators to complete liquidation within a certain period.
- Set up principles and a fund for (partial) essential claims.
- Develop a market/exchange for assets of liquidated stock enterprises and "unwanted" (ancillary) assets of other state enterprises.
- Possibly introduce an additional voucher scheme allowing mass purchase of those assets. Assets of liquidated stock enterprises could be made more attractive by developing streamlined procedures (special courts) to accelerate decisions on land and building titles.

Reform of the Financial Sector

Financial sector reform is crucial in Poland's transformation to a market economy. Real resources cannot easily be relocated without credit, and efforts to bring financial discipline and a hard budget constraint to state enterprises will be fruitless without stronger financial markets. The government's strategy has been to introduce competition and private sector activity to financial markets; to strengthen both the central bank and nine Treasury-owned banks that resulted from the break-up of the old monobank in the late 1980s; to create a framework resolving portfolio problems inherited from before; and to establish the regulatory and institutional framework for a securities market. Meanwhile, macroeconomic stabilization policies, including positive real interest rates, are expected to result in the remonetization of the economy; so is the progressive reduction (in line with disinflation) in reserve requirements imposed on the banking system.

In this section we review progress in the implementation of this strategy. We argue that:

- Incomplete macroeconomic stabilization, and the resulting high rate of inflation, are the main reasons for the stunted growth of credit and the virtual lack of long-term credit.
- Progress has been made in restoring sound balance sheets for the Treasury-owned commercial banks, with a positive contribution to enterprise restructuring.
- Considerably less progress has been made with agriculture and housing credit; elaborating a strategy for reform and privatization of the specialized banks is the next item on the government's agenda.
- The troubles experienced by a number of private banks underscore the importance of strengthening supervision.
- Encouraging the development of non-bank financial intermediation can be fostered by appropriate policies.

Financing the Needs of the Economy: Monetization and Intermediation

Financial markets remain relatively shallow in Poland. Total broad money, at about 31 percent of GDP, is lower than in other Western economies. Its increase relative to GDP in the past three years is attributable almost entirely to increases in foreign exchange deposits, which at end-1993 accounted for 29 percent of the money supply (table 3.2). Złoty money, on the other hand, after a substantial increase in 1991, has remained roughly constant as a share (about 22 percent) of GDP and fell in real terms toward the end of 1993. Banking intermediation — which accounts for most financial intermediation, measured as broad money net of currency holdings — increased by 4 to 5 percentage points between end-1991 and end 1993, to about 26 percent of GDP. But again, about half of this increase come from the rise in foreign currency deposits. Złoty deposits, on the other hand, after rapid increases in 1990-91, stagnated in real terms in 1992 and dropped in the second half of the 1993, the result of reduced enterprise deposits (both in Złoty and foreign exchange), perhaps because of the large wage awards in late 1993 (although there is also a long-term trend toward better management of assets and liabilities).

Table 3.2: Poland - Monetary Aggregates
(Zloty Trillion)

	1990	1991 1/	1991 2/	1992	1993
Broad Money	190.6	281.0	257.1	411.1	559.2
(real % increase) 3/	-43.1	-8.1	-15.9	10.8	-1.1
(% of GDP) 4/	24.4	29.3	29.1	29.4	30.3
Zloty Money	130.8	215.5	192.7	309.2	398.3
(real % increase) 3/	42.1	2.7	-8.1	11.2	-6.4
(% of GDP) 4/	14.5	22.0	21.8	22.0	22.2
Currency	39.3	56.4	56.4	78.0	99.8
(real % increase) 3/	14.0	-10.7	-10.7	-4.1	-7.0
Bank Deposits in Zloty	91.4	159.1	136.3	231.2	298.5
(real % increase) 3/	58.9	8.5	-7.0	17.5	-6.2
Firms	58.7	71.8	..71.8	109.5	135.9
(real % increase) 3/	100.2	-23.7	..-23.7	5.7	-9.8
Households	32.8	87.4	..64.5	121.7	162.7
(real % increase) 3/	17.4	66.2	..22.7	30.7	-2.8
Foreign Exchange Deposits	59.8	65.4	64.3	101.9	160.9
(real % increase) 3/	-75.4	-31.8	-32.9	9.8	14.7
Firms	4.1	2.6	3.2	3.6	6.6
(real % increase) 3/	-94.8	-50.5	-51.0	-21.6	32.5
Households	55.7	62.8	61.1	98.3	154.3
(real % increase) 3/	-52.3	-30.4	-31.7	11.5	14.1

1/ former NBP methodology
2/ recent NBP methodology
3/ Deflated by CPI
4/ Average end-of-month stock divided by nominal GDP

Sources: NBP, World Bank calculations.

Credit to the Economy. Total domestic credit rose by about 10 percent in real terms in 1993 (deflated by the producer price index). As in 1991 and 1992, however, most of the increase is attributable to growth in credit to the general government, which absorbed almost 60 percent of credit (table 3.3). As a result, banks dramatically increased their lending to the government, mainly by purchasing Treasury bonds. Between end-91 and September 1993, real holdings of Treasury bonds increased 35 percent in the banking system (200 percent in the nine commercial banks, and more than 800 percent in the private banks, but a real decrease of 16 percent in the specialized banks). In the same period, Treasury bonds as a share of bank holdings increased from 7 percent to 24 percent for the nine commercial banks, from 17 percent to 21 percent for the specialized banks, and from 3.5 percent to 14.7 percent for the private banks.

Table 3.3: Poland - Domestic Credit
(Zloty Trillion)

	1990	1991 1/	1991 2/	1992	1993
Net Domestic Credit	109.1	245.7	279.4	438.9	632.2
(real % change) 3/	0.3	66.0	88.8	19.5	6.4
General Government	-9.2	54.0	92.7	190.0	300.3
(Change as % of total)	....	....	....	30.6	9.7
Non Government	118.2	191.8	186.8	248.9	332.0
(real % change) 3/	31.3	19.5	16.4	1.4	-1.5
SOE	101.0	145.6	103.8	117.7	142.5
(real % change) 3/	...	6.2	...	-13.7	-10.6
Private Enterprises	11.3	36.5	75.8	119.2	166.8
(real % change) 3/	...	137.7	...	19.6	3.4
Households	5.9	9.7	7.2	12.0	22.6
(real % change) 3/	84.2	21.5	-9.9	27.2	38.8

1/ former NBP methodology
2/ recent NBP methodology
3/ deflated by PPI
As there is a series discontinuity, the absolute composition of non-government credit is not reported for 1990

Sources: NBP, World Bank calculations.

Credit to the enterprise sector (state and private enterprises) declined some 2 percent in real terms in 1993. As in the previous three years, this reflected diverging trends, as credit to state enterprises continued to decline substantially (by 8.7 percent in 1993, after a fall of 14 percent in 1992), whereas modest increases in real terms were posted for private enterprises (16 percent in 1992 and 6 percent in 1993). Credit to private enterprises exceeded credit to state enterprise at end-1993. Finally, credit to the household sector increased rapidly in 1992 and 1993, but remains relatively low.

The reorientation of credit toward the private sector, seemingly in synchrony with developments on the real side, is more complex than raw figures suggest. First, there is a statistical illusion, owing to the reclassification of state enterprises as they become private. Second, as interest rates on bank loans were substantially positive in real terms (perhaps 7-10 percent on working capital loans), the net real resource transfer from the banking sector to private enterprises (and *a fortiori* to state enterprises) — defined as net new loans minus interest payments — was probably considerably negative (particularly in 1993). Finally, the composition of credit itself has shown worrisome trends (table 3.4).

The fastest-growing component of credit, in fact — for state and private enterprises alike — was unpaid interest, including interest on nonperforming loans (substantial for state enterprises) and capitalized interest under the housing and construction credit capitalization scheme. For private firms (including the building cooperatives that benefit from the interest capitalization scheme), this item now accounts for 13 percent of loans, and explains entirely the growth in exposure of the banking sector.

The counterpart for enterprises has been a sharp decline in working capital credit, which in 1993 fell in real terms, by 18 percent for state enterprises and 3 percent for private enterprises. More encouraging is the small but noticeable increase in long-term credits to private enterprises (except housing).

Table 3.4: Composition of Credit to Non-Government
(Percent)

	1991	1992	1993
State Enterprises	100.0	100.0	100.0
Working capital	67.3	50.9	45.8
Construction	8.2	0.2	0.1
Other long-term	24.5	27.9	32.8
Other (unpaid interest)	0.0	6.0	9.1
Private Firms	100.0	100.0	100.0
Working capital	51.6	39.3	36.0
1-5 years	18.8	16.2	17.2
Construction	25.5	28.5	24.5
Other long-term	4.2	9.1	9.3
Other (unpaid interest)	0.0	6.9	13.1
Households	100.0	100.0	100.0
Short-term	47.0	52.7	46.8
1-5 years	35.7	28.2	34.1
Housing	16.1	16.4	15.3
Other long-term	1.2	0.8	0.8
Other (unpaid interest)	..	2.9	3.0

Source: National Bank of Poland; World Bank calculations.

What conclusions can be drawn from these figures? First, the narrowness of monetary aggregates, together with the apparent shift toward dollar-denominated deposits, is the main constraint on the development of financial intermediation in Poland. Increased financial deepening is likely only if macroeconomic conditions continue to improve and only if the remuneration of financial assets (relative to other uses of wealth) is maintained at appropriate levels. Second, lending to the productive sector is severely constrained by lending to the government, which has crowded out the productive sector. Real lending to the nongovernment sector is unlikely to increase until public accounts are brought under control. Finally, until inflation and nominal interest rates are brought down, the composition of credit will probably deteriorate further, partly because no genuine long-term lending is possible when rates imply heavy real repayment of principal in the early life of a loan, and partly because of the snowball effect the housing finance scheme will probably continue to inspire (with capitalized interest taking progressively more of the permissible increase in credit).

Structural Reform of Banking

While the main constraints on the growth of financial intermediation remain macroeconomic, it is legitimate to ask whether and to what extent the banking sector has increased efficiency in resource allocation. Progress is apparent: the Polish banking system has started to move away from the monopolistic, backward structures that prevailed only a few years ago, when Treasury-owned commercial banks (TOCBs) controlled most of the enterprise sector market; the four specialized banks dominated the financing of housing, agriculture, trade, and exports (and foreign exchange deposits); and the private banks were just emerging. Two Treasury-owned banks were privatized in 1993, bringing the private banks' market share to about 23 percent of nongovernment credit and 18 percent of deposits at year-end (table 3.5). About half of the trade finance market has been captured by Treasury-owned banks and private banks, breaking down the monopoly of the specialized bank previously operating alone in this market. About 150 new bank branches opened in 1992. And new banking or quasi-banking services — such as credit cards, export insurance, corporate services, leasing, and brokerage — are increasingly being provided to the public.

Table 3.5: The Polish Banking System
(Billion U.S. Dollars)

	Total deposits				Nongovernment credit			
	Amount		Percent of total		Amount		Percent of total	
	end-92	end-93	end-92	end-93	end-92	end-93	end-92	end-93
Specialized banks	11.04	12.13	53.2	54.0	6.81	6.92	43.1	43.3
Commercial banks (ex-NBP)	6.08	6.33	29.3	28.2	5.45	5.04	34.5	31.6
Nonprivatized	4.49	4.54	21.6	20.2	4.31	3.94	27.2	24.6
Privatized	1.59	1.79	7.7	8.0	1.14	1.11	7.2	6.9
Other private banks	1.93	2.30	9.3	10.2	2.21	2.83	14.0	17.7
Cooperative banks	1.70	1.72	8.2	7.7	1.35	1.19	8.5	7.5
Total banking system	20.76	22.48	100.0	100.0	15.81	15.99	100.0	100.0

Source: NBP.

Segmentation. These changes are promising, but much more remains to be done to move away from segmentation of the banking system. The private banks that were licensed in 1989-90 to introduce competition increased their market share of deposits only moderately in 1992-93, from 9 percent to 10 percent; they showed more substantial gains in lending (from 14 percent to 18 percent of credit). But, as 60-odd small entities, they remain fragmented. Even the two largest private banks, with networks of 20 to 25 branches, cannot yet compete directly with the nine commercial banks, and are simply niche players. So far, a similar strategy has been followed by the 10-odd foreign banks in Poland, except for the recent breakthrough of a foreign bank that took a "strategic" stake in one of the private banks.

Many old problems remain unresolved. Segmentation, both sectoral and geographic, is strong. Only specialized banks have nationwide networks; general-purpose commercial banks have a limited geographic scope. Segmentation limits the efficiency of credit markets because without an efficient interbank market, credit is allocated across sectors, regions, and bad or good borrowers for criteria other than careful debtor or project assessment. Financial intermediaries are also less able to diversify their portfolio and spread risks.

Large Lending Spreads. Segmentation and lack of competition may have helped widen the spreads observed in Poland since mid-1993. The spread between the prime rate and that paid on six-month deposits in złoty increased to about 1500 basis points, as banks lowered deposit rates more than lending rates after the National Bank lowered the refinance rate in April 1993. Such high spreads result partly from the implicit taxation of the financial sector in the form of relatively high reserve requirements (23 percent for demand deposits, declining to 10 percent for longer maturities). But the observed *increase* probably reflects the banks' need to finance branch expansion, provide against bad loans, and computerize banking operations. Escalating salaries also raise operating costs.

Big spreads not only make the financing of production and investment more expensive, but add to the burden of monetary and macroeconomic policy. The policy-maker must choose between giving deposit-holders negative real interest rates or seeing homeowners charged high real interest rates. Little can probably be done in the short run to remedy the problem. The increased use of market-based instruments of monetary policy will allow the gradual reduction of required reserves, increasing the sector's profitability and alleviating the need for high margins. Improving the quality of portfolios will in time reduce the need for provisioning. But only through increased competition, especially from efficient foreign financial intermediaries, will banks be forced to lower their operating costs. The prudential and supervisory environment must be improved to allow strong new firms to enter the sector.

Banking Crises and Quasi-Fiscal Deficits

This snapshot of banking intermediation in Poland reflects a rapidly changing reality, in which reform has profound effects but unexpected problems surface. Many resources have already been devoted to restoring solvency in the financial system. Shortly after reform began, people became aware of problems with foreign exchange deposits on the balance sheet of the institutions (mainly PKO SA) responsible for their collection. Foreign exchange-denominated bonds equivalent to US$2.5 billion were issued in 1991 to cover the foreign exchange losses of those institutions. But soon other problems emerged. After state enterprise profits swelled in 1990, because of hyperinflation and poor accounting standards, the enterprises' financial situation deteriorated quickly. Not surprisingly, bank portfolios followed suit.

Enterprise Restructuring and the Commercial Bank Crisis. In Poland in late 1991, as in most former socialist countries, the portfolio of the banking system deteriorated substantially. The government was confronted by the fiscal implications of large losses (in Poland's commercial banks, some 40 percent of assets) and with a double challenge. It wanted to find a solution that minimized the loss of jobs and productive capacity, but it must do so despite the weakness of the government machinery itself, the court system, and the banks. After considering relative risks, the government decided to delegate to the Treasury-owned commercial banks the task of restructuring the enterprises that had failed to adapt to the new market conditions, and to recapitalize the commercial banks for that purpose. One year into program implementation, indications are that the commercial banks passed the test and acquired much-needed skills and a stronger market orientation along the way.

By the March 1994 deadline spelled out in the law on the Enterprise and Bank Restructuring Program (EBRP), the commercial banks had dealt effectively with the 600-odd larger enterprises that accounted for the most of their bad portfolio in Złoty.[7] About 200 of these enterprises — the third that accounts for more than half of the bad loans — entered into conciliatory agreements with their creditors under a streamlined, out-of-court Chapter 11-type procedure created by the EBRP Law. The conciliatory agreements that have been signed typically entail:

- Transforming state enterprises into joint stock companies.
- Rationalizing and reorienting troubled enterprises activities by redefining product lines, closing unproductive units, and reducing the workforce.
- Reducing or rescheduling their financial obligations, to make them financially viable.
- In about 50 cases, significantly diluting state ownership through debt-equity swaps, permitted under the EBRP Law.

Many enterprises (roughly 150, or about 25 percent of the total) are undergoing liquidation or bankruptcy. The others regained creditworthiness, or their debts have been auctioned off by the banks, or their collateral has been executed.

The EBRP program has strengthened financial discipline and forced the commercial banks to develop risk and customer assessment capabilities. An infusion of technical assistance helped to build up institutional skills in the Treasury-owned commercial banks. This was an impressive start, but the enterprise sector's adjustment to market conditions is an ongoing task. The commercial banks must actively address certain problems in the near future:

- New "bad" customers have emerged since the universe of bad loans targeted by the EBRP Law in 1991. Their debts may account for 10 percent of the banks' portfolio, which will require much attention from the banks and their owner, the Treasury. The same applies to bad loans to smaller enterprises that held loans below the Zł 1 billion threshold and so were not included in the original bad-loan portfolio.
- Implementation of the 200-odd novel restructuring agreements concluded under the EBRP must be monitored closely by the commercial banks, which must take early remedial action if debtors do not meet program targets.
- Equity holdings exchanged for bad debts are concentrated in four to five commercial banks, which may pose problems in terms of their management and the banks' compliance with regulatory requirements. This issue must be addressed quickly — for example, by setting up ad hoc holding companies that would receive technical assistance or be run under management contracts and that could later be floated on an ad hoc segment of the stock exchange.

The agenda for the commercial banks is substantial. In the next few months, the government must monitor the implementation of the EBRP, as well as refine its strategy for the privatization/break-up or consolidation of the remaining public banks. The other Treasury-owned commercial banks should be privatized as rapidly as is feasible, with an ownership structure conducive to effective governance, either through strategic bank investors or a core of stable investors. Selected Treasury-owned commercial banks should be encouraged or directed to merge, preferably with already-privatized banks taking over public ones.

---

[7] About 1300 enterprises with loans below US$50,000 remain to be dealt with. A number of these enterprises, however, reportedly belong to the private sector and are expected to undergo the regular commercial code procedures.

Emerging Threats to Financial Soundness

It soon became evident that reform and restructuring did not resolve problems in the specialized banks. Indeed, the current crisis in the agricultural and cooperative banks (and to a lesser extent the savings bank) has potential ramifications for the budget and the soundness of the deposit base that could dwarf the problems of the commercial banks in 1991-92. Immediate decisive action is required.

BGZ: A crisis in the making. Problems faced by the Bank for the Food Economy (BGZ) and part of the cooperative banking system have their roots in the agriculture crisis, especially in the state farm sector. BGZ's portfolio has deteriorated in the past three years because of loans to bankrupt agriculture enterprises. Audits of the 1993 accounts are expected to show substantial losses, resulting in a negative net worth of perhaps US$1.6 billion. By comparison, the recapitalization needs of the seven commercial banks under EBRP (which brought them back to an 8-percent weighted capital ratio) were limited to some US$650 million. BGZ has other serious problems, besides its financial performance. These include:

- High administrative costs.
- A nondiversified lending strategy with about 75 percent of lending to the high-risk agriculture, food processing, and forestry subsectors.
- Important obstacles (inadequate skills and competitiveness) to effective diversification.
- An unwieldy structure, with more than 100 branch managers dealing with several headquarters departments on important decisions so managers feel little responsibility for their branch's performance.
- Continuing losses in quality staff.
- Operation in such a politicized arena that it is difficult to stop lending to large bad customers.

The government recognizes the seriousness of the situation and has began to take action.

In 1991, many of BGZ's debtors — the state-owned farms — were taken over by the State Agriculture Property Agency, which has the mission of restructuring and privatizing them. This mission has not improved the servicing of BGZ claims, which have reportedly deteriorated in most cases. In December 1993, BGZ got an infusion of fresh capital under the EBRP Law: Treasury bonds amounting to about US$200 million. This was well short of the amounts needed to restore solvency and did not address the issue of BGZ governance. BGZ is linked to the cooperative banking system, the more than 1,600 banks that serve rural cities and villages. BGZ received most surplus funds from the cooperatives until 1990, when those banks were freed from compulsory association with BGZ. A number of them have flourished, developing new business ties with the communities they serve, but about 300 of them are in serious shape because of imprudent loans. Their negative net worth is an estimated US$200 million, and the public may be getting nervous about the cooperative system, which holds deposits of more than US$1.5 billion.

A law for restructuring BGZ and the cooperative banking system passed Parliament in July 1994. Under this law (i) BFE is to be transformed into a joint-stock company and, thereupon function as the cooperative apex bank (ii) six to nine new regional banks are envisaged to be established, and (iii) and the cooperative banks' range of activities will be limited. Little is said, however, about restructuring BGZ, except to provide for its full recapitalization. The intent of the law is laudable, but the law needs improvement. The crux of the matter is BGZ's insolvency and near-illiquidity. Given the probable high costs if BGZ is not properly restructured, no option should be ruled out, including placing BGZ in bankruptcy and proceeding with an orderly liquidation, retaining as much value as possible — protecting all depositors, making BGZ's excellent branch structure and regionalized personnel available both to a regional cooperative banking system and, selectively, to any commercial banks that purchase pieces of it. The government's view, however, is that, if recapitalized, regionalized and fundamentally restructured, BFE could play a major role in reorganizing Poland's important cooperative banking system. That could become a reality only if, as a pre-condition, the cooperative banks are completely insulated from BFE's probable future financial problems.

Several options are possible. One option is to separate BFE's assets and liabilities as well as activities into three distinct sections and assigned to three companies, i.e., "bad loans" company; a regional bank holding company that would provide support services to the six new regional banks; and downsized "residual" BFE agricultural bank to deal with all remaining parts of BFE.

The Bad Loan Company. BFE's large bad loans should be moved into this company to be managed by the staff in BFE's "bad loans department" augmented by technical assistance. This company should not be a bank and, hence, will not require positive net worth. The primary benefits involve stremlining, downsizing, and rationalizing BFE as the loan transfers in themselves, while reducing BFE's total capital requirement, actually increase the capital shortgfall by 92 percent of the net asset value of the transferred loans (after writedowns). Any offsetting BFE deposits owned by, and off-balance sheet liquidity associated with, these borrowers should be either transferred with or offset against these loans, thus reducing any incremental capital shortfall. Without a need to maintain capital, this bad loan company would have the flexibility to convert some of these loans *de facto* to equity through forgiveness as part of real sector restructuring programs.

Every effort should be made to insulate the new regional banks from any financial impact relating to these large bad loans and to ensure that any future funding required relative to these loans be derived only from (i) collections on this portfolio of loans; (ii) government budgetary funds; or (iii) other external-to-BFE resources. The bulk of any new restructuring bonds issued to BFE should be placed at the Regional Bank level to ensure that each of these banks is adequately capitalized to protect the viability of the country 's LCBs. Only one of the present BFE branches should be involved in serving a member Regional Bank, and BFE should not compete for banking business with the regional banks. Most regional banks could, if they consolidate with only one BFE branch, will be viable and can play their designed role of saving and strengthening the Poland's invaluable LCB system.

Regional Bank Holding Company. The regional bank holding company which would consist of a very small head office, with perhaps 10 to 20 staff in addition to any new specialized personnel associated with cooperative bank union type services. The head office of this company need not legally be a bank so that it is not subject to capital adequacy requirements. The company would act as a conduit for fund flows between regional banks and NBP (mandatory reserves, refinancing, etc.) on an agency basis (i.e. off balance sheet so it would not need substantial capital). Financial statements of LCBs, when consolidated, would be at the regional bank level. and not at the holding company (national) level. Six new regional banks would be set up, each associated with only one present BFE branch, whose own assets will have been made as "clean" as feasible through transfer of most of the classified loans and appropriate levels of high cost deposits to other BFE branches.

The Residual BFE. A residual BFE would have total asset of about Zł 7 tr., total deposits of Zł 10 tr. and negative net worth of Zł 9 tr. It obviously must have additional capital in order to achieve positive net worth. Consideration should be given to (i) recapitalizing only to, say, 1 percent of total asset in order to keep BFE "on a short leash" so that the amount of new capital that may be lost will be limited if BFE cannot turn it self around; (ii) requiring that BFE downsize administratively as a precondition to receiving the new capital, e.g. in accord with a business plan that would reduce administrative cost to reasonable level, say 2 percent of total assets; and (iii) using roughly half the

Box 3.2: Housing and Housing Finance Problems in Poland

Under the old system, housing was considered a social good that the state should provide to all citizens at a notional cost. Most households received an assigned dwelling for which they paid only 3 to 6 percent of monthly income. So long as consumption of housing bore no relation to income or to production costs, demand outstripped the delivery capacity of the state-controlled supply system. Housing became a national issue because of enduring shortages, exorbitant grey market prices, waiting lists of 10 to 15 years, a low turnover rate, and the misallocation of living space.

Poland's current housing stock is estimated at nearly 11 million dwellings, 10 percent short of the number of households. Four types of investors have operated in the past 40 years: the state or *gminy* (municipalities), the enterprises, the cooperatives, and the private sector. Forty-six percent of all units are privately owned, most located in rural areas. In the cities, about 40 percent of the housing stock is communal rental units, subject to rent control. Rent control applies also to enterprise-owned housing, and rent covers only about 35 percent of operation and maintenance expenditures (and none of capital costs). Housing construction declined considerably in the early nineties, with the number of completed apartments falling from about 200,000 in the mid-1980s (excluding individual construction), to 134,000 in 1990 to less than 90,000 in 1993.

Housing is heavily subsidized. Some of these subsidies are on the budget and can be easily identified. Housing subsidies accounted for 2 to 3 percent of GDP and 8 to 13 percent of total budget expenditures in the 1980s. In addition, substantial subsidies go unmeasured, the most important being the difference between the rent paid by the household and the rent that it would be charged at market prices. These subsidies are regressive, and they mainly benefit urban dwellers, incooporative-enterprise- provided and public housing regardless of family income and size.

Housing finance was simple until 1988. The National Bank of Poland (NBP) gave investors 43-year loans at 2 percent interest, financing the loans with transfers from the state budget. After a three-year grace period in which the interest during construction was capitalized, loans were converted to repayment over 40 years. Except for a small portfolio of loans issued to individuals (less than 4 percent of the total), housing finance was mostly loans made to about 4,000 housing cooperatives.

In 1989 NBP transferred all cooperative housing loans to PKO BP. PKO was soon overwhelmed by the new burdens. Problems arose with rapidly escalating construction costs, high inflation, and a jump in interest rates, which became adjustable in January 1990. These events jeopardized the housing portfolio and forced the government to intervene. Most construction loans had to be renegotiated for ever-increasing amounts because building costs were rising even faster than inflation.

Below-market interest rates were abolished on January 1, 1990, and all housing loans have since been charged positive real rates. But these rates have made loan payments unaffordable for virtually everyone, prompting the government to have PKO BP capitalize the interest and refinance much of it quarterly with government debt. PKO's cash flow has not been impaired, but the government has rapidly acquired much of the bank's housing portfolio — an estimated 50 percent by the end of 1994. Although in principle the government's portion of the loan carries the same terms and conditions as PKO's portion, there is a widespread feeling that the government will eventually forgive repayment.

Housing loans could become a major fiscal issue. The government tried to tackle this issue in early 1992 by canceling construction loans that had not yet turned into long-term housing or quasi-mortgage loans, but this decision was reversed in 1993 and repayment conditions were subsequently softened. So the challenge the government faces today is not qualitatively different from that confronted in 1990: to find a non-inflationary way to restructure the housing loan portfolio while developing a housing finance system based on market principles. The crucial first step will be to adopt sound underwriting and servicing standards and to deal with issues of inflation and affordability through choice of lending instruments. The longer-term objective is to introduce and enforce a legal and regulatory framework that recognizes mortgages as sound collateral for real estate loans.

Slow action in resolving the housing finance issue is likely to slow progress toward market-based housing finance. Policymakers have accepted the principles of dual adjustable mortgage loans (variable-rate loan payments which are tied to a specific index such as Poland's average wage index), which are being introduced through the Housing Project, supported by loans from the World Bank, USAID, and EBRD. There is a risk that such loans must compete with schemes that have explicit or expected subsidies.

bonds to pay off deposits such that BFE's net loan to deposit ratio is reduced to less than 100 percent and its balance sheet is reasonably prudently structured.

To prevent spreading a crisis of confidence in the cooperative banks the National Bank of Poland and the Ministry of Finance should make appropriate declarations and should arrange for the orderly takeover of troubled cooperatives. Whatever option is chosen for BGZ, the government should improve supervision mechanisms to tackle the problems generated by so many institutions. Perhaps compulsory participation in a national association of cooperatives would facilitate supervision.

Housing finance and PKO-BP. PKO BP, the housing bank, is Poland's largest bank, measured by assets (US$3 billion), złoty deposit base (US$4.5 billion), and size of network (about 500 branches). Its lending activities, including commercial lending, have slowed down in recent years because of unaffordable new mortgage loans and the illiquidity of the outstanding portfolio.[8] Commercial mortgage lending under conventional market conditions probably cannot resume until inflation is substantially reduced. Housing loans, largely from PKO BP, became massively non-performing after 1989-90 as inflated construction costs, high nominal interest rates, and lower real wages rendered most of them unserviceable.[9] Outstanding loans were transformed into a kind of dual-index mortgage, but the relationship between the average size of a loan and the borrowers' capacity to pay is such that these loans are unlikely ever to be repaid. By the end of 1991, roughly 80 percent of housing loans were considered to be unrecoverable. The government moved to stem losses, mandating stricter financial parameters for new housing loans, but the problem of what to do about the stock of bad loans was largely unaddressed. And problems continue with loans made since 1992.

PKO-BP's restructuring is a thorny issue because the nature of Polish households (the end-debtors) clearly limits the possibilities for portfolio restructuring and because PKO-BP has a close link with the housing cooperatives (box 3.2). So far, the problem of PKO-BP's stock of bad loans has not been addressed, in terms of either banking or the real sector. In 1991, 1992, and 1993, the authorities provided PKO-BP with a total of about US$1.5 billion in Treasury bills to refinance accrued and capitalized interest and make up for part of PKO-BP's shortfall in cash flow.[10] Another US$1.5 billion been budgeted in 1994, continuing the bank's de facto recapitalization.

To some extent, PKO-BP is undergoing spontaneous restructuring. The bank has apparently decided to downsize its balance sheet by aggressively lowering interest rates on deposits. Moreover, if the Treasury's "purchase" of capitalized interest on outstanding housing loans continues, PKO-BP will soon have replaced its assets with government paper, transferring the problem of its insolvent mortgage portfolio to the government. There are inherent dangers in the government's *do-nothing* approach. Few if any conditions have been put on bank management in exchange for massive budget support, nor have strategic directions for the bank been considered. After thoroughly reviewing its policies on housing finance and subsidies, the government should analyze options available for PKO-BP, and condition any further financial support on the implementation of a clear restructuring plan.

---

8 With the sharp increase in housing costs and high nominal interest rates, households can service only about 15 to 20 percent of their installments. The budget offsets part of the shortfall by providing PKO BP with Treasury bonds.

9 For completed units, households were able to service only 15 to 20 percent of their mortgage installments. For incomplete units, the situation was even worse because of the sharp increase in construction costs in 1990-91. Any new financing would clearly have led to losses, so the construction of tens of thousands of units was literally stalled.

10 These Treasury bills were initially issued with a one-year maturity but were subsequently rolled over, with the Treasury servicing only interest. In addition, PKO BP received at the end of 1993 a Zł 4.5 trillion Treasury bond allocation so it could write off part of its commercial loan portfolio in the context of bank-led restructuring.

Private banks. Recently, a significant number of private banks have experienced severe problems. The National Bank of Poland seized three private banks as they became illiquid, and more recently 14 banks appear to (based on their own declarations to the Central Bank) to be insolvent. This crisis has arisen partly because of lax licensing criteria after 1990, and partly because of weak supervision. On the whole, the private banks seem to have a weak capital base; they have been less profitable than the commercial banks, their competitors.[11]

Two aspects of the smaller private banks' problems need to be addressed. First, the deposit insurance scheme under preparation should be rapidly established to allow the liquidation of certain banks and to create a more level playing field for the others. Then, the surviving private banks must strengthen their capital base and reach critical mass. The National Band of Poland should seriously consider devising a package of financial and regulatory incentives to attract private and foreign capital to enter this market.

Strengthening the Regulatory and Supervisory Framework

Strengthening the regulatory and supervisory framework for banking should reinforce public confidence in the banking system, and improve resource mobilization in the medium term. By imposing financial transparency and sounder practices, it should also help banks optimize their credit and financial decisions (for example, about deposit levels and lending rates). It is of course essential to the long-term viability of bank restructuring and privatization.

How good is Polish regulation and supervision? It depends on which of three functions you are considering: regulation, supervision, or the resolution of bank failure. The Central Bank has adopted a comprehensive set of regulations that meet Western European standards, regulations covering licensing requirements; capital adequacy; accounting rules governing the recognition of interest, and loan classification and provisioning; and the management of foreign currency risk. Polish supervisors will lose credibility if any of the stringent rules issued — particularly about the capital adequacy ratio — cannot be enforced effectively because of weak supervisory or bank-failure resolution capabilities. With the assistance of the IMF and the World Bank, the Central Bank has been strengthening its off-site and on-site supervisory procedures. Significance progress is needed before supervisors can carry out meaningful financial analysis of the banking system and detect potential bank failures at an early stage, but the area in which progress is most urgently needed is the third one, the resolution of bank failures. The Central Bank has been able, in the past two years, to resolve or facilitate the resolution of fifteen-odd bank failures (five of them cooperative banks), but its severely underdeveloped human and financial capacities fall short of the demands imposed by many troubled banks.

What should the next priorities be? First and foremost, gather the technical and financial means to improve the Central Bank's capability for resolving bank failures. This means finalizing the deposit insurance scheme; making broader use of the external technical assistance available for this purpose; and devising financial or regulatory incentives to attract domestic or outside investors who might take over troubled banks. Second, while maintaining the orthodox regulatory stance of the past two years, the administration may need to better phase in some of the current regulations, giving banks

---

11 Net operating income of the private banks, as a percentage of total assets, was 1.9 percent and 2.5 percent in 1992 and 1993, respectively (compared with 6.3 percent and 4.6 percent, for the state commercial banks). Net income for the private banks was a negative 0.8 percent and 0.7 percent for those two years, while state commercial banks made net profits equivalent to 2.2 percent and 2 percent of total assets.

an incentive for some banks to build up their capital base. Third, more bank supervision could be delegated to the Central Bank's regional agencies, and to national and regional counterparts in the cooperative bank system.

Clearly, the legal framework for financial activities also needs improvement. Drawing on the significant work already done to prepare a draft collateral law, the government should submit that law to Parliament. Under the new system, new instruments of collateralization would be introduced such as floating charges, mandatory registration to prevent conflicts between creditors, and procedures for direct foreclosure.

Developing Financial Markets

Financial deepening will affect the banking system mainly by mobilizing more deposits. But there are good prospects for developing nonbanking intermediation and for primary emissions to help finance investment of private and public entities. Pension reform (along the lines discussed in Chapter 2) would tremendously increase the demand for securities, which could gradually be met through private sources. First, however, inflation and inflationary expectations must be reduced.

Some of the groundwork for a stock market has already been laid: A sound regulatory framework was established for a stock market, the Securities and Exchange Commission developed market standards, and a logistically up-to-date Stock Exchange was set up. After two years of only modest activity, demand for stocks took off in 1993, spurring a tenfold increase in prices, to an average price/earnings ratio of 30 and an increase of capitalization from about US$200 million to over US$2.5 billion (US$5.5 billion after the listing of Bank Śląski's shares). In a parallel development, turnover increased dramatically — from monthly levels of US$20 million in early 1993 to about US$900 million in December. As many as 36 brokers — 22 of them banks — now operate on the Stock Exchange. Domestic investors, mostly individuals, reportedly account for 75 percent of the market; foreign investors account for the balance. The market for fixed-income securities is still limited and dominated almost entirely by Treasury issues. Outstanding Treasury securities in the hands of the nonbanking public amounted to some Zł 20 trillion at end-1993, or 1.2 percent of GDP. (Total domestic debt amounted to about 20 percent of GDP.)

Though remarkable, developments in the stock market do raise several issues. First, there is clear evidence of inadequate price-setting mechanisms at the time of initial public offerings, and of an insufficient supply. There were only six initial public offerings in 1993, down eight each in 1991 and 1992, when demand was more sluggish. Second, most public offerings were associated with the privatization of state enterprises, so the market did not bring new financing to the enterprise sector. Third, developments in the securities markets affected only stocks; interest-bearing securities (corporate or Treasury) were unaffected. Fourth, there are signs that the stock market and its participants (the stockbrokers' back offices) are logistically overwhelmed by rising demand and rapid turnover. This logistical overload could seriously constrain further development of the market — a worrisome thought, considering the potential supply of stocks when the mass privatization program gets into full swing.

Fully aware of the challenge implicit in success of the market, the authorities have begun to prepare for the future. The following improvements or developments are possible, among others:

- Improving the logistical capabilities of the Stock Exchange and its operators.
- Depending on market developments, a significant increase in the supply of stocks. This would imply accelerated preparation of state enterprises for capital privatization and the promotion of capital increases by private enterprises, be they already listed or not.

- Conducting initial public offerings through the stock exchange — in essence, auctioning off stocks. This would maximize capital raised by either state or private enterprises, would help to clear the market, and would cut short any questions about inappropriate pricing.
- A second market for stocks, created along the lines of more developed markets. By providing a vehicle for selling less-than-blue-chip private companies, such a market could significantly deepen market intermediation while clearly signaling high risk to investors.
- Developing a role for institutional investors — insurance companies, mutual funds, and eventually pension funds — either by establishing new legal entities or by revising investment guidelines to stem market volatility, enhance contractual saving schemes (such as pension funds), and diversify investor portfolios toward interest-bearing securities and corporate and Treasury bonds.
- Reviewing the tax framework for securities with an eye to providing incentives for market development and balanced access to the market (for both investors and types of security).

Issues in the Energy and Agriculture Sectors

A number of problems in the energy and agriculture sectors deserve closer scrutiny because of their potential effects on the economy.

Reforms in the Energy Sector

The energy sector presents special challenges in Poland's transition to a market-oriented economy because it affects the whole society and economy. Energy prices before 1990 were highly distorted; being mostly subsidized, they were much lower than international levels. The primary energy source was domestic coal; gas and oil were mostly imported from the USSR. The industry structure was predominantly monopolies, under obligation to produce but with little or no incentive to keep costs down. Assets were often old, even obsolete, and levels of pollution from both energy producers and consumers were unacceptably high because of technological inefficiencies and high energy intensity. With low energy prices, there was little incentive for energy conservation and efficiency.

As it embarked on reform, Poland's energy sector had several objectives: to maintain energy security; to rationalize energy supplies by increasing and diversifying supplies of gas and reducing over-reliance on coal and lignite; to improve energy efficiency (reduce the economic cost of energy production and the intensity of energy use); to reduce damage to the environment; and to transform the system by eliminating subsidies and introducing competition, commercialization, and some degree of privatization. The recession that began with the transition brought a substantial decline in energy demand, compounded by increases in energy prices, so except for gas, the security of the energy supply is not an issue. A combination of measures are needed to achieve the above objectives, the most important one being to introduce economic pricing of energy.

Economic Energy Pricing

Rational pricing leads to more economic use and more efficient supplies of energy, and less environmental harm, but in Poland today most fuels are still priced below the economic cost of production. As a result, energy enterprises lack the financial resources to invest in rehabilitation, modernization, and environmental retrofitting. Energy prices in market economies worldwide are at a twenty-year low in real terms and are unlikely to decline much further. In our view, it is important for Poland seek to raise its energy prices to economic levels and keep them there.

As part of social policy, the impact of higher energy prices on low-income households should be mitigated. One option is to have a special low (lifeline) rate for low-income consumers, limited to a consumption block equivalent to the average monthly consumption of no more than, say, about 25 percent of all households. Another option, energy vouchers to be distributed through social assistance offices, would be more effective than an across-the-board subsidy in the form of lower energy prices that benefit rich and poor alike and discourage energy conservation. Energy costs accounted for an average 8 to 12 percent of income in Poland in 1992 and 1993. Of course, low income groups spend proportionately more of their income on energy.

Recent Developments

There has been major, if uneven, progress in energy reform. All subsectors but oil and gas have been demonopolized and are being restructured, and there are plans to demonopolize and restructure those subsectors as well. It is hoped that the power generating companies — three lignite generator and four hard coal generators — will be restructured and commercialized. Not much progress has been made on privatization, which requires both political will and the government's extension of certain guarantees to private investors.

Most resources for the sector's huge investment needs must be generated domestically. Given scarce budget funds and the need for economic efficiency, these must come from the sector itself or from loans. Foreign direct investment could play a vital role but any capital, domestic or foreign, will be forthcoming only if energy prices reflect economic costs or at least a strong government commitment, a well-defined plan, and a firm target date for achieving economic costs.

Good progress has been made in adjusting energy prices. The measures introduced in 1990-93 by successive governments created hardship for part of the population, but also positive effects — among them, more emphasis on energy conservation and efficiency, budget cuts for energy subsidies (for operations, investments, and consumption), and drastically reduced air pollution. As a result, energy prices have moved from a fraction of economic levels (in some cases as low as 5 percent) to about 80 to 90 percent (for coal) and an average 60 percent for all network fuels combined (power, gas, and heat). In 1993 prices remained constant and some even declined in real terms, but in 1994 a real increase averaging about 6 percent is expected.

With the introduction and consistent application of economic pricing rules, Polish energy prices will move to appropriate levels and relationships, which will stimulate efficient energy use and fuel substitution. In Poland, the basis for relative prices is the cost of domestic coal (the predominant energy source, which determines the cost of power and heating), and the cost of imported gas and oil. Network fuels (electric power, natural gas, and district heat), which can to some extent substitute for each other, should be competitively priced based on consistent criteria. Tariff studies completed for all three network fuels offer further guidance, though the gas pricing study needs updating and the recommendations of the district heat pricing study need to be tested in one or two case studies. It is important to remember that *economic prices* depend on exogenous factors such as developments in international energy prices, changing demand for gas, power, and heat, and the elasticity of substitution between energy and other factors of production, so they are not constant and must be periodically reassessed. There is little doubt, however, that in Poland many if not most prices and tariffs are currently well below economic cost.

The Gap Between Current and Economic Energy Prices

Hard coal. Sound pricing of coal is vital for rational energy and industrial pricing. Under conditions of free trade, the price set by domestic coal producers in a competitive environment will tend to approximate the import parity (adjusted for quality). This has not yet happened in Poland, where coal prices have been regulated and kept low either explicitly or indirectly (through trade prohibition, for example, and moral suasion). Mining companies have recently been given greater latitude in setting prices. The main barrier to a rational policy has been no exit policy for high-cost mines, which still produce at a loss, depressing prices, directly or indirectly, burdening the budget with the high costs of keeping unprofitable mines operating, and of reducing operating profits in the efficient mines. Before anything else, the problem of unprofitable mines must be solved but, given the social costs and consequences of doing so, the government has chosen for the moment to allow unprofitable mines to remain open, while imposing production ceilings on all mines. This policy is certainly preferable to imposing minimum prices, but we recommend that production quotas for unprofitable mines be progressively reduced.

A restructured mining industry would be free to set its prices in a competitive environment, and domestic prices would probably fluctuate between export parity price and import parity price, but tending toward the latter. International trade, including coal imports, would not be subject to control. The possibility of coal imports should be envisaged for the medium term, as long-term export contracts may not enable the coal mines to divert enough high-grade washed coal to the domestic power and industry sectors to meet demand as environmental standards tighten.

Lignite. The transfer price from the mine to the power plant would need no regulation once the mine and power plant are linked in one company: the power tariff should cover the combined cost of the mine and power company. Of course, one would expect the transfer price to be set at the level needed to cover the mine's production costs, including environmental costs.

Electricity. The recently completed power tariff study calculated the average long-run marginal cost (at economic prices) of electric power in Poland to be equivalent to about 7.40 US cents/kWh (based on current international coal prices and the sector's future investment requirements), which is about 90 percent above the current average retail price of 3.85 US cents/kWh equivalent. A huge price adjustment is needed, since these figures assume efficiency gains. Of course, the economic price is partly a function of the assumed return on assets and of the emission and ambient air standards Poland wants to apply to its power industry. Ambient air standards that exceed European Union levels would sharply increase power sector investment costs and hence future tariff levels. The present structure of tariffs for high-, medium-, and low-voltage consumption appears to be roughly correct, although some adjustments will need to be made.

Natural gas. Present consumption is based two-thirds on Russian imports at a border cost of about 9.4 US cents/m^3 and only one-third on domestic production at a cost of about 6.4 US cents/m^3. Today's import prices should be adjusted for implicit discounts given for Poland's construction of Russian pipelines. The cost of future Russian, British, or Norwegian gas deliveries may well be significantly above present import prices, since the cost of producing and transporting the gas will be higher. *Industrial prices* should reflect gas import costs plus appropriate charges for the cost of operating, modernizing, and expanding the transmission networks. The average industrial price will probably reach a level covering current economic costs and a small profit margin in 1994. Future adjustments will be needed in line with the cost of imports. Moreover, the present tariff structure does not differentiate between firm supply contracts and interruptible supply contracts (all contracts are now interruptible). Firm contracts should be priced higher than interruptible contracts because of the higher costs of ensuring supplies. Once enough gas is available in Poland, the industrial tariff structure should be revised to reflect those differences in delivery costs.

Residential gas prices require significant real increases (of about 24 percent) to ensure full recovery of all distribution costs plus a profit margin. PGNiG estimates its costs for gas delivered to residential customers to be about 18 US cents/m^3, compared with the present price of only 14 US cents/m^3. PGNiG's (Polish Oil and Gas Company) current distribution costs do not include the cost of connecting consumers to the network, but they will from 1994 on. Tariffs will need to be adjusted to reflect this increased cost.

To further illustrate adjustments needed, compare Poland with the Netherlands, a small country with an abundant gas supply and low distribution costs. Household gas prices in the Netherlands, (27 US cents/m^3, the lowest in Western Europe), were 80 percent above those in Poland (an average 14 US cents/m)^3. Of course, the Dutch price may well be lower than the Polish economic price because of the Netherlands' small size and easy topography. Further adjustment may be needed once the cost of distribution to households is better known.

District heating. District heating costs vary widely, depending on location (distance from coal mines), heat generation mode (combined heat and power plant, large utility heat-only boilers, small dedicated boilers), size and extent of network, consumer profile, and so on. These variations are reflected in heating company prices. In the first half of 1993, prices for district heat in Poland averaged about Zł 140,000/GJ (Gigajoule) (about US$7.2/GJ), but ranged from Zł 60,000/GJ (US$3.1/GJ or 43 percent of average) to Zł 365,000/GJ (US$18.7/GJ or 160 percent of average). Subsidies for household consumers must allow for these huge variations, providing in some cases only marginal support, and in others covering more than 60 percent of the bill. The current average price of heat is about US$7.35/GJ (excluding a 7-percent value-added tax) and the average subsidy was an estimated 28 percent as of January 1, 1994.

For comparison, consider Denmark, which has among the lowest heat prices in the West and an efficient, predominantly coal-fired, CHP (Combined Heat and Power) based system. Country size is less important than for gas, because of the local nature of district heating, but the Denmark's higher CHP-generated heat ratio (60 percent) compared with Poland (45-50 percent) may well mean that Poland's price level should ultimately be above Denmark's. Staff costs represent a modest share of the full cost of heating, so this is a representative minimum economic price to use as an interim target. Poland's present contract price (between heat distributors and cooperatives) of about US$7.35/GJ covers about 60 percent of Denmark's estimated economic costs of (US$12/GJ). With the government's proposed 1994 tariff increases, all subsidies to households for heat and hot water consumption would be eliminated by end-1994.

Petroleum. The downstream petroleum sector has been granted a protected transition period to become fully competitive with Western European firms. Retail prices are now about 20 percent above U.S. retail prices but 40 to 50 percent below Western European prices. At this stage, setting appropriate retail prices is more a question of tax level than of economic pricing. In the transition period, gradual real after-tax adjustments of retail prices would allow: aligning gasoline prices to changes in the import parity price of different crude imports; increasing tax revenues for badly needed infrastructure investments; and creating pressure to use public transport instead of cars, which would also help environmental protection. In setting both taxes and the after-tax prices for retail gasoline, the government may also want to reconsider why and for how long it should subsidize gasoline purchases from consumers in neighboring countries, who make quick trips to Poland to buy cheaper gas.

Adjustments Needed to Reach Economic Prices

The foregoing review, despite unknowns, shows how much Poland's energy prices fall short of the full cost of supplying and delivering energy. It is essential that Poland develop a strategy for price increases to bridge these gaps. Authorities should also pursue a proactive competition policy in the energy subsectors to encourage efficiency and limit price increases. Efficiency can be improved by improving management and ensuring that enterprises spin off service companies and trim their work forces through attrition, for a start.

Box 3.3: Effective Protection in Agroindustry

The domestic performance of Poland's agro-industry is influenced by foreign trade policy through the effective protection tariffs and nontariff barriers confer. Estimates of effective protection have not been calculated (this requires knowledge of the weight of different inputs in processing and the taxes, tariffs, and subsidies applied). But comparing tariffs on agricultural raw materials and on the intermediate and final products processed form them provides a check on whether the tariff structure is internally consistent and provides logical price signals to potential processors, without distortions. The tariffs applied after September 1989 often had perverse effects. In the desire to adopt a free market system and to liberalize the domestic market, many tariffs were set at zero, or very low. This was politically unsustainable, as the world prices for some products (such as sugar) were so depressed that to insist on maintaining the tariffs would have sounded the death knell for the domestic industry. The government responded by gradually raising many tariffs between 1989 and 1993. In so doing, processed products were often granted negative effective protection.

The latest revisions have helped to eliminate most negative effective protection for agroindustry, but important distortions remain in the new tariff structure — for example, for modified starch products. To manufacture modified starch from native starch is not complex, and does not typically add much value to the end product. So one would expect that, even if no effective protection were intended for Polish modified starch producers, the nominal tariff on modified wheat or corn starch would be similar to that for native starch. But not in Poland. The tariff on modified wheat and corn starch is only 15 percent, compared to 30 percent for native wheat starch, and 20 percent for native corn starch. As long as domestic prices are close to their import parity levels, the tariff structure is as a disincentive to upgrade native starch into modified starch. The starch industry is full of such examples of perverse tariffs. Modified potato starch enjoys much lower levels of protection (15 percent) than native potato starch (35 percent). And glues, manufactured from dextrins, have a duty of only 15 percent, compared with 40 percent for dextrin inputs.

The sugar industry further illustrates distortions in the tariff system. Carbonated soft drinks from the EC pay import duties of 20 percent, whereas white sugar from the EC pays 40 percent. At recent world sugar prices, the import tariff on sugar approaches 100 percent. Since sugar is the most important input in carbonated soft drink production, soft drink bottlers are sometimes forced to operate with negative effective protection.

The worst distortion have been removed in recent tariff reforms, but important anomalies remain. It is a matter of urgency that the tariff structure be systematically reviewed to identify and eliminate these anomalies.

A timetable menu (table 3.6) shows the real fuel price adjustments needed to reach economic prices for each of three energy sources, depending on which timetable the government adopts. On balance, the government should aim to reach economic levels by the year 2000. Anything less ambitious would dry up funds from outside sources and the utilities would not have enough internal cash flow to finance investments in urgently needed, long-overdue rehabilitation, modernization, and environmental retrofitting. Price adjustments should come at regular intervals; quarterly adjustments are probably the most credible, practical, and acceptable way to reach economic price levels.

Table 3.6: Menus of Price Increases and Years Needed to Reach Economic Prices for Energy (Percent)

Year economic level is reached	Number of years needed	Real increase needed each year		
		Electricity	Household gas	District heat
2000	7	9.6	8.8	6.9
1999	6	11.4	10.3	8.1
1998	5	13.8	12.5	9.9
1997	4	17.5	15.8	12.5
1996	3	24.0	21.6	16.9
1995	2	38.1	34.2	26.5

Note: Based on end-1993 price levels; does not reflect proposed 1994 tariff increases.

Source: World Bank estimates.

Some countries have used an alternative approach, a one-time increase in economic prices, combined with a substantial compensation for most of the population. Taxation would prevent a windfall to the energy enterprises, and would make this approach budget-neutral. A *big-bang* closing of the price gap has some merit: It would send the right price signal to households responsive to high energy prices, and it would prevent lengthy debates every time energy prices increase. The technical details of such a proposal would have to be carefully worked out, but this could represent a way out of an impasse that is damaging Poland's long-term interests.

Regulatory Framework

It is expected that a draft energy law being prepared by the Ministry of Industry will be presented to the Sejm. If adopted, this law would establish an Energy Regulatory Agency (ERA) and a modern regulatory framework for energy. The ERA would ensure that price increases are granted where justified, based on effective control of operating costs and investments. The proposed tariff adjustment schedule would be subject to change once the ERA takes over responsibility for setting prices. Such a regulatory framework is essential if utilities, investors, lenders, and consumers are to have any confidence that future price adjustments will be fair and the process transparent. The regulator should insist on increased efficiency, because there is much scope for cost cutting. In the coal sector, high-cost mines need to be closed and mining companies need to rationalize capacity; in the gas sector, the monopoly should be abolished as soon as possible; in district heating, inefficient small boilers should be eliminated; and in the power sector, obsolete capacity should be retired and there should be enough power generating companies to ensure effective competition. In general, management should be improved and excess staffing reduced. Beyond those measures, efficiency improvements must come from investment in modern technologies, for which all energy subsectors currently lack the financial means.

Modernizing the Agriculture Sector

To some extent, the problems in agriculture are like those in other sectors; no credit, too much manpower, and similar byproducts of the transition from central planning to a market economy. As a result of drastic economic changes in the 1990s, Poland today is among the countries with the least subsidized agriculture in the world. Before, there were heavy subsidies for imports, exports, and food, plus low-interest credit and guaranteed farm prices (on a cost-plus basis). The government allocated some 10 percent of GDP as subsidies for the sector. Reform has reduced this subsidy tenfold, to about 1 percent of GDP, setting the stage for major restructuring of the sector. The emphasis now should be on government policies that permit this restructuring to take place as rapidly as possible, to maximize efficiency and incomes and put the sector in a position to eventually join the European Union. Solid progress has been made but it is important to maintain the momentum, particularly in rationalizing agroprocessing capacity and dealing with marketing problems. Failure to face up to the reality of processing overcapacity in some sectors has sharply reduced profitability in the whole sector and has caused hardship and uncertainty in rural areas.

Some 45 percent of the Polish population lives in rural areas, and 16 percent of the labor force still works in agriculture. Small, low-productivity private farms prevail, and part-time farming is common; 40 percent of those employed in agriculture hold 17 percent of the land, and 29 percent of active farmers are reportedly seeking employment. Regional disparities in yield and in farm income are considerable. At 20 percent, the unemployment rate for the nonfarm population is much higher than in urban areas. Unemployment is highest in the western and northern regions, those with proportionately more state farms.

Many of Poland's poor live in villages and small cities. Rural poverty accounts for a disproportionate 60 percent of total poverty; only 38.9 percent of the people live in rural areas. Not that rural poverty is necessarily *agricultural* poverty. Farmers are more likely to be poor than the general population, but among people living in villages fewer than half are farmers or farm workers. That poverty is overrepresented among nonfarmers living in rural areas indicates a lack of economic opportunity. Modernizing the sector means substantially reducing the agricultural labor force. Preventing increases in poverty in rural areas means finding alternative employment for young workers and farmers leaving the sector; it means developing infrastructure, trade, and services, and removing the main impediments to regional mobility, especially rigidity in the housing market. Agricultural modernization and rural revival — which in Western Europe took several generations — will be partly shaped by demographic trends but can be accelerated through well-designed, well-implemented policies.

As a result of liberalization, agriculture's position in relation to other sectors has deteriorated: The terms of trade for agricultural products (vis-à-vis nonagricultural products farmers buy) worsened by more than 60 percent in 1990-91 (improving in 1992 because of the drought). The average farmer's income fell 40 percent more than the average wage in nonagricultural sectors between 1985 and 1990.

Objectives of Reform

One cannot ignore the enormity of the adjustment ahead and the slow progress of the past four years. Progress has often come from the sector adjusting to a liberalized, market-oriented policy environment, rather than from deliberate agricultural policies. State intervention in agriculture has often been counterproductive. The state has not particularly helped to alleviate rural poverty. It has been slow and has lacked clear direction in creating effective new institutions, privatizing enterprises, reforming credit institutions, and developing an enabling environment for agroindustry.[12]

There is basic agreement on the strategic objectives for Polish agriculture. They include the following:

- Modernize farms to increase efficiency.
- Stabilize prices in agricultural markets.
- Accelerate the privatization of agroindustries and create an enabling environment for them, adapted to the market economy.

---

[12] The main agricultural institutions created in the last four years — all operating fairly independently of the Ministry of Agriculture — are the Agency for Agricultural Markets (ARR), the Agricultural Property Agency of the State Treasury (APA), and the recently created Agency for Restructuring and Modernization of Agriculture (ARMA), replacing a previous scheme to provide agricultural credit to farmers.

- Improve agricultural credit.
- Create an active private market for land (using the available stock of state farm land).
- Develop a more business-oriented research and extension system.
- Increase the number of small and medium-size services and manufacturing businesses (and hence employment) in rural areas.

Implementation has been slow partly because of wide disagreement about how best to achieve these objectives. First, people disagree about the speed and cost of agricultural reform, an issue closely connected with support and protection for the sector. Second, people disagree about the appropriate type of ownership and management of agricultural enterprises (farms, agroprocessing, trade) and the market structures that would best achieve efficiency gains. There are two main points of view. Some argue (on economic grounds) that not all farms deserve support, only those with good prospects of increasing productivity, and that most of the instruments commonly used to provide across-the-board support to agriculture distort the economy. They argue that once special treatment is given, inertia sets in and it is difficult to modify protective structures (the CAP they say, is the example not to follow). Others make a case for special treatment, arguing that a "scissors crisis" was developing as a result of price liberalization, so public funds should be used to support agricultural output prices and incomes. In the long term, they argue, many farms could become more efficient, but the sector as a whole requires subsidized credit (because risks are higher in agriculture than elsewhere), price supports (because incomes fluctuate too widely), and public funds to supplement private capital for extension services, education, technology, infrastructure, and so on.

Recent Government Interventions

Despite such disagreements, in the past three years, government policy has gradually shifted toward more active intervention, both on tariff policy and in domestic price stabilization. Results have been mixed.

Agricultural trade policy. Starting in September 1989, the Polish government reduced import tariffs on all agricultural and agroindustrial products and allowed world prices to influence the domestic market. This was seen as way to force competition on agriculture and industry. The Agency for Agricultural Market (ARR, Agencja Rynku Rolnego) continued to support domestic prices and provide export subsidies in only limited cases (such as sugar in 1991). Gradually, between mid-1990 and mid-1993, there was a movement back toward protecting the domestic market and Poland went from near-zero tariffs on agricultural products to agriculture being the second most protected sector, after automobile manufacturing.[13] The latest import tariffs were introduced in July and December 1993.

In February 1994 the Sejm adopted variable levies for major agricultural products. Still under discussion are the list of products to be subject to variable levies, the body that will have authority to set the threshold prices (the Council of Ministers or the Ministry of Agriculture), and the method for calculating threshold prices. These variable levies will have to be abolished in 1995 as a part of the GATT agreement process. In the meantime, variable levies are likely to impede the restructuring of important agroindustrial sectors.

---

13 The new tariffs adopted in July 1993 result in an average weighted tariff for processed and unprocessed agricultural products of 21 percent, making this the second most protected sector after automobiles (weighted average tariff, 24 percent). These figures do not include a 6-percent special customs payment. In December 1993, a further package of tariff duties was adopted by the Council of Ministers. The new tariff structure was produced largely to establish a standardized tariff schedule and eventually bind specific tariffs, an essential step in negotiating for full GATT membership.

Domestic market interventions. There has been a fairly heavy reliance on government intervention, notably by the ARR to solve sector problems. The ARR was created in June 1990 with the objective of "stabilizing the farm products market and protecting farm incomes." In 1992 it was given the additional responsibility of managing state food reserves. ARR activities have been financed by yearly budgetary allocations: Zł 2.3 trillion in 1991, Zł 1.8 trillion in 1992, Zł 1.9 trillion in 1993 (plus a special budget allocation of US$137 million to import grain during the 1992/93 crop year, when Poland faced a disastrous decline in domestic cereals crop), and Zł 2.6 trillion in 1994 (about 0.2 percent of GDP).

The mandate of the ARR has shifted considerably over the past three years. The agency currently undertakes market interventions, fulfills price support functions (implements minimum price policies), provides export subsidies, gives credit guarantees, and manages state reserves. It has become a major player in all major agricultural markets. The Agency could drain budgetary resources, because of the economic difficulties experienced by private farmers, state farms, and agricultural marketing and processing industries. The enabling legislation is not clear on the limits of ARR intervention. The ARR has recently expanded its activities into such areas as brokerage on commodity exchanges, the acquisition of large assets, and equity participation in privatized companies. While the government is pursuing a policy of transferring public assets into private hands, the ARR is re-nationalizing some of these assets in the hands of a public corporation that does not play the same rules of the game as private companies and could hinder the development of competition in agricultural markets.

The ARR is also the main conduit for government *export subsidies* for major agricultural commodities to processing industries that are unable to compete internationally. In most cases, processing industries receive direct export subsidies. In some cases, the government is considering variants of the EC system of variable export subsidies (in which the level of the subsidy is adjusted as world export prices change) and more elaborate schemes. In some sectors the ARR provides *credit guarantees* for troubled agricultural processors, rather than export subsidies and direct purchases from producers. Guaranteeing seasonal credits on preferential terms for some financially troubled companies could cause major distortions if other, equally troubled companies do not have access to the same guarantees.

Because it is *managing strategic reserves*, the Agency is regularly involved in most agricultural markets. There are regular programs of stock rotation of frozen meat by the date required by public health regulations, for example. The ARR enters into contracts for meat storage for its reserves, following regular bidding procedures, and makes purchases when prices are seasonally low. That is, the Agency combines an element of price stabilization with the day-to-day management of state strategic reserves. To prevent surplus stocks of meat from depressing the market unduly, the ARR also tries to develop export outlets for the meat (or other surplus foods).

ARR's governing body determines both the price at which it will intervene and by how much the intervention price will exceed the minimum price set by the Council of Ministers. Minimum prices are in effect for wheat, rye, and milk. In addition, the ARR was authorized in January 1993 to intervene to defend a minimum price of Zł 14,500 per kilo for live pigs. ARR's method of intervention introduces an element of unpredictability into the market, because the agency has the power to adjust the differential between the intervention price and the fixed minimum price, so long as the gap between the two does not exceed the limit set by the Council of Ministers. (And since ARR operates through authorized warehouses, there is also a danger that, in selecting authorized warehouses, it will be accused of favoring some companies over others.) Applying a single nationwide intervention price discourages regional arbitrage such as the transportation of cereals from surplus to deficit regions.

The ARR intervenes in the spot market, so it has not taken the opportunity to develop forward markets that would enable trading and storage companies to develop the trading skills to exploit the scope for profiting from differences between the costs of storage and the premia for forward prices over cash prices. The ARR's guarantees that authorized warehouses undertaking intervention buying on the agency's behalf will not lose any money when they subsequently sell the grain (in effect, granting a free "put" option to these warehouses) do nothing to create a forward market. Nor does ARR encourage local enterprises to profit from hedging opportunities provided by commodity markets outside of Poland — for example, taking advantage of the low costs of forward purchases on world markets.

Has Government Intervention Been Effective?

It is fair to say that, over the past three years, there has been a wide gap between the objectives of government intervention and the results, including unintended effects and economic and social costs unforeseen when the policies were implemented. There is evidence, for example, that repeated increases in tariff protection for certain products have distorted the rates of effective protection for a number of domestically produced products (box 3.2). And introduction of the variable levy system, which is bound to be dismantled soon under GATT rules, is likely to disrupt the market further.

Apprehension about the ARR and of some decisions about restructuring important agroindustrial sectors seems to be justified. The government has not been particularly effective at stabilizing prices. ARR's activities have gradually shuffled from intervention designed primarily to prevent prices from falling below some predetermined floor toward intervention which assumes that state intervention in markets is desirable in most crop years, even when domestic prices are already at levels that might be considered satisfactory to growers. Crop-growing farmers have welcomed this fund but it imposes potentially heavy costs on such groups as livestock farmers, consumers, and taxpayers.

Not only has ARR influenced average prices, but it has had the (possibly unintended) effect of dampening price fluctuations so strongly that stockists — including private farmers — have been unable to earn an economic return for providing stock-holding facilities. By supporting prices when the new harvest is depressing prices and then releasing them (or encouraging others to do so) later in the year, the ARR has tended to pull up prices near the start of the crop year and to depress them later on. These interventions have led to a flattening of the profile of price changes over the course of the crop year, and have undermined the returns from storage. At the same time, the agency has failed to use its position in many product sectors to help develop forward markets, which would be the most effective means of managing risks linked to movements in prices, exchange rates, and interest rates.

Government strategy has been least effective in the past four years in the adoption of appropriate price, trade, and antitrust policy frameworks that would have allowed grains, dairy, sugar, and other important agroindustrial sectors to surmount the difficulties of the transition. The slowness of privatization and restructuring has been compounded by enterprises' financial difficulties and by uncertainties linked to the absence of an overall policy framework that would have facilitated and accelerated the reorganization of those sectors. Decisions about the demonopolization and reorganization of the cereals sector, for example, have already taken more than three years and are far from complete. Similarly, under government stewardship, a framework for restructuring the sugar sector could have been hammered out much earlier in negotiations between factories.

Recommended Agricultural Interventions

Total real agricultural incomes have begun to increase from their 1989-90 low point, but rural agricultural households as a whole still face a crisis. In some regions, this crisis calls for special programs. It does not follow, however, that policies should use targets such as income parity for agriculture and industry; this would negate the fundamental objective of development policy, to allow resources to flow where they can generate the highest return. To address the problems of agriculture and rural areas; the best policy responses would be to:

- Improve prospects for growth by downsizing the sector and making it more efficient. Letting farms and factories face the market test, over time, will eliminate uncompetitive farms, as happened in the sugar sector. The state can help the natural process by adopting appropriate trade policies, by developing modern marketing institutions, and by importing the Western European agricultural institutions that are essential for agricultural development — everything from futures markets to grain certification — and adapting them to conditions in Poland.
- Mitigate the social costs of adjustment for vulnerable social groups through targeted social policies (such as pensions for retiring farmers, social assistance, and regional employment programs).

Instead of operating mostly through direct intervention, which inevitably generates market distortions, we recommend that the government agree to implement a program that switches the focus of ARR activities away from physical operations — such as buying, selling, and stockpiling commodities — toward using price signals to encourage other market institutions to assume responsibility for creating an appropriate framework for agricultural markets. Such a program would be consistent with the government policy of allowing market forces to determine the development of economic activities and would benefit all participants in the sector, whether farmers, traders, or processors. Five specific changes should be made in ARR's role and manner of operations:

- The ARR should be lent funds by the budget, on which it would pay interest rates similar to those paid by commercial companies, rather than being granted money, with no interest cost, for its intervention activities.
- The ARR should shift its focus to transactions on forward, rather than spot, markets, both domestically and abroad, to stimulate the development of local skills and experience in forward trading.
- The ARR's charter should define the agency's objective as defending a floor price, rather than stabilizing the market price.
- The agency's budget for unprofitable activities should be linked specifically to each activity in a way that prevents funds intended for one use from being applied to another.
- The size and the form of management of the government's strategic reserves should be reviewed — the size, to see if it should be reduced; the form, to see if large physical stocks are needed, or whether forward purchases would be an adequate alternative.

Central though the ARR is to many aspects of Poland's agricultural commodity markets, there are at least as many respects in which the structure of agricultural trading urgently needs changing, without necessarily involving the agency at all. For the health of this sector, Poland needs most to:

- Create a comprehensive legal framework for trading commodities, including procedures to ensure that contracts can be enforced.
- Establish national quality standards for agricultural products, modeled on those in effect in the European Union and the United States.
- Promote standardized commodity trading contracts that can be traded on a forward basis.
- Give domestic companies easier access to foreign commodity markets for the purposes of risk management.

STATISTICAL APPENDIX

STATISTICAL APPENDIX

Table of Contents

Table 1.1. Poland: Main Economic Indicators (1985-1993)

	1985	1986	1987	1988	1989	1990	1991	1992	1993 /1
Total Population (million)	37.3	37.6	37.8	37.9	38.0	38.2	38.3	38.4	38.5
Rate of Natural Increase (per thousand)	7.9	6.9	6.0	5.7	4.8	4.1	3.7	3.2	2.6
(percentage changes)									
Gross Domestic Product	5.1	4.2	2.1	4.0	0.3	-11.9	-7.6	1.5	3.8
Consumption /2	7.8	4.4	2.8	2.3	-1.6	-14.7	5.4	6.1	5.3
General Government	6.1	0.0	1.0	0.2	-14.1	0.2	-4.8	9.4	2.8
Private	8.1	5.1	3.9	2.6	0.2	-16.5	6.9	5.6	5.7
Investments	3.7	4.5	0.1	8.1	5.6	-24.8	-14.2	-2.5	7.8
Fixed Investments	5.1	4.5	4.1	5.5	-1.6	-10.6	-4.5	2.8	8.0
Changes in Stocks 3/	0.0	0.3	-0.9	1.1	2.0	-5.4	-2.8	-1.3	0.0
Exports (g+nfs)	0.3	4.2	5.0	9.4	2.6	15.1	-1.7	1.4	-3.0
Imports (g+nfs)	7.0	5.4	4.6	9.0	4.3	-10.2	31.6	9.2	3.7
CPI Inflation (Average)	15.1	17.7	25.2	60.2	251.1	585.8	70.3	43.0	35.3
CPI Inflation (Dec-Dec)	15.0	17.6	31.2	72.9	639.6	249.3	60.4	44.3	37.6
Industrial Production (average)	4.1	4.4	3.4	5.3	-0.5	-24.2	-11.9	3.9	6.9
(Percent of GDP)									
Current Account	-0.9	-0.9	-0.7	-0.4	2.2	1.0	-1.0	-0.3	-2.6
of which: non-interest current account	2.6	2.6	3.7	3.7	1.5	6.4	0.8	1.6	-1.2
General Government:									
Total Revenues	..	49.4	46.9	48.4	34.1	44.5	41.5	44.0	44.8
Total Expenditures	..	49.7	47.7	48.0	39.9	41.3	48.0	50.7	47.2
Balance	..	-0.3	-0.8	0.3	-5.8	3.2	-6.5	-6.7	-2.4

1/ Preliminary.
2/ Includes statistical discrepancy.
3/ Contribution to GDP growth.

Source: GUS, NBP, and World Bank estimates.

Table 2.1. Poland: Population and Demographic Indicators

	1970	1975	1980	1981	1982	1983	1984	1985	1986	1987	1988	1989	1990	1991	1992	1993
Total Population (million)	32.7	34.2	35.7	36.1	36.4	36.7	37.1	37.3	37.6	37.8	37.9	38.0	38.2	38.3	38.4	38.5
Male	15.9	16.6	17.4	17.6	17.7	17.9	18.1	18.2	18.4	18.4	18.5	18.5	18.6	18.6	18.7	18.7
Female	16.8	17.6	18.3	18.5	18.7	18.8	19.0	19.1	19.2	19.4	19.4	19.5	19.6	19.6	19.7	19.8
Urban	17.1	19.0	21.0	21.4	21.7	21.9	22.3	22.5	22.8	23.0	23.2	23.4	23.6	23.7	23.7	23.8
Rural	15.6	15.2	14.7	14.7	14.7	14.8	14.8	14.8	14.8	14.8	14.7	14.6	14.6	14.6	14.7	14.7
Under 15 Years of Age	8.7	8.2	8.7	8.9	9.0	9.2	9.4	9.5	9.7	9.7	9.7	9.6	9.5	9.4	9.3	9.2
15 - 59 Years of Age	19.8	21.3	22.3	22.4	22.5	22.5	22.6	22.6	22.6	22.7	22.7	22.8	23.0	23.1	23.2	23.3
Over 59 Years of Age	4.2	4.7	4.7	4.8	4.9	5.0	5.1	5.2	5.3	5.4	5.5	5.6	5.7	5.8	5.9	6.0
Percent Distribution																
Total Population	100.0	100.0	100.0	100.0	100.0	100.0	100.0	100.0	100.0	100.0	100.0	100.0	100.0	100.0	100.0	100.0
Male	48.6	48.7	48.7	48.7	48.7	48.8	48.8	48.8	48.7	48.7	48.8	48.6	48.7	48.6	48.7	48.7
Female	51.4	51.3	51.3	51.3	51.3	51.2	51.2	51.2	51.3	51.3	51.2	51.4	51.3	51.4	51.3	51.3
Urban	52.3	55.7	58.7	59.2	59.5	59.7	60.0	60.4	60.6	60.9	61.2	61.8	61.8	62.1	62.2	61.7
Rural	47.7	44.3	41.3	40.8	40.5	40.3	40.0	39.6	39.4	39.1	38.8	38.5	38.2	37.9	37.8	38.3
Under 15 Years of Age	26.5	24.0	24.4	24.6	24.9	25.2	25.2	25.6	25.8	25.7	25.6	25.2	24.9	24.5	24.2	23.9
15 - 59 Years of Age	60.5	62.3	62.4	62.1	61.7	61.2	61.0	60.4	60.1	60.0	59.9	59.9	60.2	60.3	60.4	60.6
Over 59 Years of Age	13.0	13.7	13.2	13.3	13.4	13.6	13.8	14.0	14.1	14.3	14.5	14.9	14.9	15.2	15.4	15.5
Per Thousand Population																
Birth Rate	16.6	18.9	19.5	18.9	19.4	19.7	18.9	18.2	17.0	16.1	15.5	14.8	14.3	14.3	13.4	12.8
Death Rate	8.1	8.7	9.9	9.2	9.2	9.6	9.9	10.3	10.1	10.1	9.8	10.0	10.2	10.6	10.2	10.2
Rate of Natural Increase	8.5	10.2	9.6	9.7	10.2	10.1	9.0	7.9	6.9	6.0	5.7	4.8	4.1	3.7	3.2	2.6

Source: GUS.

Table 2.2. Poland: Employment by Sectors (Thousands)

	1970	1980	1985 1/	1986	1987	1988	1989	1990	1991	1992	1993
Thousands of Persons											
(Yearly Averages)											
Industry	4,452.9	5,244.9	4,876.5	4,906.7	4,915.5	4,894.2	4,894.3	4,619.9	4,249.9	3,882.1	3,696.9
of which:											
Food Processing	456.0	526.1	417.5	421.9	418.1	419.7	410.6	400.4	449.1	466.0	472.0
Electro-engineering	1,233.7	1,625.1	1,414.2	1,407.7	1,390.9	1,360.6	1,300.7	1,178.3	1,077.9	932.0	881.9
Fuel & Power	474.4	548.8	609.3	630.1	657.8	646.4	661.5	607.5	562.7	544.0	545.6
Metallurgy	239.1	259.5	226.6	222.8	217.3	212.2	204.0	194.3	178.8	183.0	164.3
Chemicals	288.0	327.4	291.1	289.4	284.2	279.5	276.7	251.9	253.8	239.0	211.7
Minerals	270.0	271.4	238.5	232.5	225.0	219.6	206.5	195.5	199.4	188.0	180.1
Textile & Leather	736.5	798.4	685.1	685.4	674.7	659.9	633.9	557.5	526.2	465.0	457.5
Wood & Paper	248.8	262.9	229.7	228.1	224.6	218.5	211.0	183.1	211.1	210.0	212.9
Mining	451.6	499.7	451.0	465.0	482.0	480.0	489.9	434.0	387.0	458.9	423.9
Other	54.8	125.6	220.9	233.5	263.3	322.4	420.9	540.2	339.9	196.1	146.7
Construction	1,074.9	1,336.6	1,282.4	1,316.5	1,338.8	1,349.9	1,318.3	1,242.7	1,116.3	1,066.2	897.9
Agriculture	5,209.8	5,143.1	4,958.4	4,861.0	4,745.3	4,616.3	4,522.9	4,424.9	4,264.8	4,037.1	3,670.1
Forestry	182.5	155.0	170.3	170.8	166.5	163.1	148.5	134.0	118.0	98.9	92.7
Transport Communications	939.7	1,119.3	1,057.0	1,053.2	1,048.8	1,033.6	978.6	932.1	842.9	773.1	730.3
Trade	1,046.4	1,304.7	1,456.7	1,476.6	1,485.6	1,477.4	1,458.7	1,388.5	1,560.8	1,605.3	2,028.4
Community Services	252.3	401.3	445.6	444.4	440.5	437.2	432.2	427.4	380.8	379.0	318.4
Housing	46.4	200.4	207.4	216.3	222.9	223.7	210.0	199.3	169.5	174.3	134.3
Science	72.5	148.5	110.9	112.6	114.6	111.4	112.1	96.2	81.7	71.3	62.2
Education	596.0	747.4	905.3	911.6	917.0	927.3	1,077.7	1,100.6	1,084.5	1,045.4	1,050.6
Cultural Services	83.7	82.7	90.2	91.3	92.2	91.4	124.4	119.4	91.2	92.7	94.4
Health S. & Social Welfare	424.5	598.7	716.7	757.5	773.6	788.3	872.2	901.3	863.5	859.9	829.1
Tourism, recreation, sports	27.2	103.8	111.7	115.9	118.0	110.9	132.3	112.7	75.7	72.0	71.7
State Adm. & Justice	240.7	227.4	270.6	275.5	269.6	267.4	260.7	259.7	273.1	296.6	330.7
Finance & Insurance	134.6	157.1	162.2	158.4	162.1	165.3	172.4	181.3	179.1	198.6	223.2
Others	290.9	344.8	322.3	324.8	326.9	365.4	414.5	371.4	249.3	201.7	198.9
Total Employment	15,175.0	17,324.7	17,144.1	17,193.2	17,137.9	17,022.8	17,129.8	16,511.4	15,601.4	14,974.2	14,584.1

1/ Change in methodology in industry.

Source: GUS.

Table 2.3. Poland: Unemployment Indicators

	Unemployed in percent of Labor Force	Registred Unemployed persons (thousands)	Unemployed as a result of Mass-layoffs (thousands)	Unemployed not previously working (thousands)	Unemployed by Gender		Percent:	
					Male	Female	School Graduates	University Graduates
March 1990	1.5	266.6	15.1	..	57.3	42.7	..	..
June 1990	3.2	568.2	58.1	..	52.2	47.8	..	..
Sept. 1990	5.2	926.4	126.4	..	49.4	50.6	..	..
Dec. 1990	6.3	1,126.1	183.1	..	49.1	50.9	14.6	0.8
March 1991	7.3	1,322.1	250.5	..	48.6	51.4	11.6	0.6
June 1991	8.6	1,574.1	315.3	..	47.9	52.1	9.2	0.4
Sept. 1991	10.7	1,970.9	422.1	..	47.6	52.4	11.9	0.5
Dec. 1991	11.8	2,155.6	498.0	..	47.4	52.6	10.3	0.5
March 1992	12.1	2,216.4	539.5	404.6	47.6	52.4	9.0	0.4
June 1992	12.6	2,296.7	565.6	485.7	46.9	53.1	6.6	0.3
Sept. 1992	13.6	2,498.5	606.7	565.0	46.3	53.7	8.3	0.4
Dec. 1992	13.6	2,509.3	603.6	544.2	46.6	53.4	7.4	0.4
March 1993	14.4	2,648.7	608.2	550.6	47.7	52.3	6.6	0.3
June 1993	14.8	2,701.8	585.9	609.7	46.8	53.2	5.5	0.2
Sept. 1993	15.4	2,830.0	569.7	685.3	46.7	53.3	8.3	0.3
Dec. 1993 1/	15.7	2,889.6	562.4	644.0	47.8	52.2	7.1	0.3
March 1994 1/	16.7	2,950.1	550.3	622.2	..	..	..	..
June 1994 1/	16.6	2,933.0	484.2	732.6	..	..	..	..

1/ The estimated size of the labor force was revised downwards in 1994. The figure for December 1993 corresponding to the new methodology would be 16.4%.

Source: GUS.

Table 2.4. Poland: Social Benefits 1/

	1985	1986	1987	1988	1989	1990	1991	1992	1993
Total Pension Outlays (billion zł.)	714	914	1,229	2,055	7,685	47,918	101,825	167,838	231,910.3
Total Beneficiaries (thousands)	6,173	6,301	6,477	6,669	6,827	7,104	7,944	8,495	8,730.0
Old age pensions									
Beneficiaries (thousands)	2,169	2,187	2,214	2,243	2,264	2,353	2,775	2,982	3,081
Avg monthly benefit (zł)	11,789	14,513	19,288	30,446	110,142	669,593	1,338,097	1,768,650	2,331,500
Disability pensions									
Beneficiaries (thousands)	1,954	2,000	2,049	2,103	2,125	2,187	2,318	2,435	2,497
Avg monthly benefit (zł)	9,212	11,250	14,699	24,621	91,509	526,380	985,607	1,320,099	1,723,700
Survivor benefits									
Beneficiaries (thousands)	904	926	951	973	1,001	1,015	1,032	1,064	1,091
Avg monthly benefit (zł)	8,845	10,877	14,577	24,422	90,525	515,031	1,000,932	1,461,329	1,950,100
Other pensions									
Beneficiaries (thousands)	75	70	64	67	54	43	29	24	34
Avg monthly benefit (zł)	11,448	15,248	23,026	38,970	91,459	560,204	1,80,433	1,218,862	1,645,800
Individual farmers									
Beneficiaries (thousands)	1,071	1,118	1,199	1,283	1,356	1,506	1,790	1,990	2,027
Avg monthly benefit (zł)	6,607	9,658	11,863	19,320	72,677	477,885	794,982	970,848	1,305,100
Average Real Pension Index (1990=100):									
Old age pension	133.4	131.3	145.5	137.8	113.3	100.0	117.1	108.3	105.6
Disability pension	132.6	129.5	141.0	141.7	119.7	100.0	109.7	102.8	99.2
Survivors benefit	130.1	128.0	142.9	143.7	121.0	100.0	114.1	116.3	114.8
Other pensions	154.8	164.9	207.6	210.8	112.4	100.0	113.2	89.3	88.1
Individual farmers	104.7	122.5	125.4	122.5	104.7	100.0	97.7	83.4	77.5
Expenditure on Pensions (% of GDP):									
Total	6.8	7.1	7.3	6.9	6.5	8.1	12.4	14.7	15.0
Old age pension	2.9	2.9	3.0	2.8	2.5	3.2	5.4	6.6	6.7
Disability pension	2.1	2.1	2.1	2.1	2.0	2.3	3.3	3.9	3.9
Survivor benefits	0.9	0.9	1.0	1.0	0.9	1.1	1.5	1.9	1.9
Other pensions	0.1	0.1	0.1	0.1	0.1	0.0	0.0	0.0	0.1
Individual Farmers	0.8	1.0	1.0	1.0	1.0	1.5	2.1	2.3	2.4

1/ From 1992, pensions net of tax.

Source: GUS.

Table 3.1. Poland: GDP by Source at Current Market Prices (Billion Złoty)

	1987	1988	1989	1990	1991	1992
Gross Domestic Product	16,939.9	29,628.7	118,318.7	591,517.6	824,329.9	1,142,429.5
Industry	7,054.5	12,367.4	52,220.0	265,717.7	331,358.5	434,040.9
Construction	1,783.6	3,162.7	9,760.4	54,590.2	84,349.4	98,481.4
Agriculture & Forestry	2,049.6	3,892.3	15,290.2	49,784.6	56,495.2	84,798.2
Transport & Communications	995.8	1,651.9	5,263.1	28,717.5	46,167.3	65,029.8
Trade	2,357.3	4,058.4	19,254.6	75,293.7	107,713.7	164,742.1
Other Material Sectors	142.9	315.4	1,305.8	9,222.5	16,757.2	23,505.8
Community Services	218.1	383.8	1,176.1	9,374.3	18,928.9	25,775.0
Housing	407.4	644.3	1,214.7	16,537.9	32,918.2	45,049.5
Education	443.6	710.8	3,513.8	21,799.1	32,472.2	57,914.4
Health & Social Welfare	326.4	575.7	2,584.1	15,748.3	25,102.7	42,454.9
Other Non-material Sectors	1,160.7	1,861.0	6,735.9	74,283.3	104,070.0	123,227.3
Bank Services	..	..	..	-29,551.5	-32,003.4	-22,589.8
(Percentage Composition)						
Gross Domestic Product	100.0	100.0	100.0	100.0	100.0	100.0
Industry	41.6	41.7	44.1	44.9	40.2	38.0
Construction	10.5	10.7	8.2	9.2	10.2	8.6
Agriculture & Forestry	12.1	13.1	12.9	8.4	6.9	7.4
Transport & Communications	5.9	5.6	4.4	4.9	5.6	5.7
Trade	13.9	13.7	16.3	12.7	13.1	14.4
Other Material Sectors	0.8	1.1	1.1	1.6	2.0	2.1
Community Services	1.3	1.3	1.0	1.6	2.3	2.3
Housing	2.4	2.2	1.0	2.8	4.0	3.9
Education	2.6	2.4	3.0	3.7	3.9	5.1
Health & Social Welfare	1.9	1.9	2.2	2.7	3.0	3.7
Other Non-material Sectors	6.9	6.3	5.7	12.6	12.6	10.8
Bank Services	..	..	..	-5.0	-3.9	-2.0

Source: GUS.

Table 3.2. Poland: GDP by Source at Constant Prices (Billion Złoty - Prices of 1990)						
	1987	1988	1989	1990	1991	1992
Gross Domestic Product	622,697	648,228	649,525	574,180	530,582	538,609
Industry	313,676	328,105	321,215	250,547	207,801	213,230
Construction	60,123	63,730	63,539	54326	57,956	60,149
Agriculture & Forest	50,057	50,918	50,845	48,769	49,401	44,764
Transport & Communications	31,980	33,163	33,528	28566	22,804	23,551
Trade	66,287	70,927	74,260	74,780	80,724	80,576
Other Material Sectors	8,696	9,348	10,432	9,222	9,529	9,765
Community Services	10,120	10,534	10,450	9,363	11,696	9,806
Housing	17,774	18,573	17,515	16,499	15,704	23,367
Education	19,787	19,826	19,926	21,799	21,879	22,608
Health & Social Welfare	15,358	15,726	15,349	15,748	15,149	15,668
Other	69,747	69,328	76,400	74,108	59,213	47,232
Bank services	..	..	..	-29,551	-21,278	-12,112
(Percentage composition)						
Gross Domestic Product	100.0	100.0	100.0	100.0	100.0	100.0
Industry	50.4	50.6	49.5	43.6	39.2	39.6
Construction	9.7	9.8	9.8	9.5	10.9	11.2
Agriculture & Forest	8.0	7.9	7.8	8.5	9.3	8.3
Transport & Communications	5.1	5.1	5.2	5.0	4.3	4.4
Trade	10.6	10.9	11.4	13.0	15.2	15.0
Other Material Sectors	1.4	1.4	1.6	1.6	1.8	1.8
Community Services	1.6	1.6	1.6	1.6	2.2	1.8
Housing	2.9	2.9	2.7	2.9	3.0	4.3
Education	3.2	3.1	3.1	3.8	4.1	4.2
Health & Social Welfare	2.5	2.4	2.4	2.7	2.9	2.9
Other	11.2	10.7	11.8	12.9	11.1	8.8
Bank services	..	..	..	-5.1	-4.0	-2.2
(Growth Rates)						
Gross Domestic Product	2.0	4.1	0.2	-11.6	-7.6	1.5
Industry	3.2	4.6	-2.1	-22.0	-17.1	2.6
Construction	2.1	6	-0.3	-14.5	6.7	3.8
Agriculture	-6.8	1.5	1.0	-0.3	6.8	-12.3
Forest	2.2	2.7	-5.2	-21.9	-31.8	18.5
Transport	4.6	3.7	1.1	-14.8	-19.9	0.9
Communication	10.9	6.4	5.3	-1.9	-21.4	14.9
Trade	5.9	7.0	4.7	0.7	7.9	-0.2
Other	5.8	7.5	11.6	-11.6	3.3	2.5
Community Services	2.3	4.1	-0.8	-10.4	24.9	-16.2
Housing	1.7	4.5	-5.7	-5.8	-4.8	48.8
Education	-0.5	0.2	0.5	9.4	0.4	3.3
Health & Social Welfare	1.8	2.4	-2.4	2.6	-3.8	3.4
Other	2.8	-0.6	10.2	-3.0	-20.1	-20.2

Source: GUS.

Table 3.3. Poland: GDP by Expenditures at Current Market Prices (Billion Złoty)

	1980	1985	1986	1987	1988	1989	1990	1991	1992
Gross Domestic Product	2,511	10,445	12,953	16,940	29,629	118,319	591,518	824,330	1,142,429
Net Exports	-73	140	184	407	811	4,962	50,009	2,466	-12,369
Exports	707	1,901	2,357	3,625	6,744	22,570	160,509	190,257	242,418
Imports	780	1,761	2,174	3,218	5,934	17,608	110,500	187,791	254,787
Total Expenditure	2,585	10,305	12,769	16,533	28,818	113,356	541,508	821,864	1,154,798
Consumption	1,923	7,399	9,095	11,674	19,344	68,283	377,634	648,361	952,905
General Government	231	961	1,178	1,516	2,428	7,067	108,899	167,973	220,713
Private	1,692	6,438	7,917	10,157	16,916	61,216	268,734	480,389	732,191
Investment	662	2,888	3,740	4,883	9,657	45,533	162,887	177,284	201,167
Fixed Investment	621	2,211	2,835	3,821	6,663	19,351	116,066	155,026	190,683
Changes in Stocks	40	677	905	1,062	2,994	26,182	46,821	22,258	10,484
Gross Domestic Savings	588	3028	3,924	5,291	10,468	50,495	212,896	179,750	188,798
Net Factor Income	-104	-376	-467	-769	-1,260	-4,598	-31,882	-14,990	-19,534
Current Transfers	30	114	166	372	613	1,776	18,430	3,257	3,134
Gross National Savings	514	2,766	3,623	4,893	9,821	47,673	199,444	168,017	172,398
Gross National Product	2,407	10,069	12,486	16,170	28,369	113,720	559,636	809,340	1,122,895
(percentage composition)									
Gross Domestic Product	100.0	100.0	100.0	100.0	100.0	100.0	100.0	100.0	100.0
Net Exports	-2.9	1.3	1.4	2.4	2.7	4.2	8.5	0.3	-1.1
Exports	28.1	18.2	18.2	21.4	22.8	19.1	27.1	23.1	21.2
Imports	31.1	16.9	16.8	19.0	20.0	14.9	18.7	22.8	22.3
Total Expenditure	102.9	98.7	98.6	97.6	97.3	95.8	91.5	99.7	101.1
Consumption	76.6	71.0	69.7	68.8	64.7	57.3	64.0	78.2	83.4
General Government	9.2	18.1	17.8	17.3	16.0	13.9	18.4	20.4	19.3
Private	67.4	61.8	60.6	59.8	56.5	51.3	45.6	57.8	64.1
Investment	26.3	27.7	28.9	28.8	32.6	38.5	27.5	21.5	17.6
Fixed Investment	24.7	21.2	21.9	22.6	22.5	16.4	19.6	18.8	16.7
Changes in Stocks	1.6	6.5	7.0	6.3	10.1	22.1	7.9	2.7	0.9
Gross Domestic Savings	23.4	29.0	30.3	31.2	35.3	42.7	36.0	21.8	16.5
Net Factor Income	-4.2	-3.6	-3.6	-4.5	-4.3	-3.9	-5.4	-1.8	-1.7
Current Transfers	1.2	1.1	1.3	2.2	2.1	1.5	3.1	0.4	0.3
Gross National Savings	20.5	26.5	28.0	28.9	33.1	40.3	33.7	20.4	15.1
Gross National Product	95.8	96.4	96.4	95.5	95.7	96.1	94.6	98.2	98.3

Source: World Bank estimates based on GUS data.

Table 3.4. Poland: GDP by Expenditures at Constant Prices (Billion Złoty - Prices of 1990)						
	1987	1988	1989	1990	1991	1992
Gross Domestic Product	622,698	648,228	649,525	574,180	530,582	538,609
Terms of Trade Effect	-3,199	-1,819	18,280	..	-10,497	-8,962
Gross Domestic Income	619,499	646,410	667,805	574,180	520,086	529,647
Net Exports	16,791	17,940	16,401	50,009	12,406	1,252
Exports	124,239	135,918	139,452	160,509	157,855	160,064
Imports	107,448	117,978	123,051	110,500	145,449	158,812
Total Expenditure	605,907	630,289	633,124	524,171	518,176	537,357
Consumption	441,966	452,249	446,005	381,985	394,455	414,288
General Government	118,071	118,189	112,752	113,316	105,898	110,674
Private	323,895	334,060	333,252	268,669	288,557	303,614
Unallocated Items	..	..	..	1,472	2,941	5,349
Investments	163,941	178,039	187,120	140,714	120,781	117,719
Fixed Investment	124,035	131,602	128,838	115,877	110,692	113,802
Changes in Stocks	39,905	46,438	58,281	24,837	10,089	3,917
(Growth Rates)						
Gross Domestic Product	2.0	4.1	0.2	-11.6	-7.6	1.5
Net Exports 1/	..	0.2	-0.2	5.2	-6.5	-2.1
Exports	5.0	9.4	2.6	15.1	-1.7	1.4
Imports	4.6	9.8	4.3	-10.2	31.6	9.2
Consumption	2.3	2.6	-1.3	-11.7	3.3	5.0
General Government	0.8	0.1	-4.6	0.5	-6.5	4.5
Private	2.9	3.4	-0.3	-15.3	7.4	5.2
Investments	0.1	8.6	5.1	-24.8	-14.2	-2.5
Fixed Investment	4.1	6.1	-2.1	-10.6	-4.5	2.8
Changes in Stocks 1/	..	1.1	1.8	-5.2	-2.6	-2.6

1/ Contribution to GDP growth.
Source: World Bank estimates based on Government Authorities data - GUS.

Table 3.5. Poland: Industrial Production Indices (1990=100)							
	1985	1988	1989	1990	1991	1992	1993
Total Industry	116.7	132.6	131.9	100.0	88.1	91.5	97.2
Mining	132.8	133.1	135.1	100.0	95.2	92.0	85.4
Manufacturing	115.6	132.5	131.7	100.0	87.7	91.7	98.2
Fuel & Power	127.0	131.6	128.4	100.0	91.8	92.5	92.4
Metallurgy	127.0	130.9	124.6	100.0	77.2	74.2	74.3
Electro-Engineering	101.7	127.3	128.2	100.0	80.2	86.9	97.2
Chemical	110.9	129.2	132.6	100.0	87.3	93.1	100.3
Mineral	106.5	120.9	127.5	100.0	96.8	94.9	101.3
Wood and Paper	105.9	124.6	133.2	100.0	98.4	109.8	119.0
Light Industry	127.1	146.2	151.0	100.0	88.1	93.7	101.5
Food Processing	130.0	139.3	131.1	100.0	98.2	99.0	106.4
(percentage change)							
Total Industry	31.1	32.6	-0.5	-24.2	-11.9	3.9	6.2
Mining	-0.5	-0.6	1.5	-26.0	-4.8	-3.4	-7.2
Manufacturing	4.5	5.7	-0.6	-24.1	-12.3	4.6	7.1
Fuel & Power	33.3	31.6	-2.4	-22.1	-8.2	0.8	-0.1
Metallurgy	28.2	30.9	-4.8	-19.7	-22.8	-3.9	0.1
Electro-Engineering	25.2	27.3	0.7	-22.0	-19.8	8.4	11.9
Chemical	24.5	29.2	2.6	-24.6	-12.7	6.6	7.7
Mineral	12.4	20.9	5.5	-21.6	-3.2	-2.0	6.7
Wood and Paper	20.4	24.6	6.9	-24.9	-1.6	11.6	8.4
Light Industry	42.6	46.2	3.3	-33.8	-11.9	6.4	8.3
Food Processing	42.6	39.3	-5.9	-23.7	-1.8	0.8	7.5

Source: GUS.

Table 4.1. Poland: Consolidated Balance of Payments (US$ Million) 1/

	1980	1985	1986	1987	1988	1989	1990	1991	1992	1993
Exports of Goods	14,170	10,685	12,468	12,359	13,874	12,892	16,178	13,073	13,997	13,585
Imports of Goods	15,806	10,283	11,741	11,558	12,748	12,529	11,677	12,920	13,485	15,878
Trade Balance	-1,636	402	727	801	1,126	363	4,501	153	512	-2,293
Exports of Services	1,624	1,266	1,399	1,533	1,703	1,864	2,410	2,159	2,224	2,424
Non-Factor Services	1,485	1,093	1,205	1,301	1,399	1,427	1,794	1,591	1,612	1,846
Shipment	883	529	564	491	499	487	539	614	755	..
Travel	269	113	131	193	233	217	358	104	152	..
Other	333	451	510	617	667	723	897	873	705	..
Factor Services	139	173	194	232	304	437	616	568	612	578
Exports of G & S	15,794	11,951	13,867	13,892	15,577	14,756	18,588	15,232	16,221	16,009
Imports of services	3,944	3,656	3,929	4,298	4,548	5,107	5,759	4,757	3,534	3,347
Non-Factor Services	1,448	926	1,073	1,163	1,318	1,475	1,787	1,344	1,268	1,477
Shipment	837	473	505	569	576	634	544	348	218	..
Travel	251	174	176	201	249	232	424	125	132	..
Other	360	279	392	393	493	609	819	871	918	..
Factor Services	2,496	2,730	2,856	3,135	3,230	3,632	3,972	3,413	2,266	1,870
Imports of G & S	19,750	13,939	15,670	15,856	17,296	17,636	17,436	17,677	17,019	19,225
Net Current Transfers	672	778	949	1,404	1,423	1,234	1,940	353	528	929
Current Acc. Balance	-3,284	-1,210	-854	-560	-296	-1,646	3,092	-2,092	-270	-2,287
of which: NICA	-927	1,347	1,808	2,343	2,630	1,549	6,448	753	1,357	-1,032
Capital Account	2,882	-1,468	-3,572	-3,064	-4,197	-1,728	-4,774	-8,084	-723	1,608
Disbursements	8,840	723	1,112	659	341	267	445	786	562	921
Amortization due	5,971	2,816	4,103	3,552	4,036	1,951	3,135	6,867	1,891	1,209
Direct Foreign Invest.	-10	14	6	4	-8	41	11	117	284	580
Capital NEI 2/	23	11	-587	-175	-494	-85	-2,095	-2,120	321	1,316
Overall Balance	-1,116	-3,280	-4,709	-3,785	-4,215	-3,098	317	-10,176	-993	-678
Net Change in Res.	402	236	173	-797	-561	-356	-4,442	1,317	-1,614	-634
Gross	402	236	173	-797	-561	-356	-4,942	995	-1,614	-496
Net IMF (+ incr.)	..	..	..	..	..	..	500	322	0	-138
Debt Relief/Resched.	0	337	1,688	7,484	4,700	538	9,054	4,382	0	0
Change in Arrears	0	-10,895	2,565	-3,063	354	3,192	-2,930	4,477	2,608	1,312
Interest	0	-3,263	1,483	-2,102	583	2,379	-1,962	1,066	1,160	1,005
Amortization	0	-7,632	1,082	-961	-229	813	-968	3,411	1,448	306

1/ Includes bilateral agreements from 1986; convertible currency transactions only starting from 1992.
2/ Includes short term capital, credit extended, and other capital not elsewhere identified.

Source: NBP.

Table 4.2. Poland: Foreign Trade by Destination

	1985	1986	1987	1988	1989	1990	1991	1992	1993
(Million US$)									
Imports	11,185	11,535	11,215	12,712	10,659	9,781	15,756	15,913	18,834
EEC	1,959	2,302	2,590	3,137	3,290	4,294	7,835	8,446	10,784
East and Central Europe	5,986	5,964	5,105	5,240	3,572	2,270	2,962	2,589	2,531
Other	3,240	3,269	3,520	4,335	3,797	3,216	4,959	4,878	5,519
Exports	11,489	12,074	12,205	13,960	13,466	14,322	14,903	13,187	14,143
EEC	2,487	2,497	2,958	3,620	3,754	6,338	8,285	7,632	8,951
East and Central Europe	5,626	5,651	5,171	5,919	5,014	3,327	2,506	2,026	1,869
Other	3,376	3,926	4,076	4,421	4,698	4,657	4,112	3,529	3,323
Trade Balance									
Total	304	539	990	1,248	2,807	4,541	-853	-2,726	-4,691
EEC	528	195	368	483	464	2,044	450	-814	-1,833
East and Central Europe	-360	-313	66	679	1,442	1,056	-456	-563	-662
Other	136	657	556	86	901	1,441	-847	-1,349	-2,196
Shares Import									
Total	100	100	100	100	100	100	100	100	100
EEC	18	20	23	25	31	44	50	53	57
East and Central Europe	54	52	46	41	34	23	19	16	13
Other	29	28	31	34	36	33	31	31	29
Shares Export									
Total	100	100	100	100	100	100	100	100	100
EEC	22	21	24	26	28	44	56	58	63
East and Central Europe	49	47	42	42	37	23	17	15	13
Other	29	33	33	32	35	33	28	27	23

Source: GUS RS 1993 Handlu Zagranicznego, Table 2.

Table 4.3. Poland: Commodity Composition of Polish Export and Imports (1991-1993)

CN Category	1991 Shares		1992 Shares		1993 Shares		1991-93 Changes	
	Exports	Imports	Exports	Imports	Exports	Imports	Exports	Imports
I - Live animals	7.3	2.6	5.3	2.7	3.8	2.1	-3.5	-0.5
II - Vegetable products	6.0	3.8	5.6	4.2	3.1	5.5	-2.9	1.7
III - Various fats	0.3	0.6	0.2	0.8	0.1	0.7	-0.2	0.1
IV - Prepared foodstuffs	4.3	6.8	3.6	4.7	3.2	4.0	-1.1	-2.8
V - Mineral products	15.0	21.4	13.8	19.2	11.7	12.6	-3.3	-8.8
VI - Chemicals	8.9	8.3	7.3	11.6	5.9	11.3	-3.0	3.0
VII - Plastics and articles thereof	2.2	3.4	2.7	4.9	2.3	5.2	0.1	1.8
VIII - Leather products	1.1	0.4	0.9	0.2	1.0	0.7	-0.1	0.3
IX - Wood products	4.4	0.2	4.7	0.3	5.0	0.4	0.6	0.2
X - Pulp of wood & Paper	1.0	2.5	1.4	4.0	1.4	4.0	0.4	1.5
XI - Textiles	4.4	6.0	7.2	4.3	12.8	9.2	8.4	3.2
XII - Footwear, headgear,umbrellas	0.9	0.9	1.0	0.6	2.2	0.9	1.3	0.0
XIII - Articles of stone, plaster, cement	2.9	1.5	1.9	1.6	1.8	1.7	-1.1	0.2
XIV - Precious stones, metals	1.0	0.1	0.8	0.1	0.8	0.1	-0.2	0.0
XV - Base metals and the articles	19.0	4.2	19.5	5.2	17.6	6.0	-1.4	1.8
XVI - Machinery and mechanical appliances	9.4	24.6	11.1	25.4	10.3	23.9	0.9	-0.7
XVII - Vehicles, aircraft, vessels	5.2	7.8	8.2	5.0	11.0	6.6	5.8	-1.2
XVIII - Optical, photographic, medical	1.0	2.7	0.7	3.1	0.6	3.2	-0.4	0.5
XIX - Arms and ammunition	0.2	1.8	0.2	1.9	0.1	0.1	-0.1	-1.7
XX - Miscellaneous manufactured articles	3.2	0.0	3.9	0.1	5.0	1.8	1.8	1.8
XXI - Works of art, antiques	2.2	0.2	0.0	0.0	0.2	0.1	-2.0	-0.1
Agriculture	17.9	13.9	14.7	12.4	10.2	12.4	-7.7	-1.5
Industrial	82.1	86.1	85.3	87.6	89.8	87.6	7.7	1.5
Manufacturing	54.5	59.7	61.8	62.2	67.9	68.2	13.4	8.5
Energy and raw materials	17.0	24.0	16.0	23.3	13.9	16.7	-3.1	-7.3
Other	10.6	2.3	7.6	2.1	8.1	2.8	-2.5	0.5

Source: Data provided by the Polish authority and World Bank estimates.

Table 5.1. Poland: State Budget Expenditures
(Billion Złoty)

	1988	1989	1990	1991	1992	1993
Total Expenditures	10,960	35,655	193,185	269,366	381,890	502,771
Current Expenditures	9,380	31,585	171,549	253,072	363,477	477,994
Subsidies	4,744	12,489	43,144	41,446	37,835	58,495
Transfers	1,248	6,093	45,336	73,511	129,395	168,863
To households	308	1,252	10,176	17,015	21,661	19,251
To Social Funds	940	4,841	35,160	43,717	90,093	119,414
FUS	199	1,272	8,819	22,060	49,508	66,052
FP	40	95	3,340	7,504	16,256	19,900
Other	701	3,474	23,001	14,153	24,329	33,462
To Local Govt.	..	..	..	12,779	17,641	26,734
Other 1/	..	..	..	..	..	3,464
Wages	1,187	6,690	34,344	61,008	91,273	111,821
Wage Payments	891	4,941	24,817	45,766	68,376	81,780
Social Contributions	296	1,749	9,527	15,242	22,897	30,041
Goods and Services	1,215	2,949	27,135	62,736	68,778	77,500
Interest Payments 2/	..	..	2,227	12,564	31,303	59,610
External Debt	..	..	..	7,148	10,938	12,111
Domestic Debt	..	..	2,227	5,416	20,365	47,499
Other	986	3,364	19,363	1,807	4,893	1,705
Capital Expenditures	1,580	4,070	21,636	16,294	18,413	24,777

1/ Includes transfers to the "Extrabudgetary Economy."
2/ Prior to 1990, these expenditures were included in "other."

Source: MoF and World Bank staff estimates.

Table 5.1A. Poland: State Budget Expenditures
(Percent of GDP)

	1988	1989	1990	1991	1992	1993
Total Expenditures	37.0	30.1	32.7	32.7	33.4	31.8
Current Expenditures	31.7	26.7	29.0	30.7	31.8	30.3
Subsidies	16.0	10.6	7.3	5.0	3.3	3.7
Transfers	4.2	5.1	7.7	8.9	11.3	10.7
To households	1.0	1.1	1.7	2.1	1.9	1.2
To Social Funds	3.2	4.1	5.9	5.3	7.9	7.6
FUS	0.7	1.1	1.5	2.7	4.3	4.2
FP	0.1	0.1	0.6	0.9	1.4	1.3
Other	2.4	2.9	3.9	1.7	2.1	2.1
To Local Govt.	..	..	..	1.6	1.5	1.7
Other 1/	..	..	..	..	..	0.2
Wages	4.0	5.7	5.8	7.4	8.0	7.1
Wage Payments	3.0	4.2	4.2	5.6	6.0	5.2
Social Contributions	1.0	1.5	1.6	1.8	2.0	1.9
Goods and Services	4.1	2.5	4.6	7.6	6.0	4.9
Interest Payments 2/	..	..	0.4	1.5	2.7	3.8
External Debt	..	..	..	0.9	1.0	0.8
Domestic Debt	..	..	0.4	0.7	1.8	3.0
Other	3.3	2.8	3.3	0.2	0.4	0.1
Capital Expenditures	5.3	3.4	3.7	2.0	1.6	1.6

1/ Includes transfers to the "Extrabudgetary Economy."
2/ Prior to 1990, these expenditures were included in "other."

Source: MoF and World Bank staff estimates.

Table 5.2. Poland: State Budget Revenues
(Billion Złoty)

	1988	1989	1990	1991	1992	1993
Total Revenues	10,544	29,742	197,103	212,060	312,775	459,009
Tax Revenues	10,056	25,552	166,802	180,223	277,448	413,454
Indirect Taxes	3,806	8,546	41,262	78,245	129,873	221,326
Turnover Tax	3,203	8,546	37,537	61,195	103,099	..
VAT+Excises 1/	..	..	..	..	..	177,494
Trade Taxes	603	..	3,725	17,050	26,774	43,832
Direct Taxes	6,250	17,006	125,540	101,978	147,575	192,128
Personal Income Tax	..	..	..	..	72,261	119,424
Corporate Income tax	3,767	9,339	82,854	50,622	50,620	62,572
Excess Wage Tax	210	1,666	8,773	27,098	16,988	9,987
Wage Tax	1,043	3,290	17,924	19,548	..	..
Income Equal. + Prof.Tax	261	..	2,398	2,900	..	..
Other	1,230	2,450	13,591	1,810	7,706	145
Nontax Revenues	488	4,190	30,301	30,127	30,483	37,751
Central Bank Profits	195	1,740	9,922	6,605	7,978	14,182
Dividend Tax	..	1,663	12,830	12,581	8,232	6,914
Other	293	787	7,549	10,941	14,273	16,655
Capital Revenues (Privatization)	..	..	..	1,710	4,844	7,804

1/ The VAT was introduced in July 1992, replacing the turnover tax.

Source: MoF and World Bank staff estimates.

Table 5.2A. Poland: State Budget Revenues (Percent of GDP)

	1988	1989	1990	1991	1992	1993
Total Revenues	35.6	25.1	33.3	25.7	27.4	29.1
Tax Revenues	33.9	21.6	28.2	21.9	24.3	26.2
Indirect Taxes	12.8	7.2	7.0	9.5	11.4	14.0
Turnover Tax	10.8	7.2	6.3	7.4	9.0	..
VAT+Excises 1/	..	..	..	..	..	11.2
Trade Taxes	2.0	..	0.6	2.1	2.3	2.8
Direct Taxes	21.1	14.4	21.2	12.4	12.9	12.2
Personal Income Tax	..	..	..	..	6.3	7.6
Corporate Income tax	12.7	7.9	14.0	6.1	4.4	4.0
Excess Wage Tax	0.7	1.4	1.5	3.3	1.5	0.6
Wage Tax	3.5	2.8	3.0	2.4	..	..
Income Equal. + Prof.Tax	..	0.2	0.4	0.4	..	..
Other	4.2	2.1	2.3	0.2	0.7	0.0
Nontax Revenues	1.6	3.5	5.1	3.7	2.7	2.4
Central Bank Profits	0.7	1.5	1.7	0.8	0.7	0.9
Dividend Tax	..	1.4	2.2	1.5	0.7	0.4
Other	1.0	0.7	1.3	1.3	1.2	1.1
Capital Revenues (Privatization)	..	..	..	0.2	0.4	0.5

1/ The VAT was introduced in July 1993, replacing the turnover tax.
Source: MoF and World Bank estimates.

Table 5.3. Poland: Extrabudgetary Funds
(Billion Złoty)

	1989	1990	1991	1992	1993
FUS (Pension Fund)					
Revenues	9,691	57,833	111,703	185,205	251,194
Contributions	6,670	39,487	75,069	113,762	156,955
State Subsidies	1,272	8,819	22,060	49,508	66,052
State Contr.	1,749	9,527	14,574	21,935	28,187
Expenditures	9,746	51,755	115,057	182,084	246,830
Surplus/Deficit (-)	-55	6,078	-3,354	3,121	4,364
FP (Labor Fund)					
Revenues	95	4,584	11,928	23,127	32,455
Contributions	..	1,244	3,756	5,909	10,701
State Subsidies	95	3,340	7,504	16,256	19,900
State Contr.	..	..	668	962	1,855
Expenditures	62	3,429	12,398	22,827	31,903
Surplus/Deficit (-)	33	1,155	-470	300	552
Other Funds					
Revenues	7,085	46,046	22,362	36,315	43,716
Contributions	3,611	23,045	8,209	11,986	10,253
State Subsidies	3,474	23,001	14,153	24,329	33,462
Expenditures	8,284	40,561	22,953	33,447	43,297
Surplus/Deficit (-)	-1,199	5,485	-591	2,868	419
Total Extrabudgetary Funds					
Revenues	16,871	108,463	145,993	244,647	327,365
Contributions	10,281	63,776	87,034	131,657	177,909
State Subsidies	4,841	35,160	43,717	90,093	119,414
State Contr.	1,749	9,527	15,242	22,897	30,041
Expenditures	18,092	95,745	150,408	238,358	322,030
Surplus/Deficit (-)	-1,221	12,718	-4,415	6,289	5,335

Source: MoF and World Bank staff estimates.

Table 5.3A. Poland: Extrabudgetary Funds
(Percent of GDP)

	1989	1990	1991	1992	1993
FUS (Pension Fund)					
Revenues	8.2	9.8	13.6	16.2	15.9
Contributions	5.6	6.7	9.1	10.0	9.9
State Subsidies	1.1	1.5	2.7	4.3	4.2
State Contr.	1.5	1.6	1.8	1.9	1.8
Expenditures	8.2	8.7	14.0	15.9	15.6
Surplus/Deficit (-)	0.0	1.0	-0.4	0.3	0.3
FP (Labor Fund)					
Revenues	0.1	0.8	1.4	2.0	2.1
Contributions	..	0.2	0.5	0.5	0.7
State Subsidies	0.1	0.6	0.9	1.4	1.3
State Contr.	..	..	0.1	0.1	0.1
Expenditures	0.1	0.6	1.5	2.0	2.0
Surplus/Deficit (-)	0.0	0.2	-0.1	0.0	0.0
Other Funds					
Revenues	6.0	7.8	2.7	3.2	2.8
Contributions	3.1	3.9	1.0	1.0	0.6
State Subsidies	2.9	3.9	1.7	2.1	2.1
Expenditures	7.0	6.9	2.8	2.9	2.7
Surplus/Deficit (-)	-1.0	0.9	-0.1	0.3	0.1
Total Extrabudgetary Funds					
Revenues	14.3	18.3	17.7	21.4	20.7
Contributions	8.7	10.8	10.6	11.5	11.3
State Subsidies	4.1	5.9	5.3	7.9	7.6
State Contr.	1.5	1.6	1.8	2.0	1.9
Expenditures	15.3	16.2	18.2	20.9	20.4
Surplus/Deficit (-)	-1.0	2.2	-0.5	0.6	0.3

Source: MoF and World Bank staff estimates.

Table 5.4. Poland: Local Governments
(Billion Złoty)

	1991	1992	1993
Total Revenues	47,428	63,907	92,966
Wage & Profit Tax	5,289	..	..
Personal Income Tax	..	12,265	21,176
Corporate Income tax	..	1,372	3,308
Property Tax	7,571	11,737	13,928
Other Tax revenues	10,044	5,395	9,700
Transfers	12,779	17,641	26,734
Other Non-Tax revenues	11,745	15,497	18,120
Total Expenditures	44,788	65,137	93,356
Current Expenditures	34,968	48,870	69,008
Wages	6,475	12,868	18,526
Net	4,560	9,062	12,500
(+) Soc. Sec. Contr.	1,915	3,806	6,026
Other	28,494	36,002	50,482
Capital Expenditures	9,820	16,267	24,348
Surplus/Deficit (-)	2,640	-1,230	-340
Percent of GDP			
Total Revenues	5.8	5.6	5.9
Wage & Profit Tax	0.6	..	..
Personal Income Tax	0.0	1.1	1.3
Corporate Income tax	0.0	0.1	0.2
Property tax	0.9	1.0	0.9
Other Tax revenues	1.2	0.5	0.6
Transfers	1.6	1.5	1.7
Other Non-Tax revenues	1.4	1.4	1.1
Total Expenditures	5.4	5.7	5.9
Current Expenditures	4.2	4.3	4.4
Wages	0.6	0.8	0.8
Gross	0.8	1.1	1.2
(-) Soc. Sec. Contr.	0.2	0.3	0.4
Other	3.5	3.2	3.2
Capital Expenditures	1.2	1.4	1.5
Surplus/Deficit (-)	0.3	-0.1	-0.0

Source: MoF and World Bank staff estimates.

Table 5.5. Poland: Consolidated General Government
(Billion Złoty)

	1989	1990	1991	1992	1993
Revenues	40,303	263,365	341,909	503,003	708,250
State Budget	29,742	197,103	212,060	312,775	459,009
Local Government	280	2,486	34,649	46,266	66,232
Gross	280	2,486	47,428	63,907	93,966
(-) subsidy SB	..	..	12,779	17,641	26,734
Extrabudgetary Funds	10,281	63,776	85,119	127,851	171,883
Gross	16,871	108,463	145,993	244,647	327,365
(-) net subsidies	4,841	35,160	45,632	93,899	125,440
(-) Soc. Sec. Contr.	1,749	9,527	15,242	22,897	30,041
Other General Government	..	..	10,081	16,111	11,126
Expenditures	47,157	244,243	395,832	579,289	746,134
Current Expenditures	43,087	222,607	369,718	544,609	695,183
Wages	4,941	24,817	50,326	77,438	94,280
Gross	6,690	34,344	67,483	104,141	131,347
(-) Soc. Sec. Contr.	1,749	9,527	17,157	26,703	37,067
Goods and Services	2,949	27,135	62,736	68,778	77,500
Interest	..	2,227	12,564	31,303	59,610
Transfers	19,344	105,921	167,423	260,019	344,745
Subsidies	12,489	43,144	41,446	37,835	58,495
Other	3,364	19,363	35,224	69,236	60,553
Public Sector Savings	-2,785	40,758	-27,809	-41,606	3,067
Capital Expenditures	4,070	21,636	26,114	34,680	59,051
Surplus / Deficit (-)	-6,855	19,122	-53,923	-76,286	-37,884
Financing:	6,855	-19,122	53,923	76,286	37,884
External Financing	-273	-4,008	-936	-2,829	-6,400
Domestic Financing	7,128	-15,114	54,859	79,115	44,283
Central Bank	4,780	-12,963	23,000	30,000	24,600
Rest of Financial System	2,347	-2,151	31,859	49,115	19,683
memo: Primary Surplus/Deficit (-)	-6,855	21,349	-41,359	-44,983	21,726

Source: MOF and World Bank staff estimates.

Table 5.5A. Poland: Consolidated General Government (Percent of GDP)

	1989	1990	1991	1992	1993
Revenues	34.1	44.5	41.5	44.0	44.8
State Budget	25.1	33.3	25.7	27.4	29.1
Local Government	0.2	0.4	4.2	4.0	4.2
Gross	0.2	0.4	5.8	5.6	5.8
(-) net subsidy SB	0.0	0.0	1.6	1.5	1.7
Extrabudgetary Funds	8.7	10.8	10.3	11.2	10.9
Gross	14.3	18.3	17.7	21.4	20.7
(-) net transfers SB	4.1	5.9	5.5	8.2	7.9
(-) Soc. Sec. Contr.	1.5	1.6	1.8	2.0	1.9
Other General Government	0.0	0.0	1.2	1.4	0.7
Expenditures	39.9	41.3	48.0	50.7	47.2
Current Expenditures	36.4	37.6	44.9	47.7	44.0
Wages	4.2	4.2	6.1	6.8	6.0
Gross	5.7	5.8	8.2	9.1	8.3
(-) Soc. Sec. Contr.	1.5	1.6	2.1	2.3	2.3
Goods and Services	2.5	4.6	7.6	6.0	4.9
Interest	0.0	0.4	1.5	2.7	3.8
Transfers	16.3	17.9	20.3	22.8	21.8
Subsidies	10.6	7.3	5.0	3.3	3.7
Other	2.8	3.3	4.3	6.1	3.8
Public Sector Savings	-2.4	6.9	-3.4	-3.6	0.8
Investment	3.4	3.7	3.2	3.0	3.2
Surplus/Deficit(-)	-5.8	3.2	-6.5	-6.7	-2.4
Financing:					
External Financing	-0.2	-0.7	-0.1	-0.2	-0.4
Domestic Financing	6.0	-2.6	6.7	6.9	2.8
Central Bank	4.0	-2.2	2.8	2.6	1.6
Rest of Financial System	2.0	-0.4	3.9	4.3	1.2
memo: Primary Surplus/Deficit (-)	-5.8	3.6	-5.0	-3.9	1.4

Source: MoF and World Bank staff estimates.

Table 6.1. Poland: Monetary Aggregates

	1988	1989	1990	1991 1/	1991 2/	1992	1993
(Trillion Złoty)							
Broad Money	11.8	95.8	190.6	281.0	257.1	411.1	559.2
M2 Złoty	9.1	26.4	130.8	215.5	192.7	309.2	398.3
M1 Złoty	5.5	18.8	94.3	120.8	108.0	149.7	196.5
Currency	2.5	9.9	39.3	56.4	56.4	78.0	99.8
Demand Deposits	3.0	8.9	54.9	64.4	51.7	71.7	96.7
Time and Savings Deposits	3.5	7.5	36.5	94.7	84.7	159.5	201.9
Foreign Exchange Deposits	2.7	69.5	59.8	65.4	64.3	101.9	160.9
(Percent of GDP)							
Broad Money	39.8	81.0	32.2	34.1	31.2	36.0	35.4
M2 Złoty	30.6	22.3	22.1	26.1	23.4	27.1	25.2
M1 Złoty	18.7	15.9	15.9	14.7	13.1	13.1	12.4
Currency	8.5	8.4	6.7	6.8	6.8	6.8	6.3
Demand Deposits	10.2	7.5	9.3	7.8	6.3	6.3	6.1
Time and Savings Deposits	11.9	6.4	6.2	11.5	10.3	14.0	12.8
Foreign Exchange Deposits	9.1	58.7	10.1	7.9	7.8	8.9	10.2

1/ Old NBP methodology.
2/ New NBP methodology.

Source: NBP.

Table 6.2. Poland: Domestic Credit							
(Trillion Złoty)	**1988**	**1989**	**1990**	**1991 1/**	**1991 2/**	**1992**	**1993**
Net Domestic Credit 3/	10.8	37.1	109.1	245.7	279.4	438.9	632.2
General Government	-0.3	6.4	-9.2	54.0	92.7	190.0	300.3
Non Government	11.1	30.7	118.2	191.8	186.8	248.9	332.0
SOEs	10.0	28.7	101.0	145.6	103.8	117.7	142.5
Private Enterprises	0.4	0.9	11.3	36.5	75.8	119.2	166.8
Households	0.7	1.1	5.9	9.7	7.2	12.0	22.6
(Percent of GDP)							
Net Domestic Credit	36.5	31.3	18.4	29.8	33.9	38.4	40.0
General Government	-1.1	5.4	-1.5	6.5	11.2	16.6	19.0
Non Government	37.5	25.9	20.0	23.3	22.7	21.8	21.0
SOEs	33.8	24.3	17.1	17.7	12.6	10.3	9.0
Private Enterprises	1.4	0.8	1.9	4.4	9.2	10.4	10.6
Households	2.3	0.9	1.0	1.2	0.9	1.1	1.4
(Real Growth Rate)							
Net Domestic Credit	..	..	0.3	66.0	88.8	19.5	6.4
General Government	..	..	..	..	..	56.1	16.7
Non Government	..	..	31.3	19.5	16.4	1.4	-1.5
SOEs	..	..	..	..	-24.3	-13.7	-10.6
Private Enterprises	..	..	..	..	393.8	19.6	3.4
Households	..	..	84.2	21.5	-9.9	27.2	38.8

1/ Old NBP methodology.
2/ New NBP methodology.
3/ Defined as the sum of net credit to general government and credit to enterprises and households.

Source: NBP, World Bank calculation.

Table 6.3. Poland: Composition of Credit to Non-Government			
	1991	**1992**	**1993**
(Trillion Złoty)			
SOEs	103.8	117.7	142.5
Working Capital	62.0	59.9	65.3
Construction	7.6	0.2	0.1
Other Long-Term	34.2	50.5	64.1
Other (int. not paid)	0.0	7.1	13.0
Private Firms	75.6	115.3	161.7
Working Capital	39.0	45.4	58.2
1-5 years	14.2	18.7	27.8
Construction	19.3	32.8	39.6
Other Long-Term	3.2	10.5	15.0
Other (int. not paid)	0.0	8.0	21.2
Households	7.1	12.0	22.6
Short-Term	3.4	6.3	10.6
1-5 years	2.6	3.4	7.7
Housing	1.2	2.0	3.5
Other Long-Term	0.1	0.1	0.2
Other (int. not paid)	0.0	0.2	0.7
(Percentage Composition)			
SOEs	100.0	100.0	100.0
Working Capital	59.8	50.9	45.8
Construction	7.3	0.2	0.1
Other Long-Term	32.9	42.9	45.0
Other (int. not paid)	0.0	6.0	9.1
Private Firms	100.0	100.0	100.0
Working Capital	51.6	39.3	36.0
1-5 years	18.8	16.2	17.2
Construction	25.5	28.5	24.5
Other Long-Term	4.2	9.1	9.3
Other (int. not paid)	0.0	6.9	13.1
Households	100.0	100.0	100.0
Short-Term	47.0	52.7	46.8
1-5 years	35.7	28.2	34.1
Housing	16.1	16.4	15.3
Other Long-Term	1.2	0.8	0.8
Other (int. not paid)	0.0	1.9	3.0

1/ 1991 Data correspond to NBP new methodology.

Source: NBP.

Table 7.1. Poland: Consumer and Producer Prices

	1980	1981	1982	1983	1984	1985	1986	1987	1988	1989	1990	1991	1992	1993
CONSUMER PRICE INDEX	0.45	0.54	1.09	1.33	1.53	1.76	2.07	2.59	4.15	14.58	100.0	170.3	243.5	329.5
PRODUCER PRICE INDEX	0.49	0.54	1.19	1.37	1.57	1.86	2.19	2.77	4.43	13.84	100.0	148.1	190.3	251.0
Fuel and Power	0.26	0.28	0.95	1.07	1.23	1.49	1.82	2.39	4.06	9.68	100.0	187.0	261.6	372.3
Metallurgy	0.30	0.30	0.69	0.81	1.00	1.21	1.48	2.03	3.40	11.32	100.0	119.7	141.4	189.5
Electro-Engineering	0.73	0.76	1.51	1.70	1.92	2.26	2.62	3.25	5.05	15.30	100.0	137.6	164.2	216.3
Chemicals	0.52	0.53	1.13	1.25	1.43	1.73	2.07	2.69	4.37	12.89	100.0	140.7	171.4	220.2
Minerals	0.45	0.45	1.28	1.46	1.68	1.95	2.28	2.92	4.57	13.77	100.0	144.9	180.5	230.0
Wood and Paper	0.60	0.62	1.40	1.49	1.67	2.00	2.36	3.07	4.56	15.16	100.0	143.0	174.7	226.9
Light Industry	0.83	0.88	1.47	1.87	2.15	2.62	3.11	3.86	6.07	19.67	100.0	137.1	165.1	212.3
Food Processing	0.43	0.54	1.25	1.48	1.66	1.88	2.14	2.59	4.07	15.92	100.0	152.4	207.3	263.1
CONSTRUCTION	0.46	0.48	1.32	1.50	1.77	2.11	2.58	3.27	5.37	15.38	100.0	146.3	171.8	213.1
AGRICULTURE	0.84	1.35	2.11	2.35	2.52	2.78	3.18	3.89	7.16	23.53	100.0	128.9	203.3	270.4
(Percentage Change)														
CONSUMER PRICE INDEX	9.4	21.2	100.8	22.1	15.0	15.1	17.7	25.2	60.2	251.1	585.8	70.3	43.0	35.3
PRODUCER PRICE INDEX	4.2	9.2	122.3	15.3	14.5	18.3	17.8	26.6	59.8	212.8	622.4	48.1	28.5	31.9
Fuel and Power	1.1	8.2	242.5	12.7	15.5	20.7	22.5	31.2	70.2	138.3	933.0	87.0	39.9	42.3
Metallurgy	11.9	2.2	125.4	17.5	24.5	20.8	22.0	37.4	67.5	232.8	783.3	19.7	18.1	34.0
Electro-Engineering	1.3	3.5	99.2	12.1	13.2	17.8	15.8	23.8	55.5	203.2	553.6	37.6	19.3	31.7
Chemicals	2.7	1.3	114.2	10.5	14.4	21.3	19.7	30.1	62.2	195.0	676.0	40.7	21.8	28.5
Minerals	0.3	0.7	181.2	14.3	15.3	16.2	16.8	28.1	56.3	201.3	626.4	44.9	24.6	27.4
Wood and Paper	1.8	2.6	125.9	6.2	12.0	20.2	17.8	30.3	48.3	232.6	559.7	43.0	22.2	29.9
Light Industry	6.2	6.3	66.6	26.7	15.2	21.9	18.5	24.4	57.2	224.0	408.3	37.1	20.4	28.6
Food Processing	6.6	26.2	130.8	18.8	12.2	13.1	13.8	20.9	57.4	290.9	528.0	52.4	36.0	26.9
CONSTRUCTION	1.8	4.2	174.0	13.3	18.0	19.6	22.0	27.0	64.0	186.5	550.0	46.3	17.4	24.1
AGRICULTURE	11.9	62.2	55.6	11.4	7.1	10.5	14.5	22.1	84.4	228.4	325.0	28.9	57.7	33.0

1/ Industrial producer prices are defined by the index of sales prices for output sold; for agriculture and construction it is the price index of gross output produced.

Source: GUS.

Table 7.2. Poland: Nominal and Real Wages (Yearly Indicators, 1990 = 100)									
	1985	**1986**	**1987**	**1988**	**1989**	**1990**	**1991**	**1992**	**1993**
6 Sectors of National Economy1/									
Nominal Wage Index	2.0	2.5	3.0	5.5	20.8	100.0	173.1	237.8	315.9
(growth rate)	18.0	21.0	21.4	84.3	275.5	381.3	73.1	37.4	32.8
Real Wage Index (Defl. CPI)	149.3	153.5	148.8	171.2	142.5	100.0	101.6	97.7	95.9
(growth rate)	..	2.8	-3.0	15.0	-16.7	-29.8	1.6	-3.9	-1.8
Real Wage Index (Defl. PPI)	110.1	113.1	108.4	125.0	150.1	100.0	116.9	125.0	125.5
(growth rate)	..	2.7	-4.1	15.3	20.0	-33.3	16.8	6.9	0.5
Industry									
Nominal Wage Index	2.4	3.0	3.6	6.5	24.1	100.0	156.6	199.2	271.3
(growth rate)	19.9	22.2	20.3	80.2	274.0	314.2	56.6	27.2	36.2
Real Wage Index (Defl. CPI)	138.2	143.6	137.9	155.3	165.5	100.0	91.9	81.8	82.3
(growth rate)	..	3.8	-3.9	12.6	6.5	-39.6	-0.8	-11.0	0.7

1/ Includes Industry, Construction, Transport, Communications, Trade, and Community Services.

Source: GUS.

Table 8.1. Poland: Agricultural Production at Current Market Prices (Billion Złoty)

	1970	1975	1980	1985	1986	1987	1988	1989	1990	1991	1992	1993
Gross Production	305.5	484.6	755.0	2586.5	3091.5	3652.1	6991.8	23693.1	88805.4	112005.0	172248.0	242231.2
Vegetable Production	178.5	263.4	399.1	1406.2	1682.9	2030.2	3762.1	13592.9	44753.6	52870.3	89130.1	141204.1
of which:												
Cereals	51.6	66.3	85.8	451.7	535.4	658.8	1200.4	3632.2	17009.7	16203.2	24952.1	45875.1
Wheat	17.5	20.8	21.4	147.9	188.7	233.3	428.2	1384.2	7019.2	6994.9	11682.5	19261.6
Rye	15.4	18.5	27.4	124.0	131.6	152.0	248.5	792.2	3518.7	2624.5	3384.9	8272.7
Barley	7.4	13.2	18.6	88.5	96.9	115.0	191.0	515.5	2576.7	2603.3	3445.9	6329.6
Oats	8.5	8.3	8.7	42.8	44.9	51.9	87.3	228.9	878.4	785.7	1351.5	2592.0
Other	2.8	5.5	9.7	48.5	73.3	106.6	245.4	711.4	3016.7	3194.8	5087.3	9419.2
Potatoes	36.6	61.0	83.4	257.3	297.3	331.0	762.0	2895.4	5602.4	9212.9	25426.1	26358.9
Industrial Crops	17.3	28.5	28.7	146.5	174.2	205.3	368.7	2118.9	5016.8	4992.2	7062.4	10057.2
Sugar Beets	7.7	15.0	14.4	59.8	71.3	95.1	181.2	1656.5	2842.6	2599.3	4380.7	6841.9
Vegetables	11.8	19.2	40.8	150.1	199.4	271.9	383.0	1983.2	6051.4	6590.2	10034.9	18649.2
Fruit	6.5	11.2	22.1	91.8	111.7	108.2	318.8	993.8	3076.8	4861.5	8378.7	9936.7
Meadow Hay	11.1	16.2	28.9	54.7	63.4	79.1	112.9	272.4	1206.0	1569.5	1972.2	5684.8
Other	43.6	61.0	109.4	254.1	301.5	375.9	616.3	1697.0	6790.5	9440.8	11303.7	24642.2
Animal Production	127.0	221.2	355.9	1180.3	1408.6	1621.9	3229.7	10100.2	44051.8	59134.7	83117.9	101027.1
of which:												
Livestock Slaughtered	58.5	115.1	187.4	611.1	751.8	864.6	1669.4	5358.2	30260.8	38712.2	52007.2	63115.3
of which:												
Cattle incl Calves	14.4	32.7	49.2	194.3	226.6	262.2	487.4	1332.6	6949.2	7680.8	8825.9	11459.4
Pigs	36.5	68.0	106.9	320.0	404.8	456.7	916.4	3210.5	19030.0	25523.4	34523.2	41871.5
Poultry	5.4	9.7	22.3	64.2	83.9	102.1	200.3	660.1	3332.7	4593.0	6467.4	7995.7
Livestock Herd	-2.7	0.5	-20.4	-2.9	-14.8	-39.6	-11.6	-71.6	-1841.1	-1992.9	-2762.0	-7367.4
Cow Milk	39.2	58.4	104.7	367.8	413.7	492.3	1051.7	3323.3	9797.0	14628.3	24131.8	29746.0
Hen Eggs	12.6	17.3	28.5	99.6	107.2	131.3	223.1	599.0	3176.9	4369.7	5019.2	7633.5

Source: GUS.

Distributors of World Bank Publications

ARGENTINA
Carlos Hirsch, SRL
Galeria Guemes
Florida 165, 4th Floor-Ofc. 453/465
1333 Buenos Aires

Oficina del Libro Internacional
Alberti 40
1082 Buenos Aires

AUSTRALIA, PAPUA NEW GUINEA, FIJI, SOLOMON ISLANDS, VANUATU, AND WESTERN SAMOA
D.A. Information Services
648 Whitehorse Road
Mitcham 3132
Victoria

AUSTRIA
Gerold and Co.
Graben 31
A-1011 Wien

BANGLADESH
Micro Industries Development Assistance Society (MIDAS)
House 5, Road 16
Dhanmondi R/Area
Dhaka 1209

BELGIUM
Jean De Lannoy
Av. du Roi 202
1060 Brussels

BRAZIL
Publicacoes Tecnicas Internacionais Ltda.
Rua Peixoto Gomide, 209
01409 Sao Paulo, SP

CANADA
Le Diffuseur
151A Boul. de Mortagne
Boucherville, Québec
J4B 5E6

Renouf Publishing Co.
1294 Algoma Road
Ottawa, Ontario
K1B 3W8

CHINA
China Financial & Economic Publishing House
8, Da Fo Si Dong Jie
Beijing

COLOMBIA
Infoenlace Ltda.
Apartado Aereo 34270
Bogota D.E.

COTE D'IVOIRE
Centre d'Edition et de Diffusion Africaines (CEDA)
04 B.P. 541
Abidjan 04 Plateau

CYPRUS
Center of Applied Research
Cyprus College
6, Diogenes Street, Engomi
P.O. Box 2006
Nicosia

DENMARK
SamfundsLitteratur
Rosenoerns Allé 11
DK-1970 Frederiksberg C

DOMINICAN REPUBLIC
Editora Taller, C. por A.
Restauración e Isabel la Católica 309
Apartado de Correos 2190 Z-1
Santo Domingo

EGYPT, ARAB REPUBLIC OF
Al Ahram
Al Galaa Street
Cairo

The Middle East Observer
41, Sherif Street
Cairo

FINLAND
Akateeminen Kirjakauppa
P.O. Box 128
SF-00101 Helsinki 10

FRANCE
World Bank Publications
66, avenue d'Iéna
75116 Paris

GERMANY
UNO-Verlag
Poppelsdorfer Allee 55
53115 Bonn

GREECE
Papasotiriou S.A.
35, Stournara Str.
106 82 Athens

HONG KONG, MACAO
Asia 2000 Ltd.
46-48 Wyndham Street
Winning Centre
7th Floor
Central Hong Kong

HUNGARY
Foundation for Market Economy
Dombovari Ut 17-19
H-1117 Budapest

INDIA
Allied Publishers Private Ltd.
751 Mount Road
Madras - 600 002

INDONESIA
Pt. Indira Limited
Jalan Borobudur 20
P.O. Box 181
Jakarta 10320

IRAN
Kowkab Publishers
P.O. Box 19575-511
Tehran

IRELAND
Government Supplies Agency
4-5 Harcourt Road
Dublin 2

ISRAEL
Yozmot Literature Ltd.
P.O. Box 56055
Tel Aviv 61560

ITALY
Licosa Commissionaria Sansoni SPA
Via Duca Di Calabria, 1/1
Casella Postale 552
50125 Firenze

JAMAICA
Ian Randle Publishers Ltd.
206 Old Hope Road
Kingston 6

JAPAN
Eastern Book Service
Hongo 3-Chome, Bunkyo-ku 113
Tokyo

KENYA
Africa Book Service (E.A.) Ltd.
Quaran House, Mfangano Street
P.O. Box 45245
Nairobi

KOREA, REPUBLIC OF
Pan Korea Book Corporation
P.O. Box 101, Kwangwhamun
Seoul

Korean Stock Book Centre
P.O. Box 34
Yeoeido
Seoul

MALAYSIA
University of Malaya Cooperative Bookshop, Limited
P.O. Box 1127, Jalan Pantai Baru
59700 Kuala Lumpur

MEXICO
INFOTEC
Apartado Postal 22-860
14060 Tlalpan, Mexico D.F.

NETHERLANDS
De Lindeboom/InOr-Publikaties
P.O. Box 202
7480 AE Haaksbergen

NEW ZEALAND
EBSCO NZ Ltd.
Private Mail Bag 99914
New Market
Auckland

NIGERIA
University Press Limited
Three Crowns Building Jericho
Private Mail Bag 5095
Ibadan

NORWAY
Narvesen Information Center
Book Department
P.O. Box 6125 Etterstad
N-0602 Oslo 6

PAKISTAN
Mirza Book Agency
65, Shahrah-e-Quaid-e-Azam
P.O. Box No. 729
Lahore 54000

PERU
Editorial Desarrollo SA
Apartado 3824
Lima 1

PHILIPPINES
International Book Center
Suite 1703, Cityland 10
Condominium Tower 1
Ayala Avenue, H.V. dela Costa Extension
Makati, Metro Manila

POLAND
International Publishing Service
Ul. Piekna 31/37
00-677 Warszawa

For subscription orders:
IPS Journals
Ul. Okrezna 3
02-916 Warszawa

PORTUGAL
Livraria Portugal
Rua Do Carmo 70-74
1200 Lisbon

SAUDI ARABIA, QATAR
Jarir Book Store
P.O. Box 3196
Riyadh 11471

SINGAPORE, TAIWAN, MYANMAR, BRUNEI
Gower Asia Pacific Pte Ltd.
Golden Wheel Building
41, Kallang Pudding, #04-03
Singapore 1334

SOUTH AFRICA, BOTSWANA
For single titles:
Oxford University Press Southern Africa
P.O. Box 1141
Cape Town 8000

For subscription orders:
International Subscription Service
P.O. Box 41095
Craighall
Johannesburg 2024

SPAIN
Mundi-Prensa Libros, S.A.
Castello 37
28001 Madrid

Librería Internacional AEDOS
Consell de Cent, 391
08009 Barcelona

SRI LANKA AND THE MALDIVES
Lake House Bookshop
P.O. Box 244
100, Sir Chittampalam A. Gardiner Mawatha
Colombo 2

SWEDEN
For single titles:
Fritzes Fackboksforetaget
Regeringsgatan 12, Box 16356
S-106 47 Stockholm

For subscription orders:
Wennergren-Williams AB
P. O. Box 1305
S-171 25 Solna

SWITZERLAND
For single titles:
Librairie Payot
Case postale 3212
CH 1002 Lausanne

For subscription orders:
Librairie Payot
Service des Abonnements
Case postale 3312
CH 1002 Lausanne

THAILAND
Central Department Store
306 Silom Road
Bangkok

TRINIDAD & TOBAGO
Systematics Studies Unit
#9 Watts Street
Curepe
Trinidad, West Indies

UNITED KINGDOM
Microinfo Ltd.
P.O. Box 3
Alton, Hampshire GU34 2PG
England

ZIMBABWE
Longman Zimbabwe (Pvt.) Ltd.
Tourle Road, Ardbennie
P.O. Box ST 125
Southerton
Harare